To Rocío

SEVERAL WAYS TO DIE IN MEXICO CITY

An Autobiography

KURT HOLLANDER

The unexamined death
is not worth dying.

Several Ways to Die in Mexico City © Kurt Hollander, 2012

Published by Feral House, Inc.
All Rights Reserved

ISBN: 978-1-936239-48-1
ebook: 978-1-936239-49-8

feralhouse.com
severalwaystodieinmexicocity.com
kurthollander.com

All photographs © Kurt Hollander, 2012

Design: Rocío Mireles and Bruno Contreras

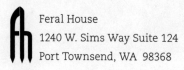

Feral House
1240 W. Sims Way Suite 124
Port Townsend, WA 98368

THE END

Death and the City

The end of our life is our final act. Unlike being born, a moment in which we are basically oblivious, death often catches us wide-awake and in our full senses, often even at the peak of our existence. While we are all born more or less at the same age and in the same way, death can come upon us at any moment, in any place, and can happen in an infinite number of ways.

There's an old Mexican saying that goes: "Tell me how you die and I'll tell you who you are." Although it is true that death is a very individual act, the way human beings meet their end, even if it is by their own hand, reflects more than just the character of a person. Human beings tend to die where they live and their death is determined in large part by the place where they have lived the longest. Given that more than half of all human beings currently live in cities, and that people tend to live longer lives now than ever before, death is determined more than ever by their urban surroundings.

In mega-cities such as Mexico City, where death-dealing elements are so highly concentrated, there is nothing natural about death anymore and human beings no longer die from 'natural causes.' Death is induced not so much by criminal activity and guns (as the media would have it) but from the way the city's more than twenty million inhabitants modify their environment.

Living in Mexico City is a two-way street. So much waste is produced in the city each day that the environment can't absorb it all, and the organic and inorganic solids, fluids and gases that accumulate inevitably make their way into our body through our nose, mouth and even our skin. The longer someone lives in Mexico City, the more material from the environment enters into and is stored within their body, thus directly affecting their health and longevity. When exposed to high levels of toxic substances for a sufficient amount of time human beings tend to get sick and die.

Hormones, pesticides and antibiotics in food, toxic additives in cigarettes and alcohol, parasites in the water or pollution in the air are on their own almost never enough to kill a human being. Together, however, they create a lethal cocktail that builds up over time within our digestive, circulatory, immune and nervous systems. Although there is no single smoking gun responsible for the majority of deaths in Mexico City today, the largest contributing factor is the human activity within the city itself.

A historical shift in the principal causes of death in Mexico City has occurred in recent decades, from diseases of poverty (such as infections, malnutrition, childbirth and maternal deaths) to chronic, degenerative, non-communicable illnesses (such as circulatory diseases, cancer and diabetes). This recent evolution of death reflects a transformation from a traditional rural existence to a modern urban consumer-oriented lifestyle characterized by an excess of man-made substances in the air, water, food, cigarettes and alcohol. These days, most *chilangos* (Mexico City inhabitants) will die slow deaths from diseases related to long-term exposure to their environment. Which is just another way of saying that living in Mexico City long enough will kill you.

The Gangs of New York

Cities have often been portrayed as hell on earth, none so much as New York City. During the 1970s, the New York City government declared bankruptcy and, unable to pay the salaries of its police, firemen and sanitation workers, garbage piled up on the sidewalks, hundreds of buildings lay abandoned or were torched by landlords seeking to collect insurance, and criminals ran free. The white upper classes fled to the suburbs and tourists huddled in a few secure areas while New York City enjoyed a reputation as the homicide capital of the world

At that time, my family and I lived in Greenwich Village inside of an industrial building that housed low-income artists. Our building fronted the Hudson River, formerly the site of the greatest shipping port in America but now home to abandoned warehouses, piers, train tracks and a defunct elevated highway. Puerto Rican, black, Italian and Irish gangs roamed the neighborhood, and to survive you had to walk the walk and talk the talk, which is why I grew an Afro and carried switchblades in my pants pockets and nunchaka sticks inside my jean jacket.

I saw my best friend get stabbed in the subway. I had knives pulled on me at least a half-dozen times. I watched kids from a local Irish gang throw bricks off the roof of my building at the gays cruising down below. I watched as Italian and Irish gangs rampaged through Washington Square Park (my hangout) beating and murdering as many black and Puerto Rican dealers as they could find (including several friends of mine). I spent 1978 New Year's Eve in Times Square watching gangs throw glass bottles into the packed crowd, and afterwards I watched a black gang mug guys and rape girls down the length of Broadway. Even though they often inflicted violence upon others, the kids in the local gangs had the lowest life expectancy of anyone in the country and they tended to die violently.

Despite the fact that many gang members are a menace to society, gangs actually serve a higher social purpose. The history of NYC is the history of gangs, and the history of gangs in NYC is the history of immigrants. Being that they always begin outside the formal economy and on the wrong side of the legal system, immigrant groups tend to be especially vulnerable and need to gang together to survive. Dangerous cities reflect the existence of dangerous governments, and immigrant and lower-working-class neighborhoods are always threatened with inadequate social services, poor housing and bleak economic opportunities, all of which serves to weaken the community. Neighborhood gangs are often a community's defense against attacks from outside, both physical and economic. In addition, by frightening off the wealthy and the tourists, gangs help keep rents low and thus allow working-class and immigrant communities to continue to live in affordable housing within the city.

At the beginning of the 1980s, old enough to go my own way, I moved to the Lower East Side. The Lower East Side was tougher than the West Side and more culturally vibrant. Still an immigrant, working-class neighborhood swarming with anarchists, Old World Jews, Puerto Ricans and junkies, the area maintained its independence from both mid-town Manhattan and mid-America.

The Lower East Side was what I wrote about when I started writing and it was the focus of the *Portable Lower East Side*, the literary magazine I created in 1983 and which I published for ten years. My magazine celebrated the oppositional culture that existed in the neighborhood (and throughout the city) with such theme issues as Crimes of the City, Live Sex Acts, Chemical City, Songs of the City, Queer City, Latin Americans in NYC, New Africa and New Asia.

My father was born and brought up in Williamsburg, Brooklyn, the son of Russian Jewish immigrants. His uncle owned a candy store on Delancey Street, a hangout for local Jewish gangs, and as a kid my father divided his free time between the candy store and Coney Island, where he made money dragging clients in to see the freak show. My mother, the daughter of Ukrainian Jews, had grown up in Los Angeles and moved to NYC when she was young, where she took jobs in factories in Lower Manhattan to organize workers into unions. When they got married, they moved into a tiny, cold-water tenement apartment on Avenue B and 2nd Street.

My father set up a lithography workshop and gallery on 10th Street, and then later moved his workshop to Chrystie Street. When my parents got divorced in the 70s, he moved into a one-room tenement apartment on Tompkins Square Park.

In 1979, I moved into an apartment on Avenue B and 2nd Street, practically next door to where my mother and father had lived. After that, I constantly moved around in search of low rent, and low rent led me to some of the most culturally rich areas of the city. I lived in illegal sublets all over the Lower East Side, including in a basement apartment in a Puerto Rican family neighborhood on Ridge Street, in an industrial building on East Canal in Chinatown and above a restaurant in Little India on 6th Street.

Low rent in the Lower East Side, however, was about to become extinct. When local and international financial markets recovered and real estate investors had bought up enough neighborhood property to control the market, the banks lifted the red lines and development took off. Even with its long history of working-class, immigrant, oppositional culture, the neighborhood fast became a a trendy neighborhood for all the upscale mid-Americans working on Wall Street or attending NYU or Cooper Union and the Euro-trash trust-funders who could afford high rents. The neighborhood flipped as chain stores replaced local businesses, contemporary art galleries replaced Puerto Rican bodegas and condos invaded rent-controlled buildings.

The Lower East Side, which had long been one of the toughest NYC neighborhoods, quickly became a global tourist destination and a high-rent district. The working-class Jews, blacks and Puerto Ricans in the neighborhood, no longer able to afford the skyrocketing rents and the steep prices of basic goods, were forced to move out of the neighborhood and into the outer boroughs or other low rent areas surrounding the city. I moved a little farther.

Me in Mexico

I came to Mexico City in the summer of 1989 to study Spanish for a couple of months. I had already traveled to the Dominican Republic and Puerto Rico and my lack of Spanish had made me feel like a stupid gringo rather than a kid from *el barrio*. It was time I learned so that, when I returned to New York City, I could read Latin American literature in the original, talk to my neighbors and order food at the corner bodega.

I knew almost nothing about Mexico City before I went there, though I had some early contact with Mexican culture. My older brothers were born in Manhattan but my younger sister and I were born in San Diego, practically on the border between the US and Mexico. My parents took us to Tijuana several times, and as kids we had piñatas at our birthday parties, played with Mexican jumping beans and ate burritos. My father had studied painting at the Esmeralda art school in Mexico City in the 50s and he often would tell us stories about helping Diego Rivera paint a mural in the Rio Lerma Water Works and about making tin lamps in El Centro to make enough money to eat in *cocinas económicas*.

In the late 70s, I worked as a busboy in Los Panchos on the Upper West Side, a Mexican restaurant that was owned and run by Spaniards and served Tex-Mex food, and in the mid-80s I went to Los Angeles, visited the Mexican section of downtown and the main market that sold Mexican goods, and crossed the border into Ensenada for an afternoon. I was a fan of Los Tigres del Norte and *Alarma!* magazine, I had seen lots of Mexican movies and read Mexican novels, but I still had no real idea what Mexico City was like.

Flying into Mexico City that first night was a scary experience, not because of the city's reputation for violence and crime (having lived in the Lower East Side so long I had no fear of so-called dangerous cities), but because I didn't know a single soul in the whole city and had no idea even where I was going to stay that first night.

A Mexican painter who crashed my going-away party the night before I left New York City had given me the phone number of his girlfriend. She didn't know who I was or what I was doing ringing her doorbell at night but she was nice enough to let me sleep on a couch in her apartment for a few days. That first night she took me to a performance by a Polish artist who lit his stomach on fire, and then on to the Covadonga, a Spanish cantina that was the after-gallery drinking spot. In the first few days in Mexico City I met more people than I had in the last years back home. The fact that I was from New York City impressed locals enough to open up doors to fancy parties and openings, despite the fact that I wore tee-shirts, ripped jeans and sneakers.

I dropped out of my Spanish classes after just a couple of weeks. Having to wake up early and battle the morning commuters in the Metro to travel halfway across the city was too much for me. Besides, I was learning the language directly from the tongue of a woman I had met and who would later become my wife and the mother of my three children. It was because of her, and the social life I had fallen into down here, that I went back to NYC, quit my job teaching World Literature at City College, packed up my few possessions, kissed my mom goodbye and moved down to Mexico City.

I moved to Mexico City in 1989 but it felt like I had been transported even further back in time. Without American chain stores or fast food restaurants, without condos and boutiques, without yuppies or Euro-trash, the city still had its own unique, local culture. *Lucha libre* arenas, boxing gyms, huge old cinemas, giant old dance halls with live salsa and *cumbia* bands filled up with locals almost every night. Funky old buses with landscape paintings on the back window circulated throughout the city, while a cheap, clean, silent Metro snaked underground. Street stands sold an incredible selection of Mexican slash-and-burn and porno magazines, books and comics. Taco and quesadilla stands served cheap delicious eats on almost every corner at all hours of the day and night, while dignified old cantinas and *pulquerías* served fine spirits in funky atmospheres. Local brands of alcohol, beer, cigarettes and sodas had incredible designs and labels inspired by Aztec civilization or Colonial Mexico and hand-painted signs hung outside every small shop. Unlike NYC, local working-class culture in Mexico City was still alive and well and flourishing.

My first years in Mexico City were the happiest, most carefree years of my life. I learned a new language, had direct contact with a culture that stretched back thousands of years, and traveled all around the country, getting to know it better than I did the United States. The woman I lived with, originally from the coast of Chiapas, was part Spanish, part Lebanese, part indigenous, with raven-black hair, black eyes and golden-brown skin. Smart, beautiful and sexy, she was comfortable talking to anyone from all classes and regions of the country, and she knew how to get around the city better than most taxi drivers. Her face and body graced the cover of several magazines but she was also the woman who designed the magazines. Unlike the millions of Mexicans risking their lives crossing the northern border, she had no desire to leave her city and live the American Dream. She had a great life in Mexico City and she was willing to share it with me.

Much of our socializing revolved around the city's art galleries, which at that time mostly showed the work of local painters, all of whom my wife knew and many for whom she had designed exhibition catalogs. I didn't like the work, too colorful and too full of nationalist icons, a cross between 80s European painting and Frida Kahlo marketing, far removed from the funky streets of the city, but the free beer and tequila made it a great scene.

Around the same time as me, several young artists from Europe, the US and South America had arrived in Mexico City. Most of them lived in giant, incredibly cheap apartments in *El Centro* (the historic center of the city) and most of them worked the city into their art with found objects, objects sold on the street and in markets, and garbage. Although they weren't Mexican, by incorporating objects and places specific to Mexico City, their work was much more Mexican than the work of the painters being exhibited in the commercial galleries. I wrote about their work, I helped organize exhibitions in their apartments. With my wife, I started up *Poliester*, a contemporary art magazine of the Americas, where we showcased their work alongside artists doing similar work in NYC, Rio de Janeiro, Havana and Bogotá, and I co-curated an exhibition of 70 up-and-coming Latin American artists at the best contemporary art museum in Mexico City.

Even with the highlife that the art world provided, I never lost my love for working-class culture. I fell in love with three-cushion billiards (*carambola*) and the hustler culture within the funky old billiard halls. I bought a 70-year-old billiards hall in my neighborhood, cleaned it up and put in decent bathrooms, made it accessible to women (up until recently there were signs in all billiard halls that read: "No dogs, police or women allowed"), added a sound system on which I played funk music, and called it *Billares Americo* in honor of my recently born first son. A few years later, I wrote and directed *Carambola*, a semi-autobiographical film shot entirely within my billiard hall, starring Mexican actors (including Diego Luna and Roberto Cobo, the main actor from Luis Buñuel's *Los Olvidados*), cultural figures (Super Barrio), pool hustlers and Mexico's five-time world champion three-cushion billiard player. A few years later, I bought a 70-year-old Spanish restaurant/bar where we often ate lunch, cleaned it up and put in bathrooms, made it accessible to single women, and added live Cuban and funk music.

Both the billiards hall and the restaurant took off right away, the first 'trendy' businesses of their kind in the Condesa neighborhood. For years I made more money than I had ever dreamed of, traveled often all over Latin America and raised a family (my older son Americo and the twins Maximo and Primo). I had found my place on this planet. Moving to Mexico City was the best decision I had ever made. Life was great for me and I was truly happy. That is, until I got sick.

Time To Get ill

During my first ten years in Mexico City I almost never ate at home. Eating out was fun, exciting, an adventure. Hundreds of street stands sold cheap tacos, tortas, tamales and quesadillas, neighborhood markets offered an incredible range of seafood and meat dishes, small *fondas* served *comida corridas* (four-course meals of simple home-cooked food), nearby restaurants offered lime soup from the Yucatan, thick mole from Oaxaca, seafood from Sinaloa and grilled fish from Veracruz, and cantinas wheeled out a large selection of free *botanas* and finger food with the purchase of just a couple of beers. An inevitable outcome of eating out every day, often three times a day, were the bouts of the weird shits (popularly known as Moctezuma's Revenge). Eating out in Mexico City was always a crapshoot, but somehow everything would just pass through me without doing any lasting damage.

Everything changed, however, during a trip to Peru. I rented a car and drove south from Lima without a fixed destination, and wound up running around a white-sand desert, skiing down dunes and snorting near-pure cocaine, feeling incredibly healthy and alive. Then, when I was driving back up north to Lima, all of a sudden and without warning my guts exploded and shit came gushing out of me. I screeched to a halt on the side of the road, pulled my pants down and stared in amazement and horror at the mix of blood and pus and brown mush spilling out of my underwear. I cleaned myself as best I could with the road map and then drove another couple of hours back to my hotel, sneaking past the reception desk, jogging past the Beverly Hills Gym and slamming the door behind me in the safety of my elegant hotel room.

Perhaps it was the sushi at an art opening, the roast chicken at a restaurant in downtown Lima, or the sweet potato and raw scallops I ate in a bar on the Pacific Ocean. In any case, that night I broke out in a cold sweat, shivering uncontrollably, my jaw clenched and all the bones in my body feeling like they were about to crack. I had to drag myself several times an hour from my bed across the room to the bathroom, where I would hug the toilet and vomit out blood at the same time as slime oozed out of my ass. It seemed as if my body was turning itself inside out to rid itself of an alien invader. Every time I closed my eyes and tried to sleep horrible scenes of ultra-violence would be projected onto the back of my eyelids.

I somehow managed to get to the airport the following day, board my plane and make it back to my home in Mexico City. The intense fever and bone chills died down after a few days. This was by far the worst bout of the weird shits I had ever experienced, but I was strong, I could hold out long enough for my body to deal with whatever it was that was attacking me. I could get my shit together all by myself.

For the next couple of weeks, all that was solid melted in my large intestine and I shit my guts out up to twenty times a day, with as little as thirty seconds warning before my intestines let loose. It was dangerous for me to leave my house and I often had to race back to my bathroom after getting less than a block away. In my sickened state, the city became reduced to a series of pit stops strung along my route, with crowds and traffic getting in the way of an easy access to a toilet. I got to know intimately restaurant, bar, cafe, museum, gas station and parking lot bathrooms all over the city. The dirtiest, most disgusting toilets, overflowing with human waste, without toilet paper or running water, were almost holy refuges to me. Even places that weren't designed to receive human excrement worked just fine in a pinch.

One day I weighed myself and saw that I had lost a substantial percentage of my body weight. It was then that I realized that whatever was inside me wasn't going to go away on its own. Unlike all the microorganisms I'd ingested since I moved to Mexico City, whatever it was that was attacking me was more than my body's defenses could handle.

I went to a doctor. I told him about my trip to Peru and described my symptoms. I told him about the long translucent strands that floated in the toilet along with the diarrhea and the blood. He asked a few questions, took my blood pressure and prescribed some medicine for the worms he believed had colonized my colon. I took the medicine, the pharmaceutical equivalent of napalm, and imagined the bloodsucking worms inside me being blown to bits, them and their whole family. It was a good feeling to be on the road to recovery and I wondered why I had waited so long to seek help.

A week later I hadn't gotten any better and my life force continued to ooze out my ass. I filled up small plastic jars with my urine and shit and took them to a nearby lab. Three days later the results of the analyses came back: no worms. Just thinking about the poison I had taken to kill off worms that never existed and what that had done to my already weakened system made me feel even sicker. According to the lab report, what I had was salmonella. A ten-day dose of antibiotics got rid of all the salmonella in my body. Although that should have fixed me up, I still suffered from the weird shits and blood continued to drip out of me.

I went to have a colonoscopy in order to find out what was really going on in there. A fiber-optic camera was shoved up my ass and took a fantastic journey deep inside my large intestine, videotaping the whole thing. As I was coming out of the anesthesia, still groggy and disoriented, a doctor gave me the lowdown of what he had found. When I got home and looked chronic ulcerative colitis up in a medical handbook, I felt even sicker. Like AIDS, chronic ulcerative colitis is an immune disorder, and it shares with AIDS many of the same symptoms and, at times, the same prognosis. Also known as irritable bowel syndrome, chronic ulcerative colitis produces diarrhea, pus, fever and anemia, and can lead to septicemia and shock. In severe cases, a person's nose, eyes and ears can swell up horribly due to intestinal pain.

According to what a gastroenterologist later told me when I showed him the colonoscopy video (or the colitis-scope, as I now called it), the salmonella that had invaded my body kicked-started a latent genetic aberration buried inside the last segment of my digestive tract, causing my body's defenses to consider my large intestine as an alien that must be attacked. He put me on a steady diet of anti-inflammatory medicine and a very high dose of cortisone. The drugs helped diminish the blood and slime and tightened up my bowel movements a bit, but I was still scrambling to the bathroom several times a day. To make things worse, I always seemed to run a low-level fever, I felt weak and I continued to lose weight. In addition, the cortisone weakened my knees, summoned up zits on my neck and upper arms, and made my tits swell.

Nothing I ate, drank, smoked or sniffed helped my condition, while lots of these things triggered or increased the intensity of the colitis. I was ordered to give up all spicy foods, chocolate, coffee, black tea, carbonated liquids, cocaine, amphetamines and even alcohol, as they all irritated my large intestine and worsened my condition (depressing news, as many of these substances are designed to combat the depression that chronic illness generates).

In New York City my friends called me Skinny and in Mexico City I was *Flaco*. From the day I got sick I started to lose weight and I continued to lose weight for years, going way beyond skinny and ending up merely thin skin wrapped around emaciated bones. The long tube that stretched from my mouth to my asshole, that is, my digestive system, designed to provide me with enough energy to live and prosper, had serious plumbing problems and the leakage drained my body of energy. Often, the expensive pills I took to lessen my intestinal inflammation (and thus to give my body time to absorb nutrients from the food I ate) reappeared intact floating in the toilet. Life dripped out of me and I couldn't for the life of me figure out how to stop it. The long-term result of losing weight seemed inevitable. For the first time in my life, trapped in a sick, genetically flawed body, I felt what it was like to be dying.

Adapt Or Die Although not responsible for the salmonella bacteria that was wreaking havoc within my digestive system, I blamed Mexico City (or Make-Sicko Shitty, as I began to call it) for its poor quality air, food and water that aggravated my illness and prevented me from getting healthy. As my Russian Jewish grandmother would have put it, Mexico City disagreed with me.

When Darwin coined the term survival of the fittest he didn't mean the strongest or the most intelligent, he meant those who could best adapt to their surroundings. In order to live a healthy life in a mega-city such as Mexico City where death is everywhere, you must adapt even faster. Not only must you adapt to the local food, water, air and alcohol, but also to its twenty million inhabitants, to their sense of time and obligations, and to the way they walk and talk.

Speaking a new language takes time, and during the learning process you are basically an idiot unable to communicate your thoughts and needs. If you learn a language late in life, like me, communicating never really becomes completely natural, you're always translating internally and your accent never sounds native. (Since I already spoke French, having lived in Paris for a year, I at least don't suffer from a gringo accent.) Mexicans tend to inject *brillo* into their conversation, working it to the max and gesticulating emphatically. I speak Spanish well but tend to mumble, speak flatly and without flair. My stumbling in Spanish is often seen as a lack of fluidity or knowledge of the language, but I do the same in English. And I refused to be ultra-polite and use the formal *usted* instead of *tu*, both of which are essential parts of being Mexican. All of this, of course, labels me as an outsider and adds a bit of stress to my everyday interactions.

Learning how to drive in Mexico City is also a process of adaptation. Either you drive like a *chilango*, king of the road and scourge of all pedestrians, or else you end up constantly honking your horn and cursing everybody. The road is divided between *pendejos* (idiots) and *ojetes* (assholes), and you must decide which side of the street you're on and how much stress you're willing to take just to make it to your destination. Having seen several hit-and-runs, having seen dozens of cars wrapped around lampposts or encrusted within other cars, having seen my share of pedestrians scraped off the street after an accident, I can't help but slip into attack mode when I cross paths with someone who drives like an asshole on wheels.

There are certain fundamental things that keep me from fully adapting and blending in, though. For one thing, I'm taller than most Mexicans and with my shaved head I stick out like a sore thumb. I'm Jewish in a Catholic country and atheist in a religious culture. I'm a writer in a country with one of the lowest literacy rates in the Americas. I can speak the language, walk the walk, and I know the ins and outs of street life, but I am not from here and it's obvious.

Being an individual, however, even in a foreign culture, is all about breaking the rules, creating your own style, trashing the traditions. So why should I, a true individual, bother to adapt to the Mexico City way of life? To live longer, that's why. Not adapting to local cultural styles wears you down and puts an extra strain on your heart and on your immune system. Basing your identity on the differences between yourself and those that surround you takes its toll, and going head-to-head with a city as large and intense as Mexico City, trying to change it or loathing it for how it is, is a lost battle. For many of the millions of immigrants (including all those from the Mexican countryside) that move to the big city, daily life is a constant battle that serves only to speed us to our grave. Ambrose Bierce once said that being a gringo in Mexico is a form of euthanasia, and I'd have to agree with him, especially in regards to Mexico City.

Before I got sick I never really took death very seriously. When people I knew dropped dead around me I considered their deaths an extension of their character. A Chilean friend (my editor at the weekly cultural supplement of *La Jornada*) crashed his car into a lamppost while driving drunk at four in the morning. A Mexican curator, unable to handle the alcohol she constantly poured into her body, died from pancreatic cancer. A Mexican editor threw himself in front of a Metro train and a Mexican artist threw himself off a roof. Several local and imported artists and photographers simply drank and smoked themselves to death.

Only now that I'm sick do I realize that the character of the deceased had nothing to do with the cause of death. Their deaths were all intimately tied to the fact that they couldn't really adapt to Mexico City.

Mexico In Me

I could be Mexican. Being married to a Mexican, having children born in Mexico, having lived in the country for so many years, all make me eligible for citizenship. I need only fill out a short form, pay a modest fee, take a simple history test and I'd be Mexican. But whom would I be fooling? I'm not Mexican nor ever will be, despite any future changes in my legal status. Right now I'm a permanent resident in Mexico, an immigrant, and that suits me just fine. Like the title of the movie in which *La India María* (Mexico's indigenous version of Charlie Chaplin) crosses the border into the US: *ni de aquí, ni de allá* (not from here, not from there).

In the end, though, being Mexican isn't really about having a Mexican passport, nor is it about speaking the language with a particular accent or even having a certain skin color. It's what's inside that counts. Having eaten the food, drunk the water and alcohol and breathed in the air in Mexico city almost every day for over twenty years, I have incorporated a microscopic Mexico City inside my body. In addition to the pollution and toxic chemicals that cloud my lungs and clog my arteries, several of my inner organs provide shelter to communities of bacteria, viruses, parasites and amoebas, all of them originally immigrants but now permanent residents, with me until the day I die.

Just as major cities tend to be more cosmopolitan and richer in immigrant culture, so too those of us who live in mega-cities host a truly multicultural flora and fauna. Only recently have scientists started identifying the microscopic civilizations residing within the human body, and they have found distinct communities of bacteria in the human mouth, within the nose and lungs, on the skin, inside the vagina or around the crotch, and deep inside the gut. Although some of these communities share certain species, each represents a different cultural mix, much like separate cities within a single nation. The greatest concentration of microorganisms exist inside the large intestines of humans. Just as humans are divided into blood types, so too they can be classified by the different strains of bacterial colonies within their large intestine. No two human beings have the same mix of microorganisms inside them, and inhabitants of different cities are characterized by different micro-cities of microorganisms within them. Three distinct bacteria colonies have been identified so far, although since only European intestines were examined a much greater variety within the inhabitants of more biologically diverse regions of the world, such as Mexico, must exist.

When scientists recently began to elaborate the first census of human genes, they were shocked to find that the greatest amount of genetic material within the human body is not human. A human body is comprised of approximately ten trillion cells, but within our large intestine alone there are ten times that many microorganisms. Most of these microorganisms are bacteria (as many as 1,000 different species), although viruses, amoebas, fungi and protozoa are lodged in there, as well. After having co-existed and co-evolved with humans for so many hundreds of thousands of years, and after having adapted their functions to our biological system, this vast, highly complex and socially interactive micro-mega-city now acts as a virtual organ within our large intestine. We depend upon these billions of bacteria to help up assimilate vitamins, encode enzymes, regulate the immune system and aid in the digestive process.

Scientists are only beginning to get a glimpse of how the micro-mega-city inside our gut interacts with our body. Our digestive tract has its own nervous system, a network of neurons so extensive and complex that some call it our second brain. Known as the enteric nervous system, this complex system of nerves embedded in the walls of our gut contains some 100 million neurons (more than the spinal cord or the peripheral nervous system) and is equipped with its own reflexes and senses. Contrary to what most scientists believed for so long, this second brain does not exist merely to control peristalsis and other mechanical processes. In fact, about 90 percent of the fibers in the vagus nerve, the largest direct connection between our gut and our head, carry information and instructions from our large intestine to our central nervous system, not the other way around.

The question that is currently being debated in the scientific community is what information and instructions does this second brain transmit to our central nervous system and, even more importantly, who is sending these signals? It turns out that the microorganisms that have colonized our colon use this neural connection as their own private hotline, calling in orders as well as taking calls from the upper brain. Our brain communicates with the microorganisms in our gut directly (by molecules released into the gut from neurons or immune cells) and indirectly (via changes in gastrointestinal movement and secretion, and intestinal permeability), while our gut microorganisms communicate with the human brain by means of receptor signaling, manipulating glandular activity or through direct stimulation of host cells in the gut lining.

This intimate interaction between humans and microorganisms is known as inter-kingdom communication and is much more frequent and important than previously suspected. The exchange of information and orders between the microorganisms in our gastrointestinal tract and the nerves in our brain is vital for maintaining homeostasis, that is, health and well-being, while communication breakdowns are responsible for many illnesses. (One of the most common inter-kingdom miscommunication turns out to be chronic ulcerative colitis in which, due to the misguided distress signals it receives from the bowels, the body over-reacts to the presence of non-aggressive microorganisms by attacking its own large intestine.)

Homeostasis depends upon the constant regulation of chemicals circulating between our gut and head. More than thirty neurotransmitters, including 95 percent of the body's serotonin (a chemical directly linked to depression and mood shifts), flow through our large intestine, influencing our emotional state and our mental health. The extent to which microorganisms control our behavior, feelings and thoughts is still mostly a mystery, but the fact that microorganisms, especially aggressive parasites, can manipulate us to serve their needs is widely accepted.

Parasites can gain control over us by depleting our system of needed vitamins and minerals, by excreting toxins that weaken us and by deactivating our immune system (making us even more susceptible to control by incoming parasitic viruses, bacteria and other microorganisms). Parasites modify human behavior in specific ways and for specific purposes. Parasite infection in male human beings has been correlated to memory loss, shorter attention span, greater risk-taking, decreased novelty-seeking, lower rule-consciousness, increased violence, irritability and jealousy. Certain parasites in women make them more intelligent, generous, outgoing, friendly and promiscuous. These behaviors serve to make both men and women, each in their own way, ideal vehicles for the spread and survival of these parasite species.

Acting in a direct way, certain common parasites such as *Toxoplasma gondii* (present in the majority of inhabitants of mega-cities) can cross the blood-brain barrier and directly provoke physiological changes involved in the development of schizophrenia, bipolar disorders, Parkinson's disease, Tourette's syndrome and attention deficit disorders. Psychiatric illness (especially depression and mood swings) are much more co-dependent on gastrointestinal disorders than previously thought. Because of their invisible influence, parasites could be considered our biological unconscious, responsible in large part for our personality, and for our personality flaws, as well.

Microorgansims, however, are responsible not only for certain individual behaviors and mental disorders, but also class differences (lower classes have more contact with parasites) and gender differences (men are twice as prone to parasite infections). Even the character of a particular culture depends upon the particular species of parasites present and their population density. For instance, certain parasite infestations most commonly found in large cities has been associated with a high level of neurotic behavior. As an example of a specific cultural character associated with parasites, the behavior of the typical Mexican macho, whose penchant for spitting in public or having children with multiple women, rather than stemming from a lack of education as is commonly believed, could actually be parasites' means of propagation.

Since human beings first emerged on the planet, microorganisms have used us as vehicles to perpetuate their own species, and they have always been one of the driving forces of our species' development. Although their essential and existential role in shaping our culture, religion and even the evolution of our species has been concealed until only very recently by man's own narcissism and anthropocentrism, much of our civilization has been the result of our intimate relationship with both beneficial bacteria and parasites.

As such, histories and biographies should include not only the culture in which a person lives but also the cultures living within them. In my case, microorganisms provided me with the subject of this book, came up with the book's parasite-eye view and gave the narration its paranoid tinge. Although I call this book an autobiography, that doesn't mean necessarily that I am the sole author or protagonist. I have no problem sharing my life's destiny with billions of microorganisms, nor sharing the credit of this book with so many ghostwriters.

Multiculture Although I dedicated much of my early cultural activity to promoting the multicultural mix of the Lower East Side, publishing Puerto Rican, Dominican, Haitian, Chinese, Polish, Rumanian and Jamaican writers and artists, it was Mexico City that taught me what it means to be truly multicultural. Over and above the European presence (from the families descended from the original colonizers to the newest influx of hipsters from France), the longstanding Jewish and Arab communities and the more recent Southern Cone and Central American emigrants, the immigration into Mexico City from dozens of distinct indigenous communities in the countryside has made the city truly multicultural.

Even beyond this human mix, however, Mexico City's greatest cultural wealth is its biodiversity, especially the thousands of species of microorganisms that represent the city's true indigenous inhabitants. Although microorganisms exist in all parts of the city, the working and lower class *barrios* in Mexico City (like the ghettos and slums throughout New York City's history) concentrate within them the greatest diversity of microorg those living in the most densely populated urban spaces tend to benefit from the mutation abilities and symbiosis of bacterial cultures. anisms, and this is precisely where the greatest interspecies communication occurs (low life and lower life forms have always had an intimate relation).

As a rule, wherever there is a wealth of microscopic culture there tends to be an active, local human culture, as well. Those living in densely populated urban areas tend to benefit from the mutation abilities and symbiosis of bacterial cultures. Because their gut flora, decimated by poor diet, poverty and stress, lacks the proper defenses, slum dwellers tend to suffer more from the diseases associated with parasites and thus live shorter lives. Excluded from the formal economy and vulnerable to dangerous governments and businesses, and open game for all types of aggresive parasites, the city's poor must constantly create new strategies to survive and thus slums have always been the fertile ground for cultural creation. (To give just one example, the South Bronx of the 1970s and '80s, one of the most impoverished, unhealthy and 'dangerous' neighborhoods in the world, gave rise to Salsa, rap, breakdance and graffiti).

Although slum dwellers have the closest contact to parasites, it is in fact the upper classes that are so often portrayed as parasites. Capitalists, like parasites, exploit the weakness of other organisms and communities and suck other people's life energy for personal profit. Just as antibiotics weaken gut flora and thus allow for more foreign penetrations, so too free trade agreements weaken local industry and unions and pave the way for market exploitation and neo-colonialism, forms of economic parasitism. The drive to colonize new worlds and the willingness to slaughter millions of human beings for personal profit could very well have come from the widespread presence of parasites in humans after the plagues that ravaged much of Europe.

Today, the latest trend in corporate global expansion continues to mimic parasitic activity, invading civilizations, transforming the existing structure, extracting energy and ultimately depleting health and leading to the death of the cultures. Lower classes *barrios* or slums, on the other hand, tend to resemble bacterial colonies, forging communities to pool resources and to defend their territory against invasion, and within these communities there exists greater cultural change and innovation, as can be seen in the local language, fashion, dance and music. ✝

DEATH VALLEY

A Note About My Sources

After having lived in Mexico City a few years, I took a series of photographs of everyday things (a glass of water, a bottle of rotgut mezcal, a bus going against traffic, a hole in the ground, etc) which I titled Several Ways to Die in Mexico City and which I exhibited in an alternative gallery called Salón des Aztecas. As I hadn't yet had my run-in with salmonella and colitis, the work was a play on gringo paranoia. Although none of the photographs from that series are included in this book, the idea of searching for death in the everyday life of the city was inspired by this earlier project.

Years later, after getting sick, I began writing somewhat regularly for the London Guardian Weekly. Without planning it, without even realizing it at first, most of what I wrote was about death in Mexico City, and eventually those articles gave rise to this book. In addition, the texts I wrote on popular Mexican consumer culture for my two photobooks (El Super and Sonora: The Magic Market) have been reworked and incorporated into this book, as was an article on edible insects I wrote for The Ecologist.

Besides pirating my own writing, information presented in this book comes from a wide variety of printed and digital material, in both Spanish and English, including but not limited to: newspapers (five years worth of clippings from Reforma, La Jornada and Spain's El País); academic journals (especially Arqueología); the Scientific Electronic Library Online (offering dozens of health-related journals such as Salud Pública de México); reports from El Centro Mario Molino (the Mexican Nobel scientist's research center on air pollution in Mexico City); the Human Genome Project and the Human Microbiome Project; The National Center for Biotechnology Information; Mexico City government websites (such as the Secretaría de Medio Ambiente) and Federal government websites (mortality statistics come from

29

the *Sistema Nacional de Información en Salud*); the NIH; web pages of corporations (such as Coca Cola and Monsanto) and of NGOs (such as Greenpeace); and hundreds of books (everything from the bloody diaries of Hernán Cortés and Bartolomé de las Casas' *Brevísima Relación de la Destrucción de las Indias* to the three-volume, lavishly illustrated *Memoria de las obras del sistema de drenaje profundo del distrito federal*, a history of sewers in Mexico City published in 1975). A special thanks goes out to my local bookstore, *La Librería del Fondo*, for allowing me to read through a large part of their well-stocked history, anthropology and science sections while sitting in a comfortable armchair in a well-lit space two blocks from my house.

In addition to the printed and digital sources, I conducted interviews with dozens of experts in life and death, including: the director of the Mexico City morgue; a Vatican-approved exorcist; an anthropologist who works in the Chapultepec Castle and another who works in the Metropolitan Cathedral; the custodian of the Santa Muerte altar in Tepito; caretakers in several cemeteries; shamans and traditional healers in the Sonora Market; all kinds of doctors and health care practitioners; and last but not least, bartenders in *pulquerías* all over the city.

Given that all facts and figures come with a point of view, huge differences exist in the death tolls for the most lethal events that occurred within the city, including: the number of natives killed during the Conquest; the number of heretics put to death during the Inquisition; the number of innocents murdered by the government during the 1968 student protests; and the number of victims of the 1985 earthquake. Even statistics as seemingly straightforward as the population of Mexico City have a deviance as large as the population of Acapulco. Although I haven't invented any facts and figures I can't say the same for all my sources. When in doubt I tended to choose the most dramatic figures available which, if not always the most accurate, at least err on the side of myth and make for a more exciting story, as befits the history of such an amazing, and amazingly brutal, place as Mexico City.

Death and Life of Great Mexican Cities

Although to the first nomadic tribes it surely must have looked like an earthly paradise, cradled as it was by a protective mountain range, carpeted with lush greenery, blessed with five lakes and innumerable freshwater springs, the Mexico City Valley has always been a disaster waiting to happen.

A major fault line runs right through the Mexico City Valley. Earthquakes have regularly rocked the Valley while volcanic activity has buried vast stretches of land beneath lava. Rainy seasons are characterized by torrential rainfall and severe flooding, dry seasons provoke droughts and harsh winters bring with them icy frost and hailstorms. Although Nature is as cruel as it is whimsical (a single day can include the worst of all four seasons), by far the greatest disaster to ever hit the Mexico City Valley was human beings.

The first thing the original immigrants did when they climbed up and over the mountains surrounding the Mexico City Valley and entered its lush, fertile paradise was to cut down the trees and kill off the animals that had made it such a paradise. Nomadic hunters and gatherers roamed the Valley for thousands of years, killing and eating most everything that moved. The larger mammals (woolly mammoths, mastodons, camels, bison and small horses) quickly became converted into food and whole species began to disappear.

Once the supply of meat had finally run out life got a lot harder and people were forced to huddle together in primitive agricultural settlements and to scratch the earth for their daily sustenance. Once they had settled and organized themselves enough to count on a steady supply of food, human beings in the Valley began to dedicate their time to what they do best, namely, making babies. The population of the settlements rose exponentially and villages gave birth to towns and eventually to cities.

Given the means, human communities will inevitably reach a critical population density, and the concentration of so many human mouths in one place will generate demands that nature can no longer supply. Great civilizations ineluctably cause widespread destruction of their environment, but when nature starts dying she makes sure to take lots of humans with her. Yet nature doesn't kill people so much as people kill people. The disasters that ravage mankind are, if not created by man, at least aided and abetted by his handiwork and presence. If an earthquake hits an empty valley it's a natural event. In the Mexico City Valley, which has been swarming with human beings for thousands of years, nature can't make the slightest move without provoking a disaster.

By 600 BC, Cuicuilco, originally a farming village in the south of the Mexico City Valley, became its first urban center, boasting several large pyramids within a city of 20,000 people. Eight hundred years later, an eruption of the Xitle volcano wiped out Cuicuilco (perhaps the greatest city within all the Americas at that time) and buried 80 square kilometers of land under boiling lava. Those who survived the eruption fled to the emerging city of Teotihucan in the northeast of the Valley. Teotihuacan eventually reached a population of 250,000 souls packed tightly within eight square miles, making it larger and more densely populated than any European city of the time. The great civilization of Teotihuacan ("the place where the gods live" or "the place where men become gods") was built around the Sun and

Moon pyramids, which ranked among the world's greatest cultural and architectural achievements up to that time.

Pyramids marked the center of all great cities in the Valley, their height attesting to the level of the culture's achievement, yet in no way were they mere stone monuments erected only for the edification of the gods. Pyramids were, in fact, carefully constructed death machines. Not only were hundreds or even thousands of humans sacrificed in temples on top of the pyramids, especially during the inaugurations, but the city's most eminent citizens were also buried within the bowels of these pyramids (the Sun pyramid was constructed above a cave that served as a tomb).

In addition to offering a sacred site for sacrifices and sarcophaguses, the very construction of the pyramids brought about mass death. It took over 10,000 slaves and forced laborers twenty years to build the Sun pyramid, and work-related deaths were quite common. In order to make room for the giant ceremonial city and to provide the wood needed for the fires used to make the pyramids' building materials, the surrounding forests were leveled. This massive deforestation killed off edible plants and chased off insects and animals, thus depleting the city's food sources and leading to widespread malnourishment. Forcing the city's inhabitants to work on the construction site interrupted local subsistence farming, and thus the demand for and dependency upon tributes from the empire's colonies (which stretched as far away as the Gulf of Mexico) increased. This extra burden forced upon both local and distant communities fed into the social discontent that eventually paved the way for civil war and invasions, and in the end Teotihuacan's pyramids, the embodiment of the heights this civilization had achieved, helped pave the way to the city's downfall.

The fall of Teotihuacan, perhaps the largest city on the planet at that time, gave way to a long period of invasions by the primitive Chicihmeca tribes (known as dog-eaters) from the north. The Toltecs were one of the first groups of Chichimecas to settle in the central region of Mexico, and they established their urban center Tollán in Tula, less than one hundred kilometers from the Mexico City Valley. Tollán benefited from the wave of immigration of survivors from Teotihuacan, incorporating into its own culture the Teotihuacan roster of gods, much of its arts and architecture (including pyramids), and its penchant for human sacrifice, as well. Like Teotihuacan before it, the Toltecs became an imperial civilization dominating not only the Mexico City Valley but also lands as far away as the southern Pacific coast. And just like the Teotihuacans before them, the Toltecs, a civilization based on human sacrifice and pyramids, were brought down abruptly by civil unrest that weakened the city's defenses and left it vulnerable to invasion by northern tribes.

Blood Splattered on the Walls

Beginning around 600 AD, several waves of Chichimeca tribes emigrated from the north and settled in the Mexico City Valley (some helping to topple the Toltecs). The Chichimecas in Aztlan, located somewhere in northwestern Mexico (or perhaps as far away as California), were most likely forced to emigrate for the same reasons that had promoted the earlier massive migrations (over-exploitation of resources, droughts that led to widespread hunger, civil war, or a combination of all three).

The Aztecs were the last of the nomadic Chichimeca tribes, emigrating from Aztlan sometime around the year 1,000 AD. The Aztecs wandered across the nation for over 300 years in search of a new homeland. Even when they arrived within the Mexico City Valley, though, the Aztecs continued moving from place to place for almost two hundred years, usually remaining in any one site for only a few decades as the locals rarely tolerated this tribe of uncivilized ruffians for very long (the Aztecs had a bad reputation for ultra violence and for stealing married women from other tribes).

Of all the beautiful places overflowing with fresh water and lush flora and fauna within the Mexico City Valley, the Aztecs wound up building their great imperial city, Mexico-Tenochtitlan, on a rocky island in the Texcoco Lake surrounded by swampland. Despite this humble beginning, the Aztecs knew in their hearts of hearts that their bloodline was destined to rule the Valley. To achieve their destiny, however, more blood had to be shed than ever before.

Tlaloc and Huitzilopochtli were the two founding gods of Mexico-Tenochtitlan, and both had a predilection for blood. Tlaloc, the god of water, needed blood to fall in order to ensure rain for the crops, while Huitzilopochtli, the god of the sun, required blood to give him the strength to make the journey across the night sky and to defeat the darkness that engulfed the world each day.

The Aztecs became experts in providing the blood the gods required, regularly sacrificing wolves, pumas, hawks, owls, eagles, rattlesnakes and small, hairless dogs in their temples. Besides serving up the blood of animals, Aztecs regularly slashed and pricked their own bodies. Although everyone donated blood, the most fanatical bloodletters were the Aztec priests, experts in self-flagellation and self-mutilation, who would regularly pierce the skin of their penis with cactus spines, impale their penises with dry reeds that they would then light on fire, or even go so far as to flay the skin right off their sacred organ. If a priest fainted during these acts it was understood that they were tainted with sin and would thus have to go to even greater lengths of self-torture the next time.

Several of the games played within Mexico-Tenochtitlan provided fresh blood to the gods. Tlachtli, a ball game somewhere between soccer and basketball, was so popular that over 15,000 rubber balls were imported into the imperial city each year from Veracruz. Both winners and losers were sacrificed after the games.

Gladiator-style fights also yielded fresh blood. In these ceremonial battles, slaves captured in battle were forced to fight Aztec warriors. The battle was enacted upon a large, round stone with a hole in the middle through which the slave was tied to a rope to hamper their movements and to keep them from fleeing. The Aztec warriors were given thick clubs studded with jagged obsidian shards while the slaves received sticks adorned with feathers. Each slave had to fight up to five warriors, whose job it was to wound the slaves and knock them down, at which time a priest would quickly slit their throats.

As sacrificing their own citizens for religious purposes could have led to civil war, a constant flow of victims from outside the Aztec capital was ensured by *guerras floridas* (flowery or play wars) arranged with their neighbors in Tlaxcala and other cities, designed not so much to kill enemies on the battlefield as to capture them alive and to provide participants for the ritual games and ceremonial sacrifices.

Human sacrifice was at the heart of Aztec society, and the city's architecture was literally built around the act. The first major construction in Mexico-Tenochtitlan was the ceremonial center called the Templo Mayor. Much more than just a large temple, as its name indicates, the Templo Mayor grew to become a small city made up of more than 70 constructions, including 25 pyramids, nine houses for priests, two ball courts, three bath houses, arsenals, workshops, a prison for the conquered gods of other tribes, seven walls constructed of skulls and two basements where the skin that had been flayed off of the sacrificial victims was stored.

For the inaugural ceremonies of the Templo Mayor in 1487, thousands of prisoners and slaves, as well as a few dozen hunchbacks, midgets and freaks, had their blood splattered on the walls to consecrate the pyramid temples. The victims met their end through a variety of methods: shot full of arrows, stuck with spears, clawed or sliced to death, stoned or crushed, skinned alive, disemboweled, dismembered, burned or buried alive, or any combination of these techniques. Babies and children were sealed in caves or taken for a ride in a canoe and drowned in a lake. The most common and the most sacred human sacrifices was the cutting out of the heart from a victim's chest while he or she was tied down and stretched out upon a sacrificial stone. On special occasions, the victim would first be roasted over an open fire and then pulled out by a large hook before their still-beating heart was extracted.

Homicidal Maniacs

Even with all the wars, capital punishment, human sacrifices, droughts, earthquakes, floods and disease, the population in the Mexico City Valley during the Aztec empire grew to around one million souls, with an estimated 300,000 alone in the capital city. When Hernán Cortés and his men first set eyes on Mexico-Tenochtitlan, soon after their arrival in Mexico in 1518, the city had been around for less than 200 years but had already grown into the greatest imperial power in the New World, and perhaps the most densely populated city in the world at that time, as well.

Moctezuma (as his name is correctly spelled), the Aztec emperor at the time of the arrival of the Spaniards, threw Cortés a royal welcome upon his entrance into the city, one that befitted a god. In return, Cortés kidnapped Moctezuma and paraded him around as his patsy to fend off resistance. To make sure the locals got the message, the Spaniards massacred most of the Aztec nobility during a peaceful ceremony in the Templo Mayor. The Conquistadores, many of who had started their killing sprees in the holy wars against Moslems, could easily be described as homicidal maniacs or psychopaths, and were therefore well prepared to carry out such acts of violence.

After the massacre, however, the Aztecs gathered in force and the Spanish retreated from the city. On the so-called *Noche Triste* (Sad Night), hundreds of Spaniards and over one thousand of their indigenous allies were hunted down by Aztec warriors (with their pockets full of plundered treasure, many of the Conquistadores drowned in the lakes as they tried to escape), and more than two hundred Spaniards were captured alive and sacrificed to the Aztec gods the following day. After this military setback, the Spanish regrouped and rearmed, building large ships, laying siege to the city and cutting off its supply of food and fresh water. After months of siege, the Spaniards finally seized the Templo Mayor and captured Emperor Cuauhtémoc, thus ending the reign of the mighty Aztec civilization.

As mighty as it was, the Aztec empire was designed to conquer and control distant colonies, not to protect the heart of its empire. Before the war-hardened Spanish arrived, no one had been crazy enough to dare attack Mexico-Tenochtitlan. With the Aztec emperor in their control, Cortés and his 900 men, backed up by 150,000 indigenous allies, set to work massacring around 40,000 men, women and children within the city.

By the time Mexico-Tenochtitlan had finally been 'pacified' by the Spaniards, the city's population had been reduced to a mere 30,000 souls, one-tenth of what it might have been before the conquest. During the fifty years after the Spanish first set foot in the new continent the vast majority of Aztecs and other cultures were killed off, leaving only around three million natives in all of Mexico. (During the same period, the population in Spain increased by 50%, due in part to the riches flooding in from the newly conquered New World.) The large-scale massacre within Mexico-Tenochtitlan and throughout the country, however, was only partially the work of the cannons and swords of the Conquistadores. The Spaniards' local allies, especially the Tlaxcaltecas, numbering in the hundreds of thousands, did the lion share of the fighting, but even they couldn't claim the greatest number of kills.

The hundreds of Conquistadores that accompanied Cortés were not the only living creatures brought from Spain to wage war. The large horses and ferocious dogs the Spaniards brought with them proved to be great weapons against the Aztecs, not just striking horror in their hearts but also trampling them to death under their hooves or ripping large chunks of flesh out of their bodies with their fangs. The greatest weapon the Spanish conquistadores brought with them, however, was not a sword, cannon, wild horse nor mad dog, but rather something so small as to be invisible.

A Plague upon You The billions of microorganisms that had stowed away on the lice, rats, grazing animals and humans aboard the Spanish ships on their the long voyage from the Old to the New World should in fact be credited as the true conquerors of Mexico. After thousands of years of commerce and wars with nations spread out far and wide throughout several continents, Spain itself had been colonized by a mix of European, Asian and African parasites. Continually shuttling back and forth between domesticated animals and the humans that raised and consumed them, these parasites had evolved in their mastery over all species and represented new and improved biological weapons waiting to be unleashed on other cultures.

The Aztecs introduced the Spaniards to some of their own homegrown microorganisms, including those responsible for syphilis, intestinal diseases (Moctezuma's revenge), malaria and warts, but due to their prolonged exposure to microorganisms which had killed off millions of Europeans during the plague years, Conquistadors were mostly resistant to the local parasites and viruses of Mexico. Although these microorganisms sickened and even killed some they in no way wreaked the wholesale destruction that the Spaniards' microorganisms did amongst the natives.

Although the Aztec codices mention several potentially lethal parasites, Aztecs were not nearly as infested as Europeans. An efficient waste disposal system and abundant clean water, healthy hygienic habits and the fact that few Aztecs lived in close contact with animals kept parasites from flourishing. Unfortunately, their very healthiness and freedom from parasite infestation paved the way to the Aztec's downfall.

The Catholic Church viewed the plagues that decimated the native population as proof of their sins. The natives, on the other hand, were aware that their families and loved ones were being killed by the diseases that the lice-ridden Spaniards had brought with them to Mexico, and thus avoided physical contact with the Spaniards as much as possible. In addition to the Spaniards' 'lethal handshake', bathing babies in baptismal waters, eating the wafer from the hand of the priest or praying in churches surrounded by dead, festering bodies were ideal ways for natives to get sick and die. (Until the plagues ceased, natives saw the Catholic church not as the house of God but rather as the house of death, and thus resisted entering.)

Parasites imported from Europe to the New World produced the colds, flu, smallpox, diphtheria, typhoid fever, bubonic plague, leprosy, and scarlet and yellow fevers that swiftly decimated the majority of the indigenous population. The smallpox virus reached central Mexico in 1520 (purportedly carried by a sick African slave), traveling across Mexico even faster than Cortés and his troops. Before Cortés launched his attack against Mexico-Tenochtitlan, the virus had already begun wreaking death in epidemic proportions amongst the inhabitants.

The Aztec emperor Cuitlahuac, the man who had replaced Moctezuma after he was killed by his own people for not standing up to the Spaniards, died from smallpox, as did thousands of Aztec soldiers. The epidemic struck down entire households, adults as well as children, and with so many sick at the same time there was no one to provide food, water or care, and thus many who fell ill died not of smallpox but of hunger and dehydration.

When the Spaniards laid siege to Mexico-Tenochtitlan, cutting off the supply of water and food to the city, European viruses ravaged the city's population and did much of Cortés' dirty work for him. More than all the advanced European technology and military strategy, more than all the guns, swords, attack dogs or horses, diseases caused by microorganisms gave the greatest edge in combat to the Spanish.

The fall of Mexico-Tenochtitlan was by no means the end of the fighting, nor was it the end of disease. The Conquistadores opened a Pandora's box of aggressive microorganisms that quickly spread throughout the Mexico City Valley. Measles struck Mexico City for the first time in 1531, and smallpox returned in 1532 and 1538. European diseases such as smallpox, measles, and typhus have long been suspected as the sole cause of the native population collapse, but recent studies show that *matlazahuatl* or hemorrhagic fevers caused by an indigenous virus were responsible for some of the destruction, as well. Symptoms for this disease included high fever, headaches, vertigo, black tongue, dark urine, dysentery, severe abdominal and chest pain, large nodules behind the ears or on the neck and face, acute neurologic disorders and profuse bleeding from the nose, eyes and mouth, and death usually occurred within four days. The plague that swept through Mexico City in 1545 lasted three years and managed to kill as many as 15 million inhabitants, around 80% of the native population in Mexico, one of the worst catastrophes in human history. Yet another epidemic in 1576 killed an additional 2 to 2.5 million, or about 50% of the remaining native population.

Mumps, influenza and other epidemics continued to sweep through Mexico, and in the last century of colonial rule, smallpox epidemics erupted every fifteen to twenty years. When smallpox hit Mexico in the epidemic of 1779-1780, one of every ten died, and in Mexico City the disease killed off more than twelve thousand people. With the succeeding outbreak in 1797, smallpox killed only half as many, thanks to improved health care in the city (and perhaps to the fact that there were so few left to kill). Measures to stop the spread of smallpox and other epidemics included banning the display of corpses by beggars seeking alms, barring public burials for plague victims, prohibiting the sale of victims' clothing and imposing quarantines and vaccinations.

The scourge of *matlazahuatl* did not return with the same intensity until 1736, when it once again wreaked havoc throughout much of Mexico, with major cities losing up to one-third of their population. Another bout in 1761 was preceded by an outbreak of smallpox, and although it only killed off one-quarter of the population this time it was still ranked as one of the great disasters of the eighteenth-century. A half-century later, in 1813, while the War of Independence raged in central Mexico, a great typhus epidemic erupted, killing off one-tenth of the population of Mexico City in just a few months. In 1892, another typhus epidemic killed off 80 thousand souls in Mexico City alone.

In addition to these epidemics, Mexico City constantly suffered from floods and droughts and these harsh climate conditions helped pave the way for future epidemics. In 1629, due to torrential rain, the lakes in Mexico City flooded and much of the city was buried underwater for five years, provoking the death of over 30,000 inhabitants (the vast majority indigenous).

From 1785 to 1787, due to a serious lack of corn and other basic food stuffs, up to half a million Mexicans perished from starvation and disease. In Mexico City, food became so expensive only the wealthy could afford to eat well. Things got so desperate that the government had to pass laws to have all dead cats and dogs buried to keep locals from eating them. Starvation in the countryside led to a massive emigration to Mexico City, which led not only to greater hunger and disease but also to a wave of crime and social uprisings against the Church, State and Colonial rule. The Spanish tactic of clearing out small towns and driving country folk into the cities to help stop the spread of disease only brought higher levels of death to the cities, such as in 1833 when a cholera epidemic killed more than 1,200 in Mexico City in just two days.

Since the creation of the first cities in the Mexico City Valley, death has ceased to be natural. The mortality rate from plagues during and after the Conquest reflects not so much the virulence of certain imported microorganisms as the devastating effects of invasion and colonization. The destruction of the local environment and agriculture, the wholesale dismantling of cities, massive land theft, the closing of local medical and religious institutions, the forced separation of families and their enslavement, the radical transformation of diet, the introduction of distilled alcohol and the impoverishment of native communities all gave rise to the wholesale destruction of the natives' immune system, particularly important in defending against foreign parasites. If the Aztecs had defeated the Spaniards and thus still had their health and medical institutions, their families and religious centers, their food and natural remedies, the European microorganisms unleashed in Mexico would not have caused such deadly plagues, the natives would have been much better prepared to resist and adapt more quickly to the imported parasites, and the death toll would have been a minor disaster instead of near total genocide.

The local population before the arrival of Europeans could have been as high as 25 million. By 1550, less than fifty years after the Spanish first set foot in Mexico, the population had been reduced to around three million, and by 1581 it dropped to less than two. Depending on estimates of the initial population, the indigenous civilization of the Central Mexico Valley may have declined by up to 90% within 60 years of the first contact with Europeans, the worst wholesale destruction of a culture up to that moment. What had been the greatest, most populated city on earth became practically a ghost town, and it wouldn't be until the beginning of the 20th century, over four hundred years later, that Mexico City recovered the peak population of the Aztec city of Mexico-Tenochtitlan.

United Front   The Conquest of Mexico represented not only the near extermination of one human race by another, it was also a generalized invasion and destruction on all levels of life. Besides the Spaniards and their microorganisms, European cattle, sheep, pigs and horses also invaded and helped conquer the New World. Old World grazing animals, unleashed upon an environment without any natural competitors, and prodded by Europeans' constant demand for meat, fat and other animal products, helped convert forests and jungles into grazing land, which over time and from over-grazing became barren, arid land. The expansion of livestock in Mexico led to very profound changes in land use, including the creation of vast tracts of grassy plains for grazing animals, and the replacement or destruction of native crops with wheat, barley and rice used for animal feed. The decimation of the native population in the Mexico City Valley allowed European grazing animals to expand unchecked throughout the region, while the spread of grazing animals helped disrupt sustenance farming and thus weakened native communities and their ability to defend against future attacks by the Spaniards.

By eating up all the local grass and shrubs, grazing animals allowed Spanish ferns, thistle, nettles, nightshade and other imported plant life to quickly dig in and put down roots, advancing almost as fast as the Spanish army. Cortés declared that every Spanish ship en route to Mexico "should carry a quantity of plants and should not set sail without them because it will be a great thing for the population and its perpetuation," and this policy was eventually made obligatory. Elms, poplars, ash, olive and willow trees were imported to Mexico City from Europe, although the Spaniards also brought species from their Caribbean, Central and South American colonies, as well.

The introduction of European plants in Mexico was accompanied by imported technology to facilitate their cultivation and to help them compete with native varieties. Monasteries often existed not only to convert indigenous souls to Catholicism and to concentrate large groups of natives to be used in the mines or plantations when required, they also served as nurseries for imported plants before being sent out to spread their species throughout Mexico.

The destruction of flora within Mexico City led to the extinction or at least marginalization of several species of fauna that had flourished during the Aztec empire. The extermination of plants and trees created widespread undernourishment and death amongst those native animals and humans who depended upon them for their survival. As European immigration increased in Mexico City, and with the rise of a *mestizo* (racially mixed) urban population that tended to follow a European diet, vast areas that had been used by the natives for hunting and gathering were transformed into agricultural and livestock zones. The conquest of Mexico occurred on every level of life, with the destruction of each level making it easier to conquer all the others.

Tortured Souls In addition to the animals and plants that accompanied the Spanish on their voyage to Mexico, other, even more powerful allies swelled their ranks. Figures and paintings of the "one, true" God, his son Jesus Christ and a whole army of saints brought from Europe rode alongside the Conquistadores during their military forays. Military victories were often credited to these holy figures, and crosses littered the Mexican countryside, marking not so much the few Spanish casualties but rather the new land conquered and dedicated to these religious warriors.

Whenever and wherever they attacked, the Spanish pointed their weapons not only at the natives but also at their gods, destroying every idol, figure and temple they could find. When Mexico-Tenochtitlan fell, so too did the Aztec gods. To make sure the Aztec gods would stay dead, Catholic churches were erected upon the still smoldering ruins of the temples, statues of the Virgin Mary appeared everywhere Aztec idols had stood, and natives were forced to reject their own pantheon of gods and accept Jesus Christ into their lives. To keep natives from backsliding, Catholic priests systematically destroyed almost all the Aztec writing, libraries, murals and idols.

After the Conquest, the Catholic Church presided over all aspects of life and death. Mexicans were born into the Church, and it was the Church that gave them last rites and oversaw their funeral services and burials, as well. To help keep the hearts and minds of Europeans, Africans, natives (and any and all combinations thereof) directed toward the one, true God, and to punish those who dared believe otherwise, the Catholic Church imported the much-feared Spanish Inquisition to Mexico, just one year after the fall of Mexico-Tenochtitlan. Under the Inquisition, the Church's mission was to teach everyone the errors of pagan practices and the benefits of Catholicism, and to punish them for their inability to tell the difference.

These differences, however, were not always so clear-cut. Although it fiercely attacked the Aztec pagan belief system and its barbaric practice of human sacrifice, the Catholic Church itself was of pagan origin and had as its founding act the crucifixion of Jesus Christ. The cannibalism of Aztecs was deemed a heinous sin, yet the Church's holiest rite of communion was based upon the eating of Christ's flesh and the drinking of his blood. And many of the Church's houses of worship were built on the same site as (and with the very stones taken from) the Aztec temples and pyramids..

In 1571, the Inquisition was officially inaugurated in the New World with a ceremony outside the Metropolitan Cathedral in which Mexico City's entire population over twelve years of age was forced to attend. Those present had to swear under oath that they would denounce anyone suspected of heresy and would help hunt them down like 'rabid dogs.' A grace period of six days was announced to allow all those who were practicing heresy and blasphemy to repent and have their souls saved, after which time any individual failing to do so would suffer the wrath of God.

From that day forth, converted Jews, Moslems and Protestants, that is, all those who posed a threat to Catholicism in the New World, were persecuted for signs of religious backsliding (half of all the cases were brought against Africans or mulattos). Those convicted were forced to announce their sins publicly, and crowds were encouraged to insult and attack the sinners. Recalcitrant heretics were forced to wear black robes adorned with brightly colored images of flames or devils, while converted Jews caught practicing their former religious rites were forced to wear yellow robes adorned with a red cross on their chest and back (perfect targets for public ridicule and abuse).

Huge *auto da fe* ceremonies were held regularly in Mexico City's Alameda Park in which hundreds of people would confess their guilt in front of crowds. During these mass shows of faith, all those accused were supposed to admit their sins, even though they were never informed of what they had been accused. If there was no confession or if the sins mentioned were not sufficient, torture was often employed to loosen their tongues.

In all its public acts of torture, the Church religiously avoided shedding blood or opening up human bodies (the sacred site of the soul). This seemingly humane policy, however, led to the invention of a series of simple, elegant means of causing excruciating pain without piercing the flesh. Popular methods of torture included the use of the rack, stringing human beings up by their hands tied behind their back and with heavy weights tied around their feet, water tortures and the roasting of feet over hot coals (an old Aztec technique the Spanish had used on the emperor Cuauhtémoc to try to get him to reveal the whereabouts of Moctezuma's treasure).

Besides religious sins, such as idolatry, witchcraft or fasting on Saturday (a sure sign of Jewish recidivism), certain forms of sexuality, such as seduction, bigamy and homosexuality, were also considered a cardinal sin and were often punished by capital punishment. Sodomites (the biblical term for gays), at least the ones who weren't well connected to the Church or State and especially those who weren't European, were either strangled, hung, burnt or condemned to slave in the galleys of ships for the rest of their lives. In one case in 1650, fourteen men were caught having sex together and were roasted on a bonfire. (Spaniards often claimed that indigenous men were all sodomites, and they often used this as an excuse for conquering and enslaving them.)

Many natives committed suicide, often in large groups, to escape betraying their beliefs, but even they couldn't escape the long arm of the Inquisition. After parading the suicides around town, the authorities would hang the corpses of the sinners in public and onlookers were encouraged to throw stones at them to dissuade others from following their example.

The grandson of Nezahuacoyotl (the last emperor of Texcoco), accused of heresy and blasphemy for continuing to sacrifice humans to his pagan gods, was the first victim of the Inquisition. Burned at the stake in a public execution, his death was a warning that the Catholic Church was the only one authorized to conduct human sacrifice. Two years after the Inquisition claimed its first victim, natives were proclaimed exempt from heresy (not so much because they were recent converts and knew no better, which applied to Africans, as well, but because of the violent uprisings that followed this first public execution).

During its most active period, up to one hundred public executions were carried out by the Inquisition each year. Those found guilty of a capital offense would be dragged through the streets chained to a horse-drawn cart or mule, then either burned at the stake or hung. Those who repented and kissed a Catholic cross in public were granted the luxury of being strangled before their body was set afire. Certain enemies of the Church were given special treatment after death, such as being stuffed into a barrel with a live animal and rolled through the city and then dumped into a lake. The Inquisition reigned for almost 300 years in Mexico and was responsible for hundreds of deaths, but so as to not bloody its hands, the Church had the State execute the sentences.

Besides serving as a tool to maintain the Church's religious and moral monopoly, and a legal way to confiscate the land and wealth of many natives and Europeans accused of heresy, the Spanish government that ruled in Mexico for hundreds of years also utilized the Inquisition to persecute those who were a threat to its rule. Many of the Conquistadores who had fought alongside Cortés were arrested and tried by the Inquisition for treason, and two sons of Hernán Cortés were killed and had their heads stuck on stakes in the main plaza after a failed uprising against the Spanish Crown in 1568.

In 1811, Miguel Hidalgo was executed for treason and heresy by the Spanish Inquisition, as was José Maria Morelos in 1815, for their roles as leaders of the Independence movement. Morelos had the honor of being the last to be sentenced to death by the Inquisition (he was shot by a firing squad and had his mutilated body and severed head displayed in public). In 1820, three hundred years after it was imported to the New World, Mexico finally won its independence from Spain and the Inquisition was laid to rest.

Pro-Creation In Mexico's War of Independence, fought between 1810 and 1820, only twenty-five thousand soldiers actually managed to kill each other, though almost half a million Mexican civilians died in the crossfire. The War of Independence, as well as later civil wars and foreign invasions (first by the United States in 1846 and then by France in 1863), completely changed the demographics of Mexico City, which received the majority of those displaced by the fighting. Even with all the disease, murders, executions and armed struggle, the country's population expanded from some five million inhabitants in 1800 to eight million by 1855, and then to over 15 million in 1910.

The deadliest war of all was the Mexican Revolution, a decade of civil struggle that began in 1910 and lasted ten years, provoking the death of almost one million Mexicans. During the heaviest fighting of the Revolution, Mexicans in the countryside flooded into the capital to escape the horrors of war. In Mexico City, however, where few armed battles were fought, life was just as tough, as thousands of homeless roamed the city, food and water was scarce, and the dead and wounded brought back from the war carpeted the streets.

Once again, parasites and microorganisms caused more deaths during the war than all the bullets and machetes. A typhus epidemic spread throughout the city during the second half of 1915, and the Spanish influenza pandemic reached Mexico in 1918. In order to reduce contagion, cinemas and theaters were ordered to close, and churches were permitted to hold services just one hour on weekdays and two on Sundays. Alcohol was banned, the city's inhabitants were prohibited from keeping pigeons, hens, dogs or any other animals inside their homes, and the poor and homeless were prevented from circulating in public places.

When the Revolution ended, the city's inhabitants once again returned to doing what they have always done best, that is, multiplying. During pre-Hispanic times, procreation was a State affair, and almost no girl reached the age of twelve without marrying, sterility was a deadly sin and infertile couples were often sacrificed to the gods. Aztec women gave birth to an average of nine children (though it was very rare that all survived childbirth and childhood).

This high birthrate continued and existed throughout all classes in Colonial and Modern Mexico, with even upper-class non-European women in the 19th century averaging around eight children. As recently as 1990, Mexican women with no schooling who survived to menopause averaged around seven children, in large part a result of the inflexible stance of the Catholic Church against birth control and abortion.

Due to increased longevity, a still relatively high birthrate and the constant migration of Mexicans from the countryside, the city's population continued to grow from around one million people in 1930 to three million in 1950, nine in 1970, over fifteen in 1995, and over twenty million in the first years of this millennium.

The only disaster, natural or man-made, to actually lower the city's population in the 20th century was an earthquake. Dozens of minor earthquakes shake up the city every year, and in the last one hundred years there have been 13 sizable ones, but in 1985 Mexico City was rocked by one of the strongest earthquakes ever. Thousands of buildings (including several hospitals, public schools, factories, housing projects and a major hotel) crumbled to pieces, and somewhere around 40,000 people died. This full-scale disaster didn't just stem the influx it actually led to a loss of the urban population as survivors fled Mexico City. This population dip, however, lasted only briefly and occurred only in the hardest-hit areas (precisely the neighborhoods, such as the Condesa, Roma and the Historic Center, that today, less than 30 years later, are experiencing the greatest real estate and commercial development).

The megalopolis as a whole, however, even after the earthquake, continued and continues to grow. As ever more human beings are packed tighter into ever more concrete constructions throughout the expanding city (especially in marginal zones constructed on land vulnerable to mudslides, flooding and earthquakes), and given the fact that three out of every ten buildings built in the last decade have structural flaws or damages, future disasters within the Mexico City Valley will surely play a part in regulating the city's population.

Apocalypse Now According to some paranoid gringos (Mel Gibson among them), the ancient Mayans predicted that the world would end in 12/21/12 (even the date, almost a perfect double 666, seems to foreshadow a cataclysm). Although the Mayan prediction referred only to the end of one life cycle and the beginning of a new one, and although Aztecs themselves had their own 52-year cycles in which the world had to be renewed, the first half of 2012 seemed to foreshadow the end of Mexico City. During the first months of this year, thick, dark clouds of toxic pollution hung just above the city. The government issued daily warnings about the extremely high levels radiation that was zapping the city. The dry season was drier than ever, hailstorms blanketed the city in ice, and historic precipitation provoked massive flooding throughout the city. The strongest earthquakes in the last few decades rocked the city and the Popocatepetl volcano spat more fire and brimstone than in any other year in recent history. None of these events, however, provided enough mayhem and manslaughter for an apocalyptic Hollywood movie.

The closest Mexico City has come in the last few years to being the setting of a real-life disaster film was in March 2009, when the city found itself without warning at the mercy of an invisible alien invader, a mutated virus that converted Mexico City into the site of the greatest number of infected human beings and the greatest number of casualties. Being that Mexico City is one of the most populated and most densely packed urban areas on this planet (a perfect Petri dish for cultivating and distributing viruses and other airborne microorganisms), experts around the world quickly predicted that this new virus would wreak havoc within the city and spread across the continent and around the world, leaving a trail of death in its wake.

During the weeks of crisis, when death seemed to hover in the air, Mexico City enjoyed a stretch of beautifully clear, hot days. The streets were exceptionally clean and quiet, few cars circulated, there was no lack of empty seats in the Metro or in city buses, kids stayed home from school and almost no one worked. For most inhabitants, however, this was no holiday. The city's residents had been warned to stay in their homes and to avoid contact with other humans at all costs. Fear kept *chilangos* glued to their television sets, their paranoia rising along with the casualty figures announced during each broadcast.

Mexico City quickly became isolated from the rest of the world as more and more countries halted flights in and out of the city and issued travel warnings. Several *chilangos* who fled the city in search of safety were attacked in their cars or in buses on the highways, while Mexicans abroad (as far away as Argentina and Chile) were beaten and chased out of town.

One credible theory floating around at that time claimed that this mutated killer virus originally came from a giant pig farm in Veracruz owned by a US company (the world's largest pig breeder). The toxic spill-off from the pig farm had already polluted the local water supply of a nearby town, half the town's population suffered from respiratory illnesses and the first one to die from this new killer virus was a local child. (The virus, originally called a mutant strain of swine flu, became referred to merely as A H1N1 after the US pig farmer lobby threw its weight around Washington.)

Others claimed that this latest crisis was in fact chemical warfare, that the CIA (still controlled by the Bush clan) had planted a weapon-grade virus in Mexico City to test its effectiveness, to divert attention from possible indictments of its high-level officials involved in torture in Guantánamo, to hit Mexico's economy so hard that the bailout package would include the privatization of its oil industry, and/or that it was part of an assassination attempt on the life of President Obama who was in Mexico City just as the news of this deadly virus broke.

In the end, after the panic died down, this mutated virus claimed only as many lives as the common flu (around 150 in all of Mexico during the first and most deadly month), but it nonetheless devastated Mexico's tourist industry and wound up costing Mexico City millions and millions of dollars in vaccines. That a single virus could shut down one of the largest cities in the world, that it could summon up such fear, hatred and paranoia, and that it very nearly toppled the country's economy, reveals how important a role microorganisms play within human society, and how economic interests tend to amplify disaster for personal profit.

No matter how many earthquakes, volcanic eruptions or floods might shake, rattle and roll it, or how many viruses or parasites might attack it, the probability that Mexico City and its inhabitants will ever be wiped from the map is very remote. The possibility that Mexico City might see its own culture destroyed and its economy absorbed by an aggressive, more powerful nation after the fallout from a similar crisis, however, is a clear and present danger. As this most recent crisis illustrates, more than any act of God it is human activity (corruption, greed, exploitation) that continues to provoke the greatest disasters in Mexico City. ✝

AIR

Death is in the Air

Before I moved to Mexico City I never really thought about air. I mean, what's there to think of? Air is perhaps the most inert, innocuous thing that could exist, the filler between things, something that tickles my nose hairs, an invisible substance worried only by the wind. There is no real reason to ever think about air, that is, until it becomes a threat to your life. During the last couple of decades the quality of air that has circulated through the lungs of all of us who live in Mexico City has represented a serious health problem (nearly a million people in Mexico City suffer from respiratory illnesses and thousands of premature deaths each year are attributable to the city air).

How did air evolve from the most basic sustenance of life on earth into a danger to human existence? The relatively recent and rapid transformation of Mexico City's clean, clear mountain air into a lethal miasma is a faithful reflection of the development of the city that lies below. By the time the city had become inhabited by millions of human beings it had also populated its air with a quantity and quality of pollution never before seen on this planet. In 1992, the United Nations declared Mexico City the most polluted city in the world, and for many years running Mexico City was awarded this same distinction in the Guinness Book of World Records.

When I take a deep breath I fill up my lungs with air, but what I breathe here in Mexico City and what human beings in other parts of the planet breathe, however, is not necessarily the same thing. Air is not a simple, homogenized element, but rather a gaseous cocktail of nitrogen (about 78%) and oxygen (about 21%), with the remaining 1% made up of mostly of argon (0.93%), carbon dioxide (0.03%) and other gases such as neon, helium, methane, krypton, hydrogen and xenon. What this list of ingredients doesn't take into account, though, is the vast quantities of other gases and substances suspended in the air above large urban concentrations.

Although it would be an exaggeration to claim that in Mexico City I inhale with each breath more pollution than oxygen, I can definitely say that I introduce into my lungs a greater quantity and diversity of gases and substances than most human beings on this planet.

Regardless of how clear and blue the sky appears on any given day, there are around one hundred thousand tons of toxic substances suspended in the air above Mexico City (a lot of weight for something as light as air). Carbon monoxide is the main pollutant, but ozone, PM10s (micro-particles), lead, nitrogen oxides, sulfur oxides, sulfates and nitrates are also heavily represented. If that is not enough to take one's breath away, toluene, xylene and benzene, all proven to be highly carcinogenic in any concentration, and formaldehyde (embalming fluid) form part of the air I inhale daily.

Besides these inorganic substances, hundreds of species of living organisms can also be found hanging out in the city air. Being that the homes of at least eight million people in Mexico City are not connected to any sewage system, human shit has a way of ending up on the street or in empty lots, eventually drying up and going airborne, taking with it hundreds of thousands of microorganisms. In addition, chilangos tend to throw their used toilet paper into wastebaskets instead of flushing them down the drain to keep from clogging up the pipes, and this shit-smeared paper winds up in the city dumps and eventually it too goes airborne.

Humans are not the only living creatures that shit in the city. An estimated three millions dogs (one-third of them strays) live in Mexico City, and many of these eat anything they can sink their teeth into, including raw or rotten meat and even shit from other animals, and they often drink untreated sewage water, all ideal sources of parasites. In Mexico City, dogs dump around 300 tons of shit into the city every day (about ten times the amount produced in Paris). Stray dogs always crap in public places and few owners pick up the shit their dogs leave on the streets and in the parks, and thus canine parasites also eventually ascend into the air. The large population of stray cats and rodents (including squirrels, pigeons and rats) also contribute their own shit and parasites to the city air. The airborne bacteria and parasites released by dried-out human or animal shit cause respiratory diseases, gastro-intestinal infections, glaucoma, hepatitis, cholera and typhoid fever in the city's inhabitants.

I am literally surrounded by shit. The shit that fills the waste baskets in public bathrooms, that which animals leave on the sidewalks, that which my two large Labradors leave for me to clean up in the patio or in the park in front of my house, and that which my two cats daintily deposit in their cat boxes. Being that my two cats tend to drink water from my toilet and that my dogs often eat the shit lying in the cat box, I'm in the middle of a perfect parasite life cycle. Keeping bits of shit and other harmful substances out of my body is the responsibility of my respiratory system. My nose hairs and mucus keep tiny solids from entering into my upper bronchi, while coughing ejects unwanted particles from my lower bronchi.

Airborne particles of shit tend to be the size of the width of a human hair, several times larger than the microorganisms, heavy metals and toxic substances that easily slip through my nose, avoid my body's defense systems and enter my blood stream and lymph system through the walls of my lungs. My bronchial passages are exposed each day to 10,000 liters of polluted air, and once inside my body many of these harmful substances will remain there for the rest of my life. The quantity of airborne chemicals, microorganisms and toxic substances that have entered my body over the last 23 years contribute to the depleted functioning of my lungs, increase the probability of my developing cancer or heart and circulatory diseases (three of the city's major killers), and will undoubtedly shave years off of my life.

Lethal Workout Even on the cleanest, clearest day in Mexico City, even without the tons of heavy metals, toxic particles, shit and parasites swimming around in the air, I would still have trouble breathing. Mexico City is located about a mile above sea level and its mountain air is thus 25% less dense than at sea level, which means that 25% less oxygen enters my lungs with each inhalation. To compensate for this lack of oxygen, my breathing rate must increase to compensate for the decrease in oxygen, and this in turn leads to a decrease in my physical and aerobic performance. In addition, my heart must increase the flow of blood through my veins, which often leads to headaches, dizziness, weakness, itching and a buzzing in my ear. At the same time, my body is forced to step up its production of blood cells, especially red ones, thus thickening my blood and hampering circulation (which over time can lead to strokes and tissue and organ damage).

There is a small park right in front of my house where I run laps, stretch or exercise in the morning, if only for a few minutes. Exercise exacerbates the effects of the decreased presence of oxygen in Mexico City's atmosphere and can cause headaches, nausea, fainting, dizziness and insomnia. In Mexico City I tend to breathe heavier, get light-headed, dizzy and weak, and often feel like a chain smoker must feel after a long day of puffing away (though without a cigarette in hand to steady my nerves). My basketball moves are slower, my stamina suffers, and I probably wheeze more during sex. To make matters worse, when I work out I inhale deeper and more often, thus sucking down into my lungs 15 times more pollution.

In winter it's even worse, for not only does the cold air make breathing more diffi-cult but constant thermal inversions concentrate the pollution lower to the ground. Which is to say, I am not the same man here than I am in sea-level cities such as Acapulco or New York City.

The 1968 Summer Olympics held in Mexico City illustrated the effects of high altitude on athletes. The high altitude and decreased air pressure led to new world records (which took many years to surpass) in non-aerobic events, such as the 100, 200 and 400 yard dash, and in the hop, skip and jump event, where leaps benefited from the decreased gravity and air resistance. The altitude, however, led to lower performance in several Olympic sports events, such as swimming and cycling, and negatively affected many of the athletes unaccustomed to such heights. In general, athletes who train for more than three weeks in high-altitude cities adapt to the decrease in oxygen in the atmosphere, while those who compete immediately after arrival are also often able to avoid the nausea, respiratory tiredness and changes in heart rate associated with high elevations. In 1968, there was still very little air pollution in Mexico City, but if the Olympics were held here today there would be not only reduced performance for many athletes but also increased acute health problems, as well.

The majority of sports associations are against holding sporting competitions in cities located at high altitudes. For instance, the World Soccer Federation re-cently banned all international soccer tournaments from being held above 3,000 meters (ruling out major cities in Colombia and Bolivia). The fact that the altitude limit wasn't lowered to 2,000 meters, which would have eliminated Mexico City as a competition site, probably has more to do with international politics than with medical issues.

Regardless of the decreased presence of oxygen and the increased presence of air pollution, *chilangos* tend to exercise and play sports outdoors. The Azteca sta-dium (home to the America soccer team) is located next to the eight-lane highway that leads to Cuernavaca and Acapulco, usually overrun with traffic on the week-ends when games are played there. There are dozens of playgrounds in Mexico City that are located next to major highways, on traffic islands or near the airport. By government order, all outdoor exercise in schools is cancelled on heavily polluted days, yet the parks, playgrounds and sports arenas remain open even during the worst days of pollution.

Chapultepec, the largest park in the city and one of the lungs of Mexico City, is a favorite recreation and sports center. Besides miles of paths where people walk, jog and bike, and endless fields where people play soccer and volleyball, there is also a professional running track, a horse-jumping club, an archery field, a water park with swimming pools and a couple of informal boxing schools. The park, however, is surrounded and in parts cut through by major avenues with constant heavy traffic, and the illusion of breathing in pure oxygen generated by the thousands of trees and plants in the park is just that, an illusion.

The combination of low oxygen at high altitude and the harmful effects of air pollution makes exercise not only not advisable but also potentially harmful, as it puts extra stress on the lungs and heart. Although it sounds like a good way to increase my body's immune system and to keep me healthy, exercising in Mexico City can be as hazardous to my health as chain-smoking.

Up In Smoke

Like everyone else in Mexico City, I inhale the equivalent of a pack or two of cigarettes each day just by breathing. If breathing the air in Mexico City is equivalent to smoking cigarettes, smoking cigarettes would be the equivalent of putting my mouth around a tailpipe and sucking down car exhaust. Although that sounds like suicide, millions of people do just that every day. I never smoked cigarettes and yet, without even taking a drag from a fag, I've managed to let more toxic cigarette smoke into my lungs than most chain smokers.

For many years, I spent almost half of my wakeful hours in my pool hall and restaurant-bar, where I received a serious daily dose of secondary cigarette smoke, sucking down more nicotine than most chain smokers. Tobacco smoke, both that exhaled from the smoker's mouth as well as the burning ash of the cigarette, is the number one contaminant in interiors, especially in places where tobacco consumers tend to congregate (like pool halls and bars).

Tobacco is indigenous to Mexico, from the same family of edible plants as the potato, tomato and chile, and also related to the hallucinogenic belladonna and nightshade. The word tobacco might come from Tabasco (a tobacco-rich state in the southeast of Mexico) or from Tobago, the indigenous Y-shaped hollow cane used to snort tobacco powder and inhale tobacco smoke. The indigenous cultures living in Mexico cultivated the weed and mostly smoked it in pipes or in cigars inserted into pipes (the Mayans called smoking *cikar*, which later gave rise to the term cigar), but it was also ground up and snorted, cured in sweet syrups and eaten. High doses of tobacco were consumed, either drunk as tobacco juice or used in enemas, by shamans and medicine men to induce altered states and visions during rituals. Tobacco has been used as a treatment for pain, headaches, flatulence and even coughs, to treat diseases of the digestive system, pulmonary disorders, dropsy, cholera and lead poisoning, and prescribed as a sedative. Tobacco leaves were also applied externally for the treatment of skin diseases, gout, rheumatism and nasal polyps.

Mayans traded tobacco throughout the Gulf of Mexico and in the Caribbean, spreading the cultivation of the plant as far away as the US and Canada. After the Conquistadors arrived, Spain maintained a monopoly on tobacco, grown exclusively in the colonies of the New World, for more than 100 years. After Mexico's War of Independence, the American Tobacco Company exerted a tobacco monopoly until 1911, when it was dismembered into several different companies. In 1923, British American Tobacco established tobacco plants in Mexico City, and in 1936 it paid $1.7 billion to purchase Mexico's largest cigarette company, Cigarrera La Moderna, one of the biggest foreign investments ever made in Mexico. Philip Morris paid $400 million for a 50 percent stake in Mexico's second largest cigarette maker, Cigatam, which had been producing Philip Morris brands under license since 1975. Government restrictions caused the foreign tobacco companies to abandon Mexico in the 1980s, but with the opening of the Mexican economy to foreign investment in the 1990s they returned with a vengeance, recapturing the world's fifteenth largest cigarette market (14 million smokers consuming over 60 billion cigarettes a year).

Cigarettes can be bought nearly everywhere in Mexico City, including supermarkets, self-service stores, hotels, restaurants, cafes, pharmacies, bars and clubs. Cigarettes are also sold on major avenues and inner-city highways, in packages or individually, often by kids who sell chewing gum and candy. By law, the sale of cigarettes to minors under 18 years of age is prohibited, but just by looking at the statistics of underage smokers (60% smoke before age 14) it's obvious that this law is not enforced very actively.

Cigarette smoke and car exhausts have much in common, including hydrocarbons, heavy metals, benzene, formaldehyde, carbon monoxide and organic acids. Cigarettes are highly toxic not only because of the smoke emitted from burning leaves but also due to the fact that cigarettes are made from a lot more than just tobacco. Besides all the stems, branches and puffed tobacco used as cheap extenders, there are almost six hundred additives approved by the US Government for use in the manufacture of cigarettes. For many years, filters contained asbestos and gunpowder was used to keep the cigarette paper burning.

Over 4,000 chemical compounds are created every time a cigarette is lit, including nicotine, lead, carbon monoxide (car exhaust), acetone (nail polish remover), naphthalene (active ingredient in mothballs), hydrazine (rocket fuel), methane (swamp gas), acetylene (blow torch fuel), polonium-210 (a radioactive substance), hydrogen cyanide (active ingredient in gas chambers), urea (piss), formaldehyde (embalming fluid), benzene (a solvent), cadmium (used in batteries), mace and pesticides.

Compared to the US and Europe, cigarettes are very cheap in Mexico City. Even so, the unlicensed, unregulated, and untaxed production of even cheaper pirate cigarettes is a very profitable industry. The pirate cigarette industry is quite sophisticated, falsifying everything from the cigarette paper and filter to the package and boxes. Most pirate cigarettes sold in Mexico City are smuggled in from China and the Philippines (usually in containers hidden beneath clothes or shoes), but there is also a healthy pirate cigarette manufacturing industry in Mexico City, as well. Pirate cigarettes, sold mostly in the markets, small stores and on the street, often contain sand and plastic as fillers and can be laced with solvents and other potentially toxic substances, making them up to five times more carcinogenic than licensed cigarettes.

Today, around one-third of all adult men in Mexico City smoke, and one out of every four deaths in Mexico City are related to tobacco. Heart disease and malignant tumors in the lungs, bronchial passages and throat, all related to cigarette smoking, are among the mains cause of death in Mexico City. Cigarette smoking also increases the risk for cancers of the lip, oral cavity, pharynx, esophagus, pancreas, larynx, bladder and kidney, with 90% of all lung cancer caused by cigarettes. Smoking raises cholesterol levels that in turn clog arteries and can lead to heart disease and heart attacks. The difference in the longevity between men and women is in large part because more men smoke more cigarettes, although this is now changing. It is estimated that tobacco will soon become responsible for more deaths that those caused by AIDS, transit accidents, homicides, suicides, alcoholism and drugs combined.

In Mexico City, men who smoke are 22 times more likely to die from lung cancer than non-smoking men, and women who smoke are 12 times more likely to die from lung cancer than non-smoking women. Smoking a pack a day increases the probability of dying from lung cancer by 100%, of developing any type of cancer by 200%, of suffering from respiratory illnesses by 400%, and of the hardening of the arteries and veins that lead to lung and cerebral stroke by 150%. With these odds, I'm afraid to calculate the lung damage I received over the years of running my smoke-filled businesses and breathing in Mexico City air.

Air Visibility With all the clouds of smoke coming from cars, buses, trucks and factories, it often looks as if Mexico City itself is chain-smoking. So much smoke is produced it makes it hard to even see the city some days. In the 1950s, average visibility was around 10 kilometers. In the 1960s it dropped to four, and since then it has hovered around two kilometers, although visibility within the city can often best be measured in blocks.

As Mexico City air began to gain color, texture and substance it began to develop its own character. In the dark days of the 1990s, air quality displaced weather as the most common subject of conversation, and it also became the butt end of jokes ("Mexico City air is so clean not a single microbe dies in it."). Which is to say, air became an active participant in the life of the city, a visible part of the culture.

On many days of the year I can actually see the city air. I can see it in my bloodshot eyes and in my green snot and thick buggers streaked with blood. I can see it when I wipe my face on a towel before washing. I can see it on my car in the morning when the windshield seems like it's been covered with volcanic ash. I can see it in the expanding and contracting gray curtain that limits the view of the urban landscape.

Lots of cities have visible air, but what makes it possible to actually see Mexico City's air is not the water or mist but instead the thousands of tons of pollution pumped into the air each day. Although airborne pollutants themselves are invisible, the dense concentration in the city's atmosphere gives them form and volume, making them, and the air itself, visible. An analysis of the air that I suck into my lungs each day would provide an accurate map of human activity throughout the city, reflecting all aspects of production, transportation and consumption.

The wind in Mexico City tends to come from the north, picking up particles from Tlalnepantla, the most industrialized zone of the city (and the country), eroded soil from the dried-out Texcoco lake, and soot from trash being burned in the garbage cities, dispersing all these particles throughout the city. The southeastern part of the city, hemmed in by nearby mountains, accumulates the highest levels of ozone, while the eastern part of the city receives the highest levels of suspended particles. Eroded soil and deforestation caused by the urbanization of forest land help create dust storms, which sometimes reach the intensity of low-level urban tornadoes, whipping up dirt and garbage and sending them flying into the air.

The particles circulating in the sky above my head filter and reflect the sunlight, and chemical reactions between the sun's ultraviolet rays and gases emitted into the atmosphere create a layer of ozone above the city, further thickening the city's atmosphere. Mexico City air should be very light due to the lower air density associated with high altitudes, but because of all the particles in the air it is among the heaviest in the world.

The classic division of the year into four distinct seasons doesn't fit so well into Mexico City's climate. Although Mexico City is colder in the winter and leaves turn brown and fall from trees in autumn, hot summer weather normally occurs between March and May and all four seasons can often be experienced within one single day in winter. More so than the weather, pollution is a seasonal event in Mexico City. During rainy season, which one might think would be the cleanest time of year, light showers serve to bring the air-borne heavy metals down from the skies in the form of acid rain, sprinkling everything with a fine layer of toxic dust, while heavy rain leads to floods that distribute sewage and garbage throughout the city. In the dry-hot season, microbes are dispersed into the air as the sun barbeques the garbage and fecal matter lying outdoors.

There are many sunny days in the city and, given that the atmosphere in this mile-high city offers 25% less of a protective filter, concentrations of ozone run high, especially around noon in the summer when the sunlight is most intense. During winter's thermal inversions, airborne metals and toxic gases are sealed under a dome of cold air. Common smog mostly occurs during cold winter days, especially at sunrise, caused mainly by the burning of industrial and domestic fuels. During the cold season coal is burned to heat homes, while the huge quantities of fireworks and rubber tires burned on Christmas and New Year's Eve make these days among the most polluted of the year.

Although much of the city is an exaggeration of saturated colors and bright paint smeared across the walls of houses, buildings and public spaces, Mexico City often appears to be a gray city. The problem is that the air itself is so dirty and dense that the reflective properties of the polluted atmosphere dim the sunlight and sap the colors of their intensity. More than just hampering perception of color, the particles suspended in the air actually eat away at the colored surfaces of city's buildings and monuments. Many of the city's pre-Hispanic and Colonial constructions have suffered significant deterioration from air pollution, and many early 20th-century outdoor murals have had their colors practically erased.

Besides the negative effects of humidity, heat and solar radiation, some of the worst damage to buildings, monuments and outdoor murals is caused by abrasion, a phenomenon in which gusts of wind whip up heavy particles and fling them against buildings. These particles tend to accumulate on the surface of constructions, smothering the work of art or architecture. Dusting or washing off these particles can lead to even greater damage as they can scratch surfaces. Oxidation and other chemical reactions eat away at man-made constructions, breaking down the materials that are then washed away by the rain, while acid rain causes deterioration of construction materials and ozone discolors dyes and pigments. Pollution even attacks metal sculptures, causing not only rust but also electrical reactions that corrode the metals. As a result of its ability to discolor everything it comes into contact with, Mexico City air has become an essential part of the city's aesthetic.

Concrete Jungle

In the 1950s, the city government began to encourage the concentration of heavy industry within the Mexico City Valley. Up until only very recently, more than half of all the industry in the country (around 30,000 factories) was located here. Mexico City was an ideal location for factories as it had an almost unlimited access to electricity, oil and other sources of energy, a seemingly endless supply of water, an efficient sewage system and solid infrastructure.

The industry most responsible for the shape and size of the city is cement. Over the last several decades, a constantly expanding sea of cement constructions has blanketed the mountain valley, stretching out in all directions and up and over the surrounding mountains. What had originally been a paradise of lakes and trees has been almost completely paved over, and in its place there now exists one of the world's largest concrete jungles.

Mexico City has been ranked amongst the worst cities in the world in terms of urban planning, development of sustainable practices, investment in basic infrastructure and proximity of workplace to living quarters. In addition, more than half of all houses in Mexico City are located in unhealthy, unsafe areas. All of these problems can be attributed to the uncontrolled construction boom. To accommodate the annual influx of three hundred thousand immigrants into Mexico City, fifty thousand new constructions are built each year. Many of these are government-subsidized low-income housing projects, vast communities of densely packed identical cement cubes. These prefab micro-cities, often constructed in arid plains far from any services (including schools, stores or adequate transportation) have changed the landscape of the outlying areas of the city.

Even with all the massive government-subsidized communities being built, more than one-third of all those who emigrate to Mexico City each year wind up illegally occupying the land they live on. These *paracaidistas* (parachutists or land grabbers) build their makeshift abodes with mostly recycled materials, including bricks, cardboard, plastic and scraps of metal. Although this self-made, outsider architecture allows the tenants to express their own individuality and create their own living space, when families attain a certain level of economic well-being they immediately lay down a cement floor and throw up four cement walls and a cement ceiling. Cement has come to be seen as a sign of superior social status, especially by immigrants from rural parts of the country. When these densely populated slums represent enough votes for local politicians to take heed, the streets are paved with concrete and cement posts are installed to bring in electrical lines. To sway local elections, bags of cement are often handed out to purchase votes.

Cement, rather than the wood, glass or steel used to build modern cities throughout the world, has been the building material of choice in Mexico City since the beginning of the 20th century. Cement became popular during the art deco architectural boom in the city mainly because it represented European modernity, but it soon became the standard construction material throughout the city because it is so cheap, resistant and easy to use.

The recent destruction of older, single-family houses of all styles (Swiss chalets, modern, Bauhaus) to pave the way for the construction of multi-apartment luxury condos has changed the face of several neighborhoods, especially the Condesa. These condos, often misleadingly advertised as lofts, are almost as uniform as the government-subsidized micro-cities and are constructed out of cement, as well.

In addition to the construction of concrete homes for people of all classes, the endless construction of huge monuments, government buildings and an ever-expanding network of avenues, highways and skyways all contribute to the thousands and thousands of tons of cement poured into the Mexico City Valley each year. The cement industry not only influences the shape and size of the city, it also directly influences its economy as the construction industry represents one-half of the gross national product.

Cement is second only to water as the most consumed substance on earth, with nearly three tons poured each year for every person on the planet. Because it is such a common substance, few people realize how much cement is involved in death in Mexico City. Cement plants alone are responsible for almost half of all industrial particulate emissions within the city. The production and use of cement disperses into the air great quantities of dust and chemicals, many toxic and carcinogenic. For several decades, and up until recently, asbestos was the insulation of choice for constructions built in Mexico City, and this toxic substance, long banned in the US and Europe, combines with the chemicals emitted by concrete to reduce the functioning and longevity of human lungs.

In Mexico, the construction industry employs 7% of the total work force. As face masks are almost never used on construction sites in Mexico City, workers' long-term contact with cement leads to a significant decrease in productive work years and an increase in fatal diseases such as lung cancer. In addition, the construction industry is responsible for 25% of all accidental deaths and injuries among workers (the biggest risks being plummeting from heights or being struck by falling objects). Poorly constructed highways and avenues are the site of innumerable traffic fatalities, while shabbily constructed concrete housing projects, hospitals and hotels lead to the greatest number of deaths during earthquakes. In Mexico City, human blood has always been mixed into the cement that covers the city.

Although cement might seem like an innocuous substance, it is in fact anything but environmentally friendly. The cement industry consumes 5% of all energy in Mexico, and 5% of all man-made carbon dioxide emissions originate from cement production. To produce the vast quantities of cement needed to construct Mexico City's ever expanding urban area, forests are leveled and agricultural land disappears to make room for quarries gouged out of the earth. Cement kilns, especially those that use car or truck tires and other garbage as fuel, emit an assortment of semi-volatile, highly toxic organic substances into the air.

The concrete that carpets the Mexico City Valley prevents the re-absorption of rainwater and increases the absorption of the sun's radiation, thus increasing the temperature within Mexico City. The average temperature within Mexico City has risen approximately six degrees Fahrenheit in the last ten years, with the gray areas of the city getting up to 10 degrees hotter than the green areas.

Over the last couple of decades, a large part of the city's industry, including cement factories, has been relocated to areas outside the Mexico City Valley in an attempt to displace the pollution and to have other regions share the environmental burden. Unfortunately, many of these new industrial zones dump their industrial wastes directly into rivers that supply Mexico City with its drinking water. What's more, migrating air pollution from these areas often makes it way back into the city, and the endless cement truck traffic going in and out of the city each day greatly increases the city's air pollution.

Although the government imposes increasingly stringent environmental measures on local industry, most factories in Mexico City merely bribe inspectors instead of implementing costly environmental modifications, and thus the factories that remain in the city still contribute a sizable portion of the city's air pollution. The cement industry in Mexico is incredibly profitable (the owner of Cemex is one of the country's dozen wealthiest). Cement, like most industries in Mexico, generates such a huge profit by not paying the true value of the natural resources and human labor it uses, and by not paying the cost of properly disposing of the waste it creates. In the end, the social costs of cement are absorbed, both economically and physically, by the inhabitants of Mexico City.

Suck My Exhaust As much as industrial smokestacks pump pollution into the air, they can't compare to what comes out of the exhausts of motorized vehicles. The four million cars, truck and buses that make over 30 million trips each day in Mexico City are responsible for up to 80% of the city's air pollution. The displacement of inhabitants away from the center of the city to the outlying suburbs causes drivers to crisscross the city several times a day, driving longer distances in ever-slower traffic, spending a greater part of their lives within their vehicle and poisoning the air every day of the week. More than half of all Mexico City inhabitants go to work in a car, one of the highest rates of a major city. Being that there is 25% less oxygen in the air in this mile-high city, gasoline doesn't burn as well as it should and consequently even more pollutants are created.

Weekends provide no relief from poor air quality, as Saturday combines day-time work traffic (most people work at least five and a half days a week) with heavy nightlife activity, almost doubling the amount of traffic for that day. Even Sunday is often no better, suffering from a pollution hangover from the whole week's activity, with the ozone and other pollutants spending the night up in the atmosphere and descending as the day heats up.

If there has ever been a perfectly designed death machine it is surely the motorized vehicle. In Mexico City, not only do cars, buses and trucks poison the air, deplete earth's precious liquids and contribute to global warming, they are also involved directly in human deaths through accidents. Mexico City ranks number one in Latin America in automobile deaths, number seven in the world. Driving a car in Mexico City not only turns people into potential mass murderers but also potential suicides. Besides those who actually commit suicide from breathing in their own car's exhaust or intentionally ramming their car into a lamppost, by keeping people immobile when they should be out walking off extra fat cars are also responsible for the high levels of obesity, one of the major causes of death in the city.

Motorcycles, cars, buses and trucks circulate on the city streets with almost total impunity. There are only a few thousand traffic lights in the whole city, which means that traffic is controlled at only a fraction of crosswalks. In addition, blackouts and brownouts are frequent occurrences throughout the city, especially on windy and rainy days, and thus the few traffic lights that do exist often don't even work. Speed limits are neither obeyed nor strictly enforced, red lights and stop signs are mere suggestions, and one-way streets exist only in theory. Recommended car-lengths between cars are measured in inches, while (rarely used) turn signals only serve to warn other drivers to block those who try to cut in front of them.

Licenses are handed out without any actual driving or vision tests, and there is no points system and nobody ever gets his or her license taken away. Even though they are cheap and ridiculously easy to obtain, most drivers in Mexico City lack a valid license. Almost 40% of all cars circulating in Mexico City are not insured, which prompts more hit-and-runs by drivers who try to escape legal responsibilities. When drivers are caught breaking the law they need only slip a fraction of the cost of a fine directly into the hands of their friendly traffic cop to drive off without legal consequences.

Chilangos are not necessarily bad drivers, but once anyone (including myself) turns on the ignition in their car in Mexico City they immediately enter into the battle of everyone for themselves and God against all. Motorcycles, cars, buses, taxis and trucks all aggressively jockey for position, the goal being to make everyone else suck your exhaust fumes.

The only thing that dares to interfere with a driver's freedom to speed ahead and the common enemy that unites all the various vehicles on the road is the pedestrian. There is a constant, deadly struggle between pedestrians and drivers on the streets of the city. The idea of a moving vehicle slowing down, let alone stopping, at a crosswalk to see if anyone is waiting to get to the other side is a foreign concept. It's not that drivers hate pedestrians (some of their best friends walk on the streets at times), but they just don't consider them on the same evolutionary level. Pedestrians are meant to respect cars like small mammals had to respect dinosaurs (perhaps dinosaurs also got a thrill from making smaller creatures scramble to safety to avoid being squashed).

As flagrant as drivers are in disrespecting pedestrians, so too pedestrians often go out of their way to disobey commonsense. Pedestrians in Mexico City insist on crossing multi-lane avenues in the middle of the street, even when there are pedestrian bridges a mere half a block away, and will often crawl through chinks in a protective fence to dodge traffic on inner-city highways. As a large part of the city's population is composed of recent arrivals from the countryside and indigenous communities, it's not rare to see whole families, grandparents as well as small children, sprinting madly across large avenues at unsafe places and often out of synch with the traffic lights, unaware of the velocity cars can attain.

Drivers park wherever they please, including on all corners of the street and on sidewalks, and combined with all the poor quality sidewalks pedestrians are often pushed back into the street. On my street, for instance, dozens of homeowners have cut ramps into the sidewalks leading to their garages, metal poles have been sunk into both the sidewalk and curb to keep cars from parking there and the roots of trees often buckle the sidewalks. More people on the street means more moving targets for speeding vehicles.

Traffic accidents represent the number one cause of non-natural death in Mexico City, and the ones who take the biggest hit are pedestrians. Almost 10 out of every 100,000 inhabitants have had a traffic accident, with half of all accidents being fatal. Although traffic fatalities rank number one for kids between 5 and 14 years old and fourth among adults, people over 75 and country folk are most at-risk while crossing the street. More than violent crime or rape, it is traffic accidents against pedestrians that make Mexico City the world's second most dangerous city after South Africa and four times more dangerous than Los Angeles.

Do the Bump In these traffic wars, however, pedestrians are not totally defenseless, having on their side *topes* (speed bumps or, as the Brits call them, sleeping policemen). In theory, speed bumps, whether they are concrete humps, metal bumps, cautionary ribbed-concrete vibrators or even thick ropes, are designed to slow cars down and give pedestrians a chance to cross the street. Speed bumps do a lot of things in Mexico City (such as helping street vendors sell their products and giving carjackers and window-smashing thieves a little extra window of opportunity), but helping pedestrians safely get to the other side isn't one of them. Drivers see speed bumps as an impediment to their liberty and the pursuit of happiness (getting out of city traffic as quickly as possible makes drivers happy), and thus they tend to speed into them, brake at the last second, bump up and over as fast as they can (risking their muffler and suspension) and then floor the accelerator to make up for time lost.

Around 18,000 speed bumps line the streets of Mexico City, most built by the City government (often using the forced labor of prison inmates). Although it is illegal to disrupt traffic in any way, thousands of unauthorized speed bumps punctuate the city streets, improvised by nervous neighbors to protect their families or, like the tiny crosses sunk in the sidewalks around the city to commemorate loved ones lost in traffic accidents, to prevent future deaths. Although many speed bumps are where they do the most good (in front of hospitals, schools, dangerous crosswalks), there are also absurdly placed ones at stoplights, in tunnels and under pedestrian walkways. Many of the speed bumps are unmarked and thus serve no function other than to ruin suspensions and mangle mufflers, while thousands of yellow and white stripes painted on roads that simulate speed bumps create confusion. Official speed bumps are all of a standard height, but unofficial ones can be vindictively high and steep.

Mexico City has one of the highest concentrations of cars in the world (more than double that of Los Angeles), and it also has the slowest average speed of circulation of all major cities (around 22 kilometers per hour, less than half of that of Los Angeles). During rush hour, the inner-city highways often resemble giant parking lots and traffic on high-speed avenues and highways is so chronically slow that it is common to see vendors casually walking between lanes selling chewing gum, water or cigarettes. The hundreds of street protests, religious pilgrimages and marathons each year, added to the thousands of potholes and constant street repairs, transforms the streets of the city into one of the world's slowest obstacle courses. To make matters worse, in the last few years the number of cars prowling the streets of the city increased by 40% while the number of main roads increased only by 16%, thus further clogging up city traffic.

In a study funded by IBM in 2011, Mexico City was considered the major city with the world's worst traffic, as judged by drivers' level of suffering, stress and loss of time, all consequences of speed bumps. Consumers buy expensive, powerful vehicles to help liberate themselves from urban problems like traffic and *topes* interfere with drivers' need for speed. The difference between a vehicle's potential velocity and the actual rate of traffic movement leads to increased road rage and class hatred (old, poorly tuned cars are still the majority on Mexico City streets).

In Mexico City, cars drive an average of 10 kilometers a day, passing over a speed bump approximately once every kilometer. Due to the effects of the thousands of *topes* located throughout the city, over one hundred thousand extra liters of gas are consumed each day in Mexico City, generating an additional cost of around 25 million dollars each year, while burning all that extra gas leads to more carbon monoxide and dioxide emissions in the air and in the lungs of the city's inhabitants.

Cars, buses and trucks, however, are not the only gas guzzling, pollutant-belching vehicles in Mexico City. Whenever I lie in my rooftop hammock I see dozens of airplanes pass overhead, taking off from and landing in Mexico City's Benito Juarez International Airport located practically in the center of the city. Even with four smaller airports in nearby cities shuttling many tourists off to the country's beaches, Mexico City's Benito Juarez airport, the largest in the country, recently expanded by 50% to meet the city's increasing air traffic demands.

From my roof, the airplanes that pass over my head appear as tiny specks of flashing metal or as wisps of smoke in the sky, but as they drop down above the neighborhoods surrounding the airport they rattle windows and shake buildings. Those living in these neighborhoods are 40% more likely to develop high blood pressure from the noise, not to mention all the extra fumes they inhale daily from the toxic trail airplanes leave in their wake.

The hundreds of flights in and out of Mexico City spread air pollutants over a large swath of the city, though mostly over the poorer neighborhoods located around the airport. Airplanes pollute even more on the ground than up in the air, with most emission coming out as they idle and taxi along the runways. Toxins from spilled jet fuel, de-icing fluids and leaked engine oil commonly flood the tarmac, filtering down into the ground water near the airport. Not surprisingly, Mexico City's airport, being a major business and tourist destination as well as a hub for the rest of Mexico and Latin America, with around 25 million people flying in and out a year, is among the largest single-source emitters of Mexico City air pollution.

Up, Up and Away Air pollution, whatever its source, affects not only humans beings but also all other living creatures, including the plants that provide humans with oxygen to breathe. In Mexico City, air pollution, acid rain, photochemical oxidants and soil erosion have been killing off the city's plants and trees for decades. The sycamore trees that lined Avenida Reforma in the 1990s all died, and in 2005 thousands of sickly trees in Chapultepec Park had to be cut down due to deterioration from the effects of air pollution. The greatest damage caused by air pollution occurs within the forests that surround the city, especially among the pine tress in the woods of Ajusco and the Desierto de los Leones, two main oxygen sources of the city.

Mexico City's endlessly growing urban blob constantly gobbles up trees from the mountains that surround the city, which in turn leads to soil erosion, loss of humidity and an increase in temperatures, all of which allow toxic particles in the air to remain there longer and to be converted into even more dangerous substances. The length of time that heavy metals, gases and other pollutants remain in the atmosphere determines their impact. In some cases, toxic compounds like methane, carbon dioxide and many halogenated organics can remain in the air for decades, traveling around the globe and spreading climatic and environmental damage. Many substances eventually reach the upper layers of the atmosphere where, in the case of compounds containing chlorine and bromine, they help poke giant holes in the stratospheric ozone layer. Mexico City contributes 20% of the country's total greenhouse gas emissions and is one of the biggest contributors to greenhouse gas emissions in Latin America.

Exported pollutants have the potential to affect atmospheric visibility, weather systems and global climate, both within Mexico and beyond. The air-streams above Mexico City carry some of the pollution formed each day out of the city across the whole country, traveling as high as ten thousand feet above sea level, and these toxic clouds can make their way in a single day to the Pacific Ocean or the Gulf of Mexico where they are joined by pollution from Europe and Asia. This new mix of pollution often returns inland, at times even making its way back into the air above Mexico City.

Over the years, several radical schemes have been offered to solve the problem of air pollution in Mexico City. In the early 1990s, scientists proposed to install throughout the city one hundred enormous gas burners that, acting like giant fans, would send the city's polluted air up into the atmosphere (without much thought about where it might then travel). Another project contemplated blasting tunnels through the southeastern mountains to allow polluted air to escape from the city. A more recent plan proposed ionic antennas to alter the electric current in the air and allow for the manipulation of rain and wind in an attempt to gain control over the direction and concentration of the city's migrating air pollution. Scientists are currently developing microorganisms that can devour toxic substances in the air, although this could eventually lead to a nightmare scenario of rogue mutated microorganisms. None of these mega-schemes have been implemented, mostly likely because the government realizes that screwing around with Mother Nature would undoubtedly bring about unforeseen cataclysmic consequences.

Making the clean-up process of air a profitable activity, like garbage collection, might be the solution to Mexico City's air pollution, and there is money to be made by converting airborne sulfur dioxide into sulfuric acid or by mining such expensive elements as cadmium, mercury and lithium from the air. Since the last decade of the 20th century, there has been a slight albeit steady improvement in the quality of the air in Mexico City. This has been due mainly to the gradual improvement of automobile fuels, the adoption of electronic fuel injection and catalytic converters, the partial restoration of the Texcoco Lake, the reforestation of some of the outlying areas of the city and the relocation of industry outside the Valley. As a result, in the last couple of years Mexico City didn't even figure in the top ten list of the world's most polluted cities.

Nothing but Clear Skies

Nowadays, when I step out of my house and fill my lungs with air or when I exercise outdoors, I breathe a little easier. The air usually seems clearer than during the dark days I lived through in the 1990s, years when I was sucking down deep into my lungs some of the most polluted air that existed anywhere in the world. There's no need for me to get nostalgic quite yet, though. Although clearer skies are part of the new, trendy Mexico City that is attracting so many international tourists and residents, having merely deleted the most visible pollution in the skies does not mean that breathing in city air is any less harmful to human beings.

With the signing of the North American Free Trade Agreement, Mexico City was forced to institute a series of measures to combat its air pollution. As a result, the pollutants most easily controlled, and those responsible for the most visible pollution, were reduced. Others, such as ozone, worsened as a consequence of these shortsighted measures. Even with the dispersion of heavy industry to outside the city, the unceasing increase in the city's population and motorized vehicles, the size of the new vehicles being purchased and the increased air traffic over the city all seriously undercut any real improvement. Nowadays, the city's air pollution is still higher than approved health levels more than half of the days of the year, and Mexico City's lower ranking in international air pollution levels might be due less to bright new horizons in air quality within the city and more to greater competition on the world scene, with newer, more polluted mega-cities topping the list.

Just as the transformation of Mexico City into a major industrial hub profoundly altered all aspects of the city's environment, so too the changes inherent in cleaning up the city, including its most visible air pollution, have changed it in a very radical way. The expulsion of heavy industry outside the Valley is not a purely eco-solution, it is also an integral part of the gentrification process of expelling the working class from the center of the city. Many industrial neighborhoods, home to some of the most important manufacturing in Latin America and a reflection of Mexico's former economic independence from the US and Europe, have now been converted into strip malls hosting Home Depots and Costcos.

The culture of urban transportation has also been impoverished by constant modernization and improvement under the eco-banner of clearer skies. When I moved to the city, the *cocodrillos* (large American cars with fins painted to resemble crocodile spikes, important local cultural icons) were being phased out and replaced by a vast fleet of Volkswagen bugs (first yellow and then eco-green) that didn't guzzle gas and polluted the city air much less. These made-in-Mexico *vochos*, the last VW bugs produced anywhere in the world, have in turn given way to homogeneous, efficient, imported four-door cars like those to be found in any major urban center around the world. Similarly, the large Ruta 100 buses, with their bucolic hand-painted landscapes exhibited on their back windows, often clouded by thick black smoke belching out from the exhaust pipes, and many of the pimped-up *pesero* jitneys with booming sound systems, have been replaced by the clean-energy, silent, more expensive and foreign-owned Metrobus.

As Mexico City air is cleaned up for tourists and foreign investors, more and more traditional urban Mexican culture seems to be breathing its last breath. Mexico City is now in a sad, transitional moment, from a producer of lung cancer to a consumer of global culture. As for me, the risk of developing lung cancer has decreased greatly since smoking was banned in public places, but the amount of toxic chemicals still stored in my body from the dark days of the 1990s might have already set in motion the seeds of cancer. Dying of lung cancer in this new, improved Mexico City, where smoking is banned and where blue skies usher in a new era of clean living, would be a cruel way to go. ✝

WATER

Our House   My wife, three sons, two dogs and two cats and I live in a two-story house in Mexico City. Built in 1945 and purchased by my wife almost 15 years ago, the house has three bedrooms, three bathrooms (two with a shower), a kitchen and a garage, while a studio, the maid's quarters (with bathroom) and a terrace are located on the roof, and a small patio is located behind the house. Which is to say, a typical house in the Condesa.

Like my body, my house is intimately connected to its environment. The same sunshine, rain and wind that come into contact with my skin also affect my house's painted surface, and just as the city's air pollution scratches my lungs, so too it can damage the outer walls of my house. Extreme weather conditions directly affect my house's longevity, while natural disasters can lead to an early demise. Like me, my house has only a certain number of years on this earth, although with proper care and attention its lifespan can be prolonged so that it outlives several generations of humans.

Besides giving me shelter, my house provides me with water. The water I need to replenish my bodily fluids and to keep myself clean is pumped in daily through an underground pipe that empties into a huge cistern buried underneath the patio. An electric pump located in the patio lifts the water up from the cistern and into the large plastic water tank located on the roof, which in turn funnels water back down into the bathrooms, showers and kitchen. In Mexico City, water is not free and every two months we must pay for the water we use. Our house produces its own hot water with a gas-powered water heater located on the rooftop terrace, and the gas must be bought from a private company that sends a truck each month to fill up a stationary tank on our roof with liquified gas.

Compared to other major cities, the quality of the water supplied to homes in Mexico City has consistently been ranked at the bottom of the list. In addition to the poor quality of city water supplied, rusty pipes, mold and old water tanks made from asbestos (prohibited since the 1970s but still used in lower-income buildings and houses) can add harmful substances to the water. Over time, poor quality water can corrode the pipes and eventually cause them to burst.

Depending on the building and on the neighborhood, water in Mexico City comes out of the tap in a variety of colors (yellow, rusty or earthy), flavors (sulfuric, chlorinated or metallic) and even textures (muddy or gritty). Water that doesn't smell, taste or look funky, however, is actually the most dangerous, for it can sucker people into believing that it's drinkable. In general, all those who have other options don't drink Mexico City tap water.

In Mexico City, the lack of free, publicly supplied clean drinking water generates great business opportunities. For many years we bought large glass or plastic jugs of water from trucks that circulate around the neighborhood. Although each jug is relatively inexpensive, the drinking water a family of five consumes can add up. These days, we filter the tap water that flows from the faucet in our kitchen by means of a costly device located under the sink that works with a double filter of ozone and carbon that must be changed every six months.

In Mexico City, it is not only drinking water that people purchase. While people in higher-income neighborhoods get cheap, government-subsidized tap water, the poorest parts of the population have no plumbing and receive no water at all in their homes. Those who live beyond the reach of the city's water pipes must buy water from trucks (called *pipas*) that distribute water out of a large hose at a high cost.

For those who have no access to hot water in their homes, or those who lack indoor plumbing, there exists *baños públicos*. These public baths, which are actually private businesses, offer for a modest fee individual and communal showers, Turkish baths, saunas and Jacuzzis (soapy massages offered by teenage boys cost extra). Public toilets represent a booming private business these days, especially in the most visited tourist sites of the city, where for less than fifty cents you receive access to urinals or toilets with paper handed to you when you pay (some WCs even operate like the Metro, with ticket windows and turnstiles). Being that most of these WCs and some of the *baños públicos* are not licensed, chances are they don't even pay for the large quantity of water used.

In Mexico City, to get access to needed water, whether it is in the shower, toilet or in a glass, you must pay dearly for it. Yet even if people in the city are willing to pay more and more for their water, there might not even be enough to go around soon.

Water World Up until around five hundred years ago, the Mexico City Valley was not a valley but rather a basin filled with a series of fresh and salt-water lakes fed by melting snow from the surrounding glacier mountains. It was precisely this endless source of fresh, clean water that allowed the Aztecs to erect the greatest empire of its time in this valley, and for which the island city of Mexico-Tenochtitlan received its pre-Hispanic nickname Anahuac (the city by the lakes).

Today, however, water is something few people would associate with Mexico City. No river runs through it, no ocean laps at its edges and no large body of water even exists within the Mexico City Valley. Besides a huge swampland near the airport and a few canals in Xochimilco overrun on weekends by gondola-like boats full of tourists and mariachis, the city is basically an immense sea of dry, dusty concrete.

Mexico City is located within a valley 2,400 meters above sea level, encircled by the Central Volcanic Beltway, smack in the middle of the country and as far from the Pacific Ocean as it is from the Gulf of Mexico. When the Aztecs began construction of what was to become the great empire of Mexico-Tenochtitlan, they did so on a swampy island in the middle of several lakes. The fresh and saltwater lakes that surrounded the island provided them with a bountiful source of fresh fish, insects and even edible seaweed, and in the freshwater lakes the Aztecs created their *chinampas*, aquatic gardens rooted to the muddy lakebed below with long tree trunks, able to provide enough crops to feed one of the most-populated cities in the world at that time. The lakes also acted as thoroughfares for the countless boats, rafts and canoes that brought to the central markets of Mexico-Tenochtitlan the fruits, vegetables and flowers from Xochimilco and other agricultural areas throughout the Valley. The lakes even provided the Aztecs with the opportunity to develop what was perhaps the first navy in the Americas.

Trapped as it is at the bottom of a mountain valley without any natural drainage system, the city suffers from constant flooding during the intense rainy season. A great flood hit Mexico-Tenochtitlan in 1450, burying the city under water. To prevent future flooding, the poet, engineer and Emperor Nezahualcoyotl from Texcoco, the largest of the port cities located just across the lake from Mexico-Tenochtitlan, constructed dikes around the island to separate the salty from the fresh water lakes, with special floodgates that allowed canoes to pass from one lake to another.

The Aztecs adopted Tlaloc, the god of rain and of agriculture, from the earlier Teotihuacan civilization and converted into one of their main gods. Provider of the rain that gave life to all crops, Tlaloc could also punish the Aztecs with flash floods that buried the city underwater, hailstorms that destroyed crops and droughts that killed off harvests. Some of the most important temples were dedicated to Tlaloc, the human sacrifices carried out in them designed to collect enough human blood, especially that from babies, to appease this god in order to ensure that the city would receive a sufficient supply of rainwater and be protected from floods.

The first Spaniards to step foot in the city described Mexico-Tenochtitlan as the Venice of the Americas, mightily impressed by the lakes and all the commerce and transport they afforded. So impressed were they with the city that they decided it had be theirs. Having been defeated in an initial attempt to conquer the city by hand-to-hand combat, the Conquistadores realized that the island was vulnerable to siege. So that the 13 ships he built could encircle and cut off all supplies to the city, Cortés destroyed the dikes that separated fresh from salty water, thus effectively ruining the supply of drinking water and food derived from the freshwater lakes, creating the conditions necessary for starvation and disease to level the local population and minimizing the need for combat.

After the Conquest was complete, Cortés ordered all material from the destroyed city that was not used to build his palaces and cathedrals, along with all the garbage generated, to be tossed into the lakes to increase the size of this island city. Determined to end nature's tyranny, the Spanish further dried out the lakes by digging canals and trenches. Although the lakes' waterline sank continually, floods still ravaged Mexico City throughout the Colonial period. When they realized that even this was still insufficient to contain the water during the rainy season, they forced 15,000 indigenous men to dig a tunnel more than five miles long and 50 meters deep through a mountain pass in order to provide an escape route for excess water to drain out of the city.

In 1629, just twenty years after the tunnel was inaugurated, the city was buried under water. The Zócalo, the main city square that housed the Metropolitan Cathedral and government palaces, was one of the only sections of the city that remained dry during the flood (it was baptized as the Island of Dogs for all the animals that sought refuge there). In the end, this flood, which lasted for five years and forced tens of thousands of Spaniards and natives to abandon the island, led to widespread disease and pestilence that killed 30,000 indigenous people. (According to local legend, only when an earthquake split the surrounding mountain wall did the water drain from the city.)

By destroying homes and ruining the crops that fed the city, floods caused widespread destruction and death. Lack of water in the city, however, could also be just as deadly, as this tended to lead to famine and disease. Recent research has brought to light the fact that mega-droughts, which seemed to have swept across all of North America in the 16th century, were responsible in part for widespread starvation and epidemics and contributed to the collapse of major indigenous civilizations.

Water Works

Mexico City has always been tormented by weather conditions that lead to either an extreme excess or lack of water. Since the fall of Mexico-Tenochtitlan and the rise of Mexico City, modern technology has been continually applied to solve the city's water problems. Inaugurated in 1900, the Great Canal, a tunnel stretching almost 10 miles and dug 100 meters underground, was designed to end flooding in the city once and for all. Twenty-five years after it was inaugurated severe flooding left large parts of the city under water. In 1949, a second tunnel of the Great Canal was added to finally assure that no floods would ever trouble the city again. One year later, a sea of mud and water left much of the city, especially the Historic Center, wallowing in a watery grave.

In 1967, the Deep Drain, with more than 40 miles of pipes running 240 meters below ground, was completed, with another 45 miles of new pipes added in 2007. Although these monumental public works projects were designed to funnel the rainwater out of the city as fast as possible, the city is still overwhelmed by water each and every rainy season. Most of the flooding within the city comes from the inability of the drainage system to absorb the massive quantity of water that falls during a heavy rain, although the city's garbage does its part to clog up the pipes (several scuba divers responsible for keeping the drains from being blocked, often by objects as large as Volkswagen beetles, were killed in action in the last few years).

Throughout the city's history there have been 25 major floods, most of them prompting new public water works to end the problem. Although no major hydraulic project has prevented flooding, they have successfully helped to dry out the mountain valley lakes that made the city so unique. The one thousand square miles of lakes in Mexico-Tenochtitlan have now been almost completely converted into approximately one thousand square miles of concrete. Parallel to the drying out of the city's lakes, the city's rivers have been converted into paved avenues, its streams have been transformed into tunnels and its canals are now used as sewers. And yet, somehow, even without all the city lakes and rivers, water still manages to haunt the city.

The rainy season's torrential rains provoke flash floods, disrupting traffic, washing away precarious homes and converting dry land into swampland, especially in the outskirts of the city where forests have recently been cut down and the soil eroded. Yet even the Condesa, the centrally located neighborhood where I live, is at risk. Like much of the city, the Condesa lies on land that used to be a lake, and traces of this body of water remain underground. When it rains heavily my back-yard patio fills up and often spills over into the kitchen, and a small river accumulates on the street in front of our front door. When we moved in we had a wooden floor installed in our living room. Six months later, the wooden slats had buckled into waves. When we had the wooden floor torn up, we discovered a deep pool of muddy water mere inches below the floor.

There are currently 322 major flood spots officially recognized throughout the city. Like an underwater unconscious, the valley's great lakes live on in the form of mud, sludge and ground water that lie dormant a mere six feet under the surface, patiently waiting to rise up during the rainy season. Yet, at the same time, the city doesn't have enough water to meet the needs of its inhabitants. Given the constant flooding, the problem of water in Mexico City is obviously not due to scarcity but rather to inefficiency and a misguided engineering strategy that began with the Spanish Conquistadors.

Despite the fact that the major bodies of water within the city have all been dried out, some rivers and springs still wend their way through parts of the Mexico City Valley. Due to a fear of flooding, instead of being conserved, rainfall and river water are funneled directly into the sewage system and sent out of the city. Not only does this deprive the city of readily available drinking water, it also denies the Mexico City Valley the opportunity to replenish its underground water basin, up until recently the major source of drinking water for the city.

Before and after the Conquest, Mexico City got its drinking water from underground water sources. The most important of these were the natural springs in Chapultepec Park (a ten minute walk from my house) whose water was transported to the inhabitants of Mexico-Tenochtitlan by stone aqueducts also constructed by Emperor Nezahuacoyotl. The Spaniards destroyed these aqueducts and built a new one that lasted 34 years (1620-1654), and a second one in 1779 (remains of which are still on view on Chapultepec Avenue). In 1806, the city boasted over five hundred private water fountains in government offices, convents, wealthy homes, public baths and bakeries, but only 28 public water fountains to service the city's inhabitants. The lack of sufficient public fountains led to the business of *aguadores* who carried water in clay pots to paying customers all over the city.

By mid-19th century, though, the springs in Chapultepec had dried out from overexploitation and other sources were desperately needed. The discovery of fresh underground springs in other parts of the city led to an obsession for digging wells. These wells, some reaching down as far as 1,000 feet below ground, eventually sucked dry most of the Valley's natural springs and freshwater lakes. Today, there are still 4,500 official wells operating within the city, alongside more than 2,000 illegal ones. Even so, the supply of water is simply not enough for the city's unquenchable demand. At present, more water is extracted from the groundwater within the Valley than is replenished, a difference of ten thousand liters per second and rising.

As holes are dug ever deeper into the earth, the water that is extracted contains more and more sediments, and thus is less potable. Deep water tends to have higher levels of magnesium and iron, substances that must be filtered out, thus making acceptable drinking water even more expensive. In addition, the deeper the wells are dug into the earth, the older the water extracted. Water from wells in Iztapalapa, a neighborhood originally built on salt flats in the mid-20th century and now the site of the most over-exploited underground water sources in the city, has been shown to be over one thousand years old. When I splash tap water onto my hands and face in my bathroom I could very well be washing myself with the same water the Aztecs used to clean themselves.

Pump it Up Mexico City uses more water each day than any other city in the world. With its own water sources overexploited, an increasingly large part of the city's water must be brought in from outside the Mexico City Valley. When I turn on the faucet, the water that fills up my bath now mostly comes from distant sources. Given that Mexico City is a mile-high mountain valley, bringing water up and into the city requires some pretty heavy-duty machinery.

Beginning in 1951, the Lerma River, located in the Toluca Valley about 70 kilometers away from the city, was the first outside water system to be tapped for use by residents of Mexico City. The Lerma Water Works located in Chapultepec Park, equipped with state-of-the-art pumps and pipes that connected the city to this distant water source, was an incredible engineering feat acclaimed by the Federal government (although dozens of workers were killed in the process), and was graced by the world's first underwater mural, *Water, The Origin of Life*, produced by Diego Rivera. For decades, the Lerma River contributed up to 15% of Mexico City's water. Over the last few decades, however, the Lerma River has largely been sucked dry. What's left of this once-great waterway is force-fed each year 170 thousand tons of toxic slime from the thousands of factories, industrial parks and irregular cities located along the banks of the river.

As the Mexico City population grew exponentially, other water sources had to be tapped to meet the increasing demand, and as its pipes sucked up water from further and further away, Mexico City's water costs increased exponentially. The

Cutzamala River, twice as far away as the Lerma River, now supplies up to one third of Mexico City's water needs. The fact that local communities are being deprived of their own water sources, essential for their survival, in order to service the capital is a cause of discontent. The Mazahua Indians who have lived around the Cutzamala River for centuries now lack access to their own river water, and violent protests have resulted. In addition, as water sources tend to be interconnected, by over-exploiting the Cutzamala River to supply drinking water to Mexico City residents, the Chapala Lake in the very distant state of Jalisco is drying up.

Lack of rainfall and higher temperatures lead to lower levels in the main water sources outside the city (dams in Cutzmala have recently been as low as 30% of their capacity), and the quality of water pumped in from the bottom of these dams is poor. In extreme cases, such as the widespread death of fish due to increased temperatures, these water sources can be poisoned. Although Mexico City as a whole depends on Cutzmala for only 30% of its water, some areas, such as the Santa Fe neighborhood in the south of the city, depend completely on water from Cutzmala and suffer droughts when its water levels sink.

Pumping more and more water up and into Mexico City requires more and more electricity. To meet this increased demand, more and more dams have been built on the country's rivers. These dams monopolize the use of local water sources and often force whole towns to move from their homeland, in turn leading to a flood of migrants into Mexico City. Many of the millions of urban land invaders in Mexico City over the past few decades are farmers who fled rural areas impoverished from an inadequate access to water.

The new, haphazard cities these forced immigrants have created in Mexico City creep up and cover the mountains surrounding the city, destroying the trees and forests that normally emit oxygen into the air and protect the soil from becoming unusable dirt and dust. The lack of trees in turn puts these areas at risk of flooding and mudslides, leading to disasters that claim several human lives each year. In addition, the new cities populated with millions of inhabitants that have sprung up around the periphery of Mexico City over the past couple of decades have put an added strain on the city's water supply.

In Mexico City, water has long ceased to be a free, readily available natural resource. The technology needed to bring water into the Mexico City Valley from far off sources converts water into a precious liquid. The government subsidizes the costs of pumping water in from outside the city, and thus water is still relatively cheap in Mexico City (cheaper than in most major cities around the country). Even so, paying money for a natural substance like water seems unnatural, which is perhaps why a good percentage of people and companies in Mexico City don't pay their water bills. If the city government should decide one day to end the subsidies and make customers pay the real cost of the poor quality liquid that comes out of their faucets, blood would flow instead of water.

The demand for water in Mexico City doubles every 20 years, twice as fast as the population growth. For each square meter of new urban construction 50 gallons of recoverable rainfall are lost each year, while for each acre of land occupied by humans the water that could be destined for more than 3,000 families is lost. With the relentless urbanization of every part of the Mexico City Valley, water is becoming less and less a renewable resource and more and more a scarce commodity.

That Sinking Feeling

Due to the overexploitation of its water sources, the city suffers from some of the worst groundwater depletion in the world. Sucking up so much water from underneath the city has undermined the earth itself. As a result, land subsidence, which occurs when porous formations that once held water collapse and lead to the settling of the surface layer, has become a major problem.

Since Mexico City was established the city has dropped more than 20 feet. At the end of the 19th century, Mexico City was sinking two inches a year, but by the mid-20th century the city was dropping down annually almost 20 inches (the depths the city has sunk to over the last century is graphically illustrated on a monument in the Zócalo that marks the original waterline).

As the ground sinks beneath the water line greater flooding occurs, which in turn leads to greater sinking, which leads to even greater flooding, which in turn leads to large-scale public work projects that only tend to make matters worse. To take just one example, Mexico City used to rise six feet above the Texcoco Lake, while today it sits more than thirty feet below the lake's water line. To compensate for this problem, a huge public works project was undertaken to sink the Texcoco Lake deeper into the earth, which in turn made the city government sink deeper into debt, which in turn led to a lack of attention to the city's infrastructure, thus feeding into a vicious cycle of disaster and neglect.

To make matters worse, the surface of the city isn't sinking in an even fashion. As the ground itself is no longer level, the buildings constructed upon it are all askance, many lacking true right angles and others that provoke vertigo in those standing inside them. The Metropolitan Cathedral underwent a complicated restoration process to level off a very extreme tilt, a process in which the higher end of the building was sunk down to the level of the lower end. Without the budget to restore them to their original angles, many centuries-old buildings and ancient monuments that form part of the country's highly valued patrimony are left teetering.

Besides creating a situation in which architecture is at odds with itself, this sinking causes structural damage to the city's already precarious infrastructure. There are currently 250 deep fissures registered in Mexico City, many located on major avenues, and large chunks of street have suddenly collapsed as much as twenty feet during heavy rainfalls, burying vehicles and human beings in open-air graves.

Sinking also increases the amount of damage brought about by earthquakes, a frequent phenomenon in Mexico City. Sinking and earthquakes not only affect structures on the surface of the city, they also tend to damage that which lies below, especially the vast labyrinth of pipes under Mexico City. In 1682, the city installed the first underground pipes to distribute water from the city's aqueduct. Being that they were made out of lead, these pipes gave rise to dysentery, diarrhea and death throughout the city. In 1731, clay pipes replaced the lead ones, but these easily broke. Many of the metal pipes that currently run underneath Mexico City are 100 years old and a large part are rusted and corroded. Old or rusted pipes crack easily when the earth shifts, either from sinking or seismic activity. The 1985 earthquake heavily damaged the city's underground water system (so much so that the blood from the tens of thousands of victims filtered into the pipes of the drinking water system), and the amount of leakage has only increased since then.

Official figures state that more than one-third of all the water that now flows through the city's water system leaks out of pipes at a rate of twelve thousand liters per second (New York City, with a water system 150 years old, loses only half as much), representing a total loss of over one billion liters a year (enough water to supply the whole population of Houston, Texas). What makes matters worse is that water is not the only liquid transported in underground pipes.

Mexico Shitty Although the shit that I and millions of other assholes dump each day into toilets throughout Mexico City takes an amazing voyage beneath the city streets, through six thousand miles of pipes, 68 pump stations and across almost 100 miles of canals, tunnels, dikes and artificial lakes, it often finds its way back to me. The disposal of human sewage (known as *aguas negras*) has always been a major problem in Mexico City. Since the Spanish colony was first established here, canals and rivers have been used as dumping grounds for human feces, with thousands of prisoners and indigenous workers forced to dredge the constantly clogged waterways. The fresh water lakes that irrigated the city's crops and provided drinking water also served as dumping grounds for humans, and this contaminated water (at one point so toxic it roasted duck feathers) spread its stench and disease throughout the city. To deal with this shitty situation, three huge, costly sewage works (the Western Interceptor in 1789, the Great Canal in 1900 and the Central Source in 1975) were built to funnel the *aguas negras* out of the city. As a result, a good chunk of the city's human sewage now rides rivers all the way out to the Gulf of Mexico or the Pacific Ocean. Most, however, remains much closer to home.

In 1971, the Federal government selected the Mezquital Valley in the state of Hidalgo, about 50 miles north of Mexico City, as the ideal destination for the majority of the capital's massive amount of human waste. (In fact, though, towns in the region had already been receiving fecal matter from the capital ever since the first sewage pipe funneled shit outside of Mexico City in 1608.) This was no act of vengeance on the locals, but instead a much sought after gift. As the land in the Mezquital Valley is arid and lacks its own water supply, raw, untreated sewage from Mexico City is used to irrigate almost 40,000 acres of cropland. The sewage sent to the area receives absolutely no treatment, even the most basic one of separating solids from liquids, and thus the Mezquital Valley, watered by the greatest concentration of *aguas negras* in all of Latin America, is commonly referred to as the world's largest outhouse.

Human sewage might help float the local economy but it does so at a price. In return for being able to use sewage as a source of water for crops, locals suffer the stench that emanates from the miasma, and hordes of flies, rats, and other vermin invade the towns in search of sustenance. Local farmers are prone to several acute and chronic health problems, especially skin and intestinal diseases caused by all sorts of especially nasty parasites, but they are not the only ones infected. The vegetables grown in the Mezquital Valley (along all the microorganisms residing within) are transported daily to Mexico City's markets and supermarkets and often make their way into my salad.

Much of Mexico City's raw sewage, however, never even leaves the city. Due to all the leaky or burst pipes, *aguas negras* constantly escape from the sewage system and leech down into the earth beneath the city. This underground sea of shitty sludge, however, has a way of surging up to the surface, especially during rainy season, flooding homes throughout the city and provoking health disasters (during the 2012 Great Black Flood 60,000 inhabitants in a single neighborhood had their homes inundated by dark rivers). In addition, due to all the rusted, cracked and burst pipes carrying water into peoples' homes, human shit often filters into the drinking water and can wind up in my sink.

Water Bugs WC Fields, the great comedian and an unrepentant alcoholic, once claimed that he never drank water because fish fucked in it. In Mexico City, it's not the fish in the water you have to worry about. Unlike tap water in major European and American cities, there is an incredible biodiversity in a single drop of Mexico City tap water.

One recent study by researchers in the UNAM university analyzed 100 samples of Mexico City tap water and found 84 microorganisms of nine different species, all of which are usually present in human and animal shit. One bacteria, Helicobacter pylori, associated with ulcers and gastric cancer, was found in all samples, while E. coli, which causes diarrhea and urinary tract infections, was also well represented. Viruses, including the Legionella virus of hepatitis A and Rotavirus, which can lead to liver and respiratory disease, also showed up in the tap water tested.

Mexico City ranks number one in the world when it comes to gastrointestinal infections (about 90% of adults in the city are infected with Helicobacter pylori) and its drinking water has been shown to be an ideal vehicle for the transmission of salmonella, dysentery and a host of other common diseases. To detect the presence of microorganisms in water, scientists need very sophisticated equipment and must constantly monitor large samples to know how many and in what quantities these pathogens are present (no governmental agency or anyone else for that matter in Mexico City bothers to do this). Although viruses are so small they can only be observed with a specialized electron microscope, bacteria and protozoa can be as much as one hundred times smaller, making their detection in water especially difficult. As the water used for public swimming pools and parks is treated water (that is, recycled sewage), the quantity of microorganisms is much higher than in tap water. Although international health standards recommend keeping the limit under one parasite egg for every liter of treated sewage water, in Mexico there is an acceptable limit of five eggs (but then again, who's counting?).

Although few humans drink treated water, most pets do (my dogs prefer toilet to tap water), and thus almost all are infected with parasites and often pass them along to their owners. For instance, one gram of dog shit can contain up to 15 thousand Cryptosporid eggs. Besides infecting humans, dogs and cats, the Cryptosporid parasite, one of the newer parasites on the scene, infects fish, birds, rats, deer, snakes, sheep, horses and pigs. Studies have found that about half of all cows raised for their milk are infested with Cryptosporid. Outbreaks of this parasite in Mexico City occur from contact with infected animals or animal products, contaminated water, in hospitals and childcare centers, and humans who engage in oral-anal sexual activity.

When humans get sick from an infectious illness, related health problems increase, especially heart disease. Secondary, chronic illnesses (meningitis, respiratory diseases, arthritis, birth defects, reproductive problems, cancer, hepatitis, and liver, kidney and heart problems) are often a legacy of gastrointestinal infections. Helicobacter bacteria can cause gastritis or colitis, which can in turn lead to ulcers and cancer, E. coli can lead to kidney failure and hemorrhages while salmonella can leave people with arthritis and colitis (as in my case). Some bacterial infections lead to thyroid immune dysfunction or neuronal paralysis, while viral infections have been shown to be involved in the onset of diabetes.

In addition to the health and hygiene problems associated with developing countries, Mexico City suffers many of the same problems as industrialized nations, including the contamination of the air, ground, food and water by toxic chemicals. Of the 4 million tons of toxic waste generated in Mexico City each year, more than 95% is dumped directly into the city's sewer system. The chemical and petrochemical industries within the city generate 2.5 million tons of hazardous waste, with only 15% treated in any way and the rest drained directly into the water supply. The most dangerous chemicals found in Mexico City water are nitrates, toxic metals, organic solvents, agricultural pesticides, herbicides and radioactive chemicals. Some of these chemicals can provoke acute and chronic toxicity while others can have harmful effects on human genes that lead to mutations and cancer.

Floating within the city's water supply are also endocrine disruptor compounds, such as certain insecticides, hydrocarbons, polyaromatics, as well as pharmaceuticals and steroids. These aggressive chemicals aren't separated out by common filters or by saturated carbon and ozone filters (like the one we use in our house), and they can disrupt the normal activity of human hormones and can affect several inner organs and even reproductive organs (causing lower sperm count or fecundity).

In Mexico City, water, like the air, is no longer an innocuous substance but has become a tricky, potentially lethal substance. My health, and the health of everyone in my house and throughout the city, is at the mercy of hundred-year-old, leaky, rusted pipes. No one in Mexico City has ever drowned in a glass of water, but drinking tap water has been the downfall of many.

Death In A Bottle

Like all gringos, when I first arrived in Mexico City I was warned about drinking the water. Nonetheless, I regularly drank *aguas de frutas* in markets and on the streets and drank drinks with ice in cantinas. Apart from several bouts of the weird shits, nothing really bad happened to me. Since my run-in with salmonella and my outbreak of colitis, however, water, the substance most present in my body and crucial for my survival, makes me very nervous. I fear that even brushing my teeth, gargling or singing in the shower could do me in.

In the 1990s, following a cholera outbreak that killed more than 500 people, the Mexico City government increased the chlorine content in tap water as a safety measure. Besides leading to health problems (such as genetic mutations) that occur from consuming chlorine or as a result of the reaction between chlorine and shit in the water pipes, the resulting unpleasant smell (much like swimming pool water) and taste made almost everyone shy away from tap water.

Although water is a naturally occurring substance, most water in Mexico City is now purchased and consumed from a plastic bottle. Mexico ranks second in the world in per capita consumption of bottled water, which is now the single most profitable product ever sold. In Mexico, bottled water is a multi-million dollar business, outselling soft drinks by 20%. Although multinational giants dominate the bottled water market in Mexico City, there are hundreds of local bottling firms, most of which are not licensed or regulated in any way, that compete for their market share.

Even though it costs thousands of times more than tap water, there is no assurance that the quality of water inside a plastic bottle is any better. Many brands in Mexico City claim to use electrolysis as a purification process, yet their bottled water is often merely filtered city tap water, with the toxic and parasitic ingredients intact. This seems to be common practice around the world, and not just among the illegal bottlers. In 1999, bottles of Coca-Cola's Bon Aqua had to be recalled due to mold and other bacterial contamination, while in 2005 Coca-Cola was caught selling London tap water containing high levels of carcinogenic substances for $5 a bottle.

The quality of ice tends to be even worse, as the ice industry is even less supervised and regulated. Besides the thousands of legal ice manufacturers there are up to 6,000 unlicensed and unregulated companies in Mexico that make ice. Industrial ice, which represents 60% of all ice produced, is usually just frozen tap water. Freezing does not kill parasites in water, but even if the water used is pure the large blocks of industrial ice transported around the city in trucks, on customized bicycle pushcarts, or dragged along the sidewalk by giant metal tongs pick up parasites on the way to the consumer. Although these blocks of ice are not made for human consumption, they are often chipped by ice picks and sold as flavored ices or used to chill drinks and food.

Drinking ice in the privacy of my own home isn't even safe. Although my refrigerator has an automatic icemaker equipped with a filter, the water used to make the ice comes directly from the tap and, being that it has never been changed or even checked during all the years we've had it, the filter has probably ceased to filter out anything smaller than a fly.

Due to pressure from The World Bank and other international institutions, water first began to be privatized in the 1980s with the sale of dams, the private control of public water and the large-scale marketing of bottled water. In Mexico, water is auctioned off wholesale to the highest global bidder, and multinational companies now lease or buy the land in which a water source is located and pay only a nominal fee to obtain unlimited access. Once they legally own the rights to water sources in Mexico, some multinational companies go to such extremes as to prohibit locals from collecting rainfall, claiming that this is their private property.

Coca-Cola, the company that most profits from water in Mexico, does everything it can to control its property. In 1994, sixteen of its companies were granted permission to use water from 15 rivers in nine states. From 2000 to 2003, ten Coca-Cola bottling plants received concessions from the government of then-President Fox (a former director of Coca-Cola in Mexico) to exploit a total of four million cubic meters of water within the country. Of the 27 permissions granted to Coca-Cola, 19 are for extracting water from water basins and eight are for dumping sewage into them. Coca-Cola's right to Mexico's water is guaranteed by the government, even against the rights of the farmers and indigenous communities who have worked the land fed by these water sources for thousands of years.

If, one day, the leaks in the water pipes were fixed and the city's water system repaired, if instead of dumping rain and river water out of the city it were collected to be used as drinking water, if consumers and corporations didn't dump their waste directly into rivers and lakes, the city might once again, as in the days of the Aztecs, have a naturally replenishing, self-sustaining, truly inexpensive supply of clean drinking water. As a result, many consumers within the city would save a substantial portion of their income, the government would save millions by not having to subsidize its supply, the ground water would be replenished and the city would stop sinking.

With the huge profits being made from the privatization of water in Mexico, however, this doesn't seem likely any time in the near future. Meanwhile, toxic substances and parasites transported around the city by different water sources continue to accumulate within my inner organs, paving the way for liver disease or cancer caused by shitty city water. ✝

FOOD

I Eat Out In New York City I ate as internationally as possible, not French and Italian but food prepared by recent immigrant groups (Polish, Dominican, Vietnamese, Philippine, regional Chinese), which not only is the cheapest but also the least Americanized, that is, the closest to what these immigrants actually ate in their countries of origin. When I arrived in Mexico City, I ate everything I could get my teeth into: street food, food prepared in markets, in traditional neighborhood dives and in elegant restaurants that had been around for decades. I quickly realized that food in Mexico is not considered Mexican food but instead regional, traditional, pre-Hispanic, holiday or anti-hangover food.

What's generally considered Mexican food around the world is actually Ex-Mex, that is, from those states in the US that once belonged to Mexico. Except in certain multinational food chains, it is almost impossible to find burritos, chimichangas, crunchy tacos or nachos in Mexico City. Even people who are familiar with food in Mexico are often confused about its origins, as much of what passes for Mexican food is merely traditional Spanish cooking, while even some of the most patriotic dishes, like *mole* or *chiles en nogada*, have roots in Asia.

Over long periods of time certain cultures co-evolve with the plants and animals that exist within their ecosystem and their digestive system adapts to better assimilate certain foods. I was not born in Mexico, nor were any of my ancestors, and thus my digestive system is genetically different than that of Mexicans. The food I best digest is not necessarily the food that has been eaten here for thousands of years, like corn, beans and chiles, yet my body has been modified by the food I have consumed over the last two decades here in Mexico City. I might never be a Mexican but I am definitely no longer the same New Yorker, at least biologically speaking, I was when I moved down here.

Just as my digestive system and I have changed over the last couple of decades, so too has my neighborhood, the Condesa, evolving from a mostly residential neighborhood into the city's most condensed international-style food emporium. Due to this transformation, the food now eaten in my neighborhood, at least in the dozens and dozens of restaurants that have opened in the last ten years, is radically different than that consumed here when I first arrived, and these changes reflect more than just culinary trends.

The Condesa wasn't yet a neighborhood when the Jockey Club's dog track and polo field were built here at the end of the 19th century. After the Revolution tore down the playgrounds of the rich across the country, the racetrack was converted into a park (Parque Mexico). A community soon grew up around the park, populated in part by European Jewish immigrants and characterized by the Art Deco architecture they brought with them from the Old World. For most of the 20th century, the Condesa was a heterogeneous neighborhood, both in terms of its mix of working-class and homeowners, residential and commercial, as well as its mix of food options.

More than just cheap, tasty food, eating out in my neighborhood brought me in contact with a whole new culture. I met my wife at an old Argentinean diner (I was munching on an empanada, she was eating the stuffed chicken) located one block away from where we now live, and together we began a long relationship of eating out every day, often three times a day.

In an effort to conserve their culture, the European immigrants started up several neighborhood restaurants (one Polish, one German, and one Hungarian) that served their own community, and although few oldtimers were left and the restaurants were often empty by the time I arrived in Mexico City, they were still in operation. Besides these traditional European restaurants in the Condesa, we ate at several *fondas*, family-run, home-style restaurants that serve *comidas corridas* (a succession of small dishes). We often ate chicken cutlets at Los Bisquets (now a large chain throughout the city), rice and beans in a local market, meat and veggie tacos in taco joints, large *tortas* (sandwiches) from street stands near the subway station, and quesadillas sold on any of a dozen street corners. We would also go to cantinas where just ordering a beer or two entitled us to several dishes.

About ten years after I arrived, tired of being merely a consumer of food, I opened a restaurant/bar. The locale had been a Spanish restaurant, famous for its *cocas* (Mallorcan pizza), furnished with a long bar and booths. I cleaned it up, installed a sound system, and decorated the joint with four long light boxes in which I exhibited photomurals I took of street scenes in Havana, Panama City, Lima, Rio and Brooklyn in place of the murals the cityscapes that had been painted on the walls. The design and concept was faithful to the Spanish restaurant that had been there for seventy years, although the food was an homage to La Floridita, an old-style restaurant/bar in Havana.

Over the last few years, however, the Condesa has since been transformed into the dining room for the whole city. Unlike the European immigrants who settled here and sought to preserve their traditional culture and diet in a strange land, and unlike the taco joints that have served the same food for decades, the new restaurants tend to reflect trendy international food options.

Although the Condesa is now often called La Fondesa, almost all of the old-style *fondas* from the neighborhood have been bought out and converted into international-style restaurants which are directly responsible for the elevated rents that have made *fondas* a thing of the past, and what is now eaten here is a globalized mishmash of fashion food, imitations of foreign fare with little relation to the original.

Glocal If I hang a left after stepping out of my house I'm immediately confronted by a hamburger joint, a hotdog restaurant, a Greek deli, a Chinese restaurant, an Argentine steakhouse and a 7/11. If I take a right and walk two blocks from my house I enter Condesa's trendy food mall, with a glut of US and European-style restaurants, bistros, *trattorias*, pubs, sushi joints, as well as Domino pizzas and Starbucks, that have nothing to do with Mexican culture (or any other for that matter).

Coinciding with the start of the 21st century, the Condesa becameone of the city's main dining destinations for the younger generations of Mexicans flaunting their own (or their parents') disposable income, for European and American corporate workers in Mexico, and for tourists. Yet despite the global consumer playground it has been transformed into, my neighborhood still retains ties to Mexico's indigenous culinary traditions. In Mexico City, the past never disappears completely and radically different economies and cultures overlap, each finding its own niche within the social strata that such a large and populated city offers. Amidst all these new culinary concepts competing for consumers, there is still food cooked with the same ingredients and in the same way as human beings have been preparing food in the Mexico City Valley for thousands of years.

Today, traditional food tends to be served on cheap plastic plates, often from homemade pushcarts, pick-up trucks or in unfurnished spaces, without waiters or table clothes, and is usually eaten standing up. One tiny hole-in-the-wall taco joint a few blocks from my house has become a legend amongst locals (immortalized by the Mexican rock band Molotov) and foreigners as well (it received a rave review in

Gourmet magazine). The tacos here bear no relation to Taco Bell tacos in the States, or to the meat tacos found in chains all over Mexico. Some are made with beef or pork or the inner organs of animals, legacies of Spain, but there are also fillings made with nopal cactus, green and brown *mole*, *huitlacoche* (corn mold), *flor de cala-baza* (pumpkin flower), *quelites* (a cross between an herb and a shrub), beans and avocado, all foodstuffs that have been grown and consumed locally since before even the Aztecs arrived on the scene.

Every Monday, a *mercado sobre ruedas* (a 'market-on-wheels' that travels around the neighborhood) sets up in front of my house. In addition to butcher meats and dairy products, this market sells indigenous fruit (papayas, mameys), vegetables (avocados, tomatoes, potatoes) and hand-made blue tortillas. Outside of a church located two blocks from my house, corn-on-the-cob and corn-in-a-cup are served boiling hot out of a large pot. A metal tent mounted on a bicycle toots its steam-driven whistle at night offering *camotes* (sweet potatoes) and fried bananas, while from a pot of boiling water on wheels with a portable loudspeaker another vendor sells *tamales* stuffed with *rajas* or *mole*. A pick-up truck that parks on a corner a couple of blocks away from my house sells regional products from Oaxaca, including bags of grasshoppers.

These food options, many which existed before Cortés ever set eyes on Mexico-Tenochtitlan, are gradually being squeezed out by the profound social and economic changes currently occurring within the neighborhood. The production and consumption of traditional foods helps preserve the indigenous cultures within Mexico, and the disappearance of these food options in the Condesa is a reflection of the extinction of the indigenous presence within the city.

Food For The Gods An increasingly dense concentration of human beings in the Mexico City Valley eventually gave rise to the first city in the Americas (Cuicuilco), which in turn gave rise to agriculture. To keep accounts of crop yields and food tributes writing was invented, to schedule the harvests calendars were created, and the preparation of food grew into a social activity that permeated the whole culture (religion, music, art). When the Aztec immigrants first arrived in the Mexico City Valley, several major cities had already come and gone, but the culture of these nations lived on, especially in the form of the cultivation and preparation of certain plants, insects and animals.

Even after hundreds of years of searching for a homeland, suffering all the misery and desperation of migrants in a harsh land, the Aztecs couldn't have been overjoyed to settle on a small, barren island surrounded by salt water lakes and swampland, especially at mealtime. It would have been hard enough for the Aztecs to survive on the food they managed to scrounge up for themselves (often only the moss growing on rocks and the spiders scudding along the lakes) but they also had to share their food with dozens of gods. The gods were always hungry, constantly clamoring for food. If their appetites went unappeased, crops or even whole harvests could be destroyed. By the time Mexico-Tenochtitlan had grown to become the greatest imperial city in the Americas, the gods responsible for this meteoric rise to power were eating to their heart's content.

Although the corn, chiles, chocolate, pulque, reptiles and birds offered up to them in their altars were tasty appetizers, the gods' often demanded richer, more substantial fare. What the Aztec gods most hungered for was blood, and there was none as delicious as human blood. To satisfy their gods' hunger, the Aztecs would regularly pierce their tongues or ears with maguey cactus thorns, and the blood that spilled onto the ground was considered payment for all they had received from the gods. The nobles and priests, who lived higher on the hog and thus incurred a greater debt, pricked their pricks with thorns.

There were times, however, when mere blood could not satiate the gods' appetite. Before wars and battles, during disruptions in the cosmic order (earthquakes, eclipses, floods, dry spells, famines, etc.), when sacred objects had been stolen from the temples or the gods had been offended, or when someone from the noble class died and wanted company on their trip to the great beyond, something even more meaty was needed to appease the gods' hunger.

Even more than blood, the gods relished human flesh. Human sacrifice had been celebrated by all of the past civilizations within the Mexico City Valley, but the Aztecs perfected the process and upped the numbers. Though prisoners of war and slaves were mostly offered for sacrifice, sick boys, babies, virgins and hunchbacks were also acceptable food for the gods.

The gods' meals were usually prepared in a temple on top of a pyramid, with the slab of meat (that is, a live human being) laid out upon a large stone that lifted their chest and their head held down by four priests. The victim's belly would then be sliced open by an "obsidian butterfly" (a double-edged knife), after which a priest would reach up into the thorax and wrench out the "precious cactus fruit" (their heart). When the heart was removed, tubes were stuck inside the body to funnel the "precious water" (blood) into a "flower" (a fountain), which was collected inside a green squash and handed to the owner of the slave or the captor of the prisoner.

No part of the body was ever thrown away, and everything was either eaten or converted into art or souvenirs. Aztec priests were not only skilled in the kill, they were also masters of dressing the bodies after the ceremony. Razor-sharp obsidian knives, as well as swordfish beaks chopped off limbs, served to flay skin, slice muscles and tendons, and separate heads from bodies. The victim's head was skinned and then displayed in the *tzompantli* (the rack of skulls that adorned the temples), while the body parts the owners, captors or priests didn't want were cut into small pieces and offered as a gift to royalty. The victim's entrails were usually fed to the animals, birds, and snakes in the zoo in Chapultepec.

Cannibal Capital Human sacrifice, the most important communal activity in all great indigenous civilizations, served more than just providing food to the gods. The sacrifices carried out atop the pyramids were public spectacles that brought communities together and helped maintain social unity. They also served as political propaganda designed to strike fear in the hearts of all the locals and the foreign dignitaries in attendance and to deter them from ever considering rebelling against the empire. Human sacrifice, however, also served an even more practical function.

Meat and other sources of proteins had become very scarce in the Mexico City Valley since around 7,000 BC, when hunters had completely exterminated mammals (woolly mammoths, camels, horses, deer and antelopes) suitable for domestication. Before these animals disappeared from the Valley, meat represented 80% of what native's ate, but once this source of protein was eliminated inhabitants' meat consumption dropped to less than 20% of their diet.

Due to the large population and class inequalities within the Aztec capital, the lower classes rarely had the opportunity to eat meat. Although fish and waterfowl were available from the lakes, most of the commoners living in the city lacked access to this protein source, subsisting mainly on domesticated plants such as squash, beans and corn. In contrast to the commoners, the Aztec elite had a diet enriched by wild game imported from outside the Valley where mammals had not been exterminated.

In the late 15th century, Mexico-Tenochtitlan was beset by five consecutive years of crop failure brought about by frosts and drought. Royal reserves were able to feed the inhabitants of the city for only a year, after which everyone was on their own. Commoners and even some nobles were forced to sell their children into slavery in order to obtain food enough to survive. This severe lack of food put great pressure on the State to find a new source of protein or else risk a civil war.

The Aztecs regularly engaged in *guerras floridas* with neighboring nations. Before battle, the Aztecs often had to send food to the warriors of their enemies, as the heavy tributes of food the Aztecs demanded from these nations kept them undernourished, and the Aztecs would further fatten up the captured warriors in an attempt to put a little extra fat on their bones before sacrificing them to the gods. Beautiful male slaves who represented Aztec gods would be wined and dined for months and given free reign amongst the slave women, all with the aim of producing juicier meat. Just before they were sacrificed, the victims were plied with large quantities of *pulque* laced with psychoactive mushrooms or peyote to steady their nerves (and perhaps to improve the flavor of their flesh).

After the sacrifice of a prisoner captured in battle, a feast would be given at the captor's house, a major event to which family and those of social standing in the community were invited. The central dish of the feast was often a stew of tomatoes, peppers and meat carved from the sacrificial victim, with a side of corn and chile. Steaming bowls of *pozole* enriched with juicy chunks of human meat or tamales large enough to accommodate a human arm or leg inside were also served, and human blood was often added to thicken *mole* sauce made from peanuts, chocolate, chiles and other spices. The victims' brain, extracted through holes drilled into the skull, a delicious, protein-packed snack, was reserved for the high priests. Although royalty got first dibs on the most succulent body parts, Moctezuma himself ate little human meat, and when he did he made sure it was well cooked and highly seasoned.

Bernal Díaz, a soldier who arrived with Cortés and wrote an account of the Conquest, witnessed the sacrifice of his fellow countrymen captured by the Aztec warriors during the Spaniards' *La noche triste*: "Then they kicked the bodies down the steps, and the Indian butchers who were waiting below cut off their arms and legs and flayed their faces, which they afterwards prepared like glove leather, with their beards on, and kept for their drunken festivals. Then they ate their flesh with a sauce of peppers and tomatoes."

Bernal Díaz also mentions that the Aztecs "used to cook the meat of young boys, and as they had so many kinds of stews and so many other things, we never checked to see if they were made with human or another kind of meat". Some human meat was sold in city markets to commoners, although this was against the law and severely punished if discovered. According to Cortés, on a long march he caught some Aztecs soldiers with a corpse they had dressed up to appear alive and upon which they would snack along the way.

Mexican archeologists excavating an Aztec sacrificial site in the neighborhood of Tlatelolco between 1960 and 1969 uncovered headless skeletons lacking limb bones and piles of human skulls broken open to extract the brains. (This excavation, which proved beyond a doubt the brutality of the Aztec regime, was carried out at the same time and in the same site as the Tlatelolco student massacre, in which hundreds of students and political activists were brutally murdered while protesting pacifically.) In a very recent dig, one hundred bodies were dragged from beneath Mexico City's Metropolitan Cathedral, sixty-seven of which had their skin, muscles or tendons ripped off, bones were found with butcher-like cut marks, many of the skulls were perforated, and cooking pots were found next to skeletons missing limb bones.

Up until a few decades ago, Mexican scholars tended to deny that Aztecs and other indigenous nations were cannibals in an effort to keep them from being viewed as a primitive and barbaric race. On the other hand, some gringo anthropologists went so far as to claim that the "cannibal empire" of the Aztecs used their enemy nations as "stockyards" of meat. These days most everyone agrees that Aztecs ate human flesh, the only question is whether it was standard fare or served up only in times of extreme hunger.

Creepy Crawlers

The cannibal nation argument is based on the claim that Aztecs needed meat and fat to provide them with sufficient protein to survive. In fact, though, during the time of the Aztec empire, the Mexico City Valley possessed one of the world's richest biodiversity, an almost unlimited variety of animals, plants and insects that could provide sufficient protein to the local populace.

Although herbivorous mammals had been exterminated in the Valley, the Aztecs domesticated wild birds, such as turkeys, as well as rabbits and hairless *cholosquincle* dogs, which were castrated, force-fed and sold in the market as meat. Big cats such as lions and pumas, as well as wild boars and bears, could still be hunted in the mountains, and there were fish in abundance within the many lakes surrounding Tenochtitlan. Several kinds of turtles, frogs, river shrimp, axolotls, lizards, iguanas and snakes, all excellent sources of protein, were readily available to be eaten, as well.

More than any of these creatures, insects provided the best source of protein for the Aztecs. The Aztecs had no specific word for insects, referring to them merely as "the meat we eat." (The meat-eating Europeans in Mexico, however, considered creepy crawlers the devil's handymen and mostly refused to eat them.)

Thousands of insect species lived (and continue to live) in the Mexico City Valley, including around 500 edible ones, with worms, ants, bees, butterflies, grubs, gnats, flies, mosquitoes, wasps, beetles and grasshoppers among the most common. (Chapultepec Park was named for the abundance of grasshoppers there.)

Insect eggs and larva were considered great delicacies, with the eggs of water flies or water spiders the pre-Hispanic equivalent of caviar.

Edible insects supply minerals, essential amino acids, iron, calcium, B vitamins, riboflavin, magnesium and, more than anything else, protein. Insects can contain up to twice as much protein as beef (a single earthworm provides the nutritional equivalent of 50 grams of meat). While only one-tenth of all food eaten by cattle is converted into meat, insects convert food to meat at a much higher rate and thus offer more protein per pound than beef or chicken.

The consumption of insects helps fight diseases of the heart, digestive system, respiratory tract, bones and nerves, and they also act as natural antibiotics and function as pain killers. Eating honey ants counteracts fevers, water bugs have anesthetic and analgesic properties and bee's poison can help fight arthritis and rheumatism.

Munching on insects instead of animals could do great things not just for our health but for that of our planet, as well. Insects are infinitely less inexpensive to breed and harvest than animals, need no chemicals or machinery to reproduce or grow, don't use great extensions of land, require no refrigeration and, because they are readily available almost everywhere on the planet, little fossil fuel is needed to transport them to market. Pound for pound, insects are the 'greenest' meat on the planet.

Insects reproduce way faster than any animal and thus provide an easily renewable source of food. A female cricket can lay up to 1,500 eggs in one month, termites lay over 30,000 eggs a day, while ants can pump out over 300,000 a day. Given that insects far outnumbered the Aztec population, it seems improbable that Aztecs would go to all the trouble of capturing and sacrificing other human beings just to get the protein that the bugs crawling across the floors of their homes or flying around their fields could have provided.

Although insects provided an excellent source of protein they were still mostly just appetizers for the Aztecs, and it was the plant kingdom that was called upon to supply the needed sustenance. The Aztec had developed advanced techniques of terracing, irrigating and fertilizing, and along with the *chinampas* that comprised 20,000 acres of artificial crop islands located within the city's lakes, they were blessed with four harvests a year and food enough to feed the whole city. Intercropping (growing several different crops on the same land) produced excellent results, particularly when beans were planted with maize corn, as the nitrogen-fixing beans helped increase corn yields. In addition, the traditional practice of planting edible wild herbs alongside squash and maize served both to deter pests and to provide additional foods before the corn harvest, a time when there could have been scarcity.

For the pre-Hispanic cultures in the Mexico City Valley corn was much more than just a food and it was referred to as 'flesh and bones.' Although by itself corn offers no protein, when prepared as tortillas and eaten with beans, squash or amaranth, these foodstuffs together provide amino acids similar to that of animal protein. Onions, red and green tomatoes, *jicamas* and sweet potatoes were cultivated in the Valley, as well, and there was also a great selection of fruit, both those grown locally and those brought into the city as tribute from coastal or tropical villages. Dozens of varieties of edible mushrooms were also available, while chiles were present at every meal.

The spiky leaves of the nopal cactus have always been a staple in the local diet and they are a rich source of readily available protein. Pulque, the naturally fermented drink extracted from the agave cactus, although mostly restricted to royalty, the elderly, the sick and warriors except during certain holidays, provided large quantities of carbohydrates, minerals and vitamins.

Even edible flowers contributed to the local diet. The *noche buena* flower (a traditional Christmas decoration), *cempoalxochitl* (the Day of the Dead flower), margaritas, vanilla bean and pumpkin flowers were all eaten in salads and soups, and flowers were used to flavor hot chocolate. The wild, edible herb *quelite*, rich in vitamin A, was another easily acquired ingredient, as were pumpkin seeds that provided more protein than egg whites. Honey from bees and cactus sap were widely used as sweeteners.

The *spirulina* algae that covered the surface of lakes in the Mexico City Valley provided a great source of protein, vitamins and minerals, could be easily collected and was abundant enough to make it part of the local diet. The Aztecs ate so much swamp grass and "rock dung" (moss), especially when they first migrated to their swamp island, that they became known throughout the Valley as the "weed eaters."

Throbbing Gristle After the Conquest, the diet in Mexico City changed radically. One of the greatest transformations in the Mexico City Valley was the introduction of pigs, sheep, goats and cows, brought to the New World to provide the Spaniards with a healthy diet of protein and fat. Just as European bacteria, viruses and parasites went wild when they first arrived in the New World, so too these grazing animals, without any other mammals of their kind to compete against, had free rein to expand and reproduce.

Throughout a large part of the 17th and 18th century, cows, pigs and sheep multiplied so much that their meat was cheap enough that most inhabitants in Mexico City (including the indigenous population) could afford to eat meat every day. In fact, after wheat and corn, meat became the third most consumed food and represented a greater percent of the daily diet than it does today. The wealthy class dined on sheep, soldiers and prisoners were fed beef, the poor had to chew their way through bull meat, but pork was affordable to most everyone. Although Aztecs originally consumed almost no fat or dairy products, after the Conquest, pre-Hispanic dishes came to depend for flavor on animal fat and were often smothered in cream and cheese produced from cow milk.

Meat and dairy products continue to represent a major part of the local diet and of the Mexican economy, as well. For the northern states in Mexico, the exportation of meat to the US is a major part of the economy, while southern states have been converted into grazing land to supply meat for Mexico City. The raising and slaughtering of animals in Mexico has been modernized and industrialized to meet the demand of so many carnivorous consumers. To increase the yield of meat per beast, farm animals are now force-fed a steady diet of tranquilizers, hormones, antibiotics and hundreds of other chemicals from before they are born to even after they die (chickens in Mexico are shipped to market floating within a cocktail of chemicals that fattens them up port-mortem).

In humans, growth hormones have been implicated in allergic reactions, prostate and breast cancer, and the premature onset of menstruation and breast development. Recent cases of food poisoning in Mexico City from the consumption of beef liver and cow's eyes (a special treat eaten in tacos) have uncovered the widespread use of clembuterol and other illegal hormones. Clembuterol is an illegal anabolic steroid and bronchodilator often used by athletes to increase muscle build-up and performance. Recently, several Mexican World Cup soccer players tested positive for clembuterol and were suspended, that is, until their lawyers convinced the authorities that the presence of steroid in the athletes' bodies came not from illegal injections but rather from chicken they had eaten the day before they were tested.

Most antibiotics manufactured today are not used to treat humans but instead are injected into the ears of healthy pigs, chickens and cows in order to fatten them up as well as to control the constant outbreak of diseases in the overpopulated and often unhygienic animal factories. The use of antibiotics (including penicillin and tetracycline) creates resistance to certain bacteria, thus threatening not just the animals but also their human consumers.

Pesticides often find their way into industrial animal feed and concentrate in animal fat and milk consumed by humans. Dioxins in the pesticides have been shown to produce cancer and disrupt hormonal activity, thus altering the reproductive, neurological and immunological systems of fetuses and newborns. In addition, natural poisons can be produced within the animal when slaughtered that when mixed with urea and uric acid within the animal can also contaminate meat. To supplement their food supply, industrial animals are often fed the meat of other animals, turning vegetarian animals into carnivores. Even worse, industrial animals are often fed the meat, or at least ground-up bones, of their own species, thus converting them into cannibals, an excellent way to spread fatal illnesses (such as Mad Cow disease).

Besides the official government-licensed slaughterhouses (in which the meat of cows, chickens and other animals is exempt from inspection), there are around 1,500 clandestine slaughterhouses in Mexico City. It is estimated that almost 80% of all animals sacrificed in the city slaughterhouses are killed in cruel, unsanitary conditions. Most animals are sliced up on floors covered in animal shit (both from the animals being slaughtered as well as from the rats, cats and dogs that scrounge for leftovers). The slaughterhouse in Ciudad Nezahuacoyotl, one of the largest in the city, was recently closed down for unsanitary conditions, though it wasn't necessarily any worse than hundreds of others still in operation. Today, most pork consumed in Mexico City comes from unregulated, garbage-fed pigs sold by local butchers in informal markets, and the origin of the meat eaten in tacos in street food stands and cheap restaurants could very well be horse, mule and donkey meat, all much cheaper than beef, pork or chicken.

In Mexico City, no part of any animal is ever thrown away and every part of the beast is consumed in some form or another. Stands on street corners in my neighborhood sell tacos stuffed with fried skin, snouts, eyes, ears, inner organs, intestines, sweat glands, uteruses and udders. Cow brain is served in quesadillas stands on the street or fried in black butter at fancy restaurants. Goat head served whole can be eaten in traditional restaurants, bull's balls are served fresh in a taco joint just outside the bullfighting ring, and *morongo* (blood sausage) is a local favorite.

Even though the Pacific Ocean and the Gulf of Mexico are hours away from the city, fish and seafood have always been a delicacy in Mexico City. During the Aztec empire, relays of runners would bring fresh fish and seafood into the city from Veracruz or Acapulco for the elaborate banquets of the royalty. These days, seafood and fish are brought into the main markets during the week by refrigerated trucks. Within the city's fish and seafood markets, there are no government sanitary controls (due to a conflict between local and federal authorities), and sanitary conditions and freshness are not always of the highest quality. In addition, thousands of street stands lack refrigeration or running water sell ceviche, sushi and raw oysters.

Animal organs, tripe and viscera, and whole fish, as well, provide an ideal environment within which microorganisms can flourish. The prevalence of rats and cockroaches, lax hygienic regulation, and the poor conservation and cooking of meat or fish combine to convert Mexico City markets and eating establishments into ideal parasite breeding grounds. Although there are strict sanitary laws and codes, there is no enforced standard water temperature for washing dishes (many restaurants don't even use hot water), for food storage or handling, nor for workers' hygiene (other than signs in the bathrooms that ask workers to wash their hands). In fact, government inspectors never actually inspect kitchens in the Condesa restaurants and no restaurant has ever been closed down or even fined because of unsanitary conditions.

Street food is even less regulated than restaurants. Food stands usually display their food without any protection against airborne microbes or pollution, most lack running water, many use ice made from tap water, and many cooks prepare and serve the food with the same hand that they receive dirty bills and coins. As a result, food eaten in the Condesa, both that which is served indoors and on the street, both local and international, comes with a healthy serving of microorganisms.

Parasite Paradise

Microorganisms have inhabited the inner organs of humans for thousands of years. Humans tend to come into contact with their local bacteria at a very early age. In general, humans and microorganisms coexist in mutual symbiosis, with humans feeding their guests who in return help by breaking down and pre-digesting certain foods humans can't assimilate.

When a new, uninvited guest slips in, though, severe turf wars can ensue, and the host tends to pay for the damage (Moctezuma's revenge, the bad shits brought on by the consumption of food rich in local parasites, is a good example of this). One out of every four *chilangos* and one out of every three tourists in the city suffer from parasites, most without even realizing what they carry within their bodies (many parasites are only discovered during autopsies). In several studies carried out in lower-income neighborhoods within Mexico City, 100% of all those tested were shown to be infested with aggressive microorganisms, and most *chilangos* carry within their bodies around 300 different kinds of worm parasites and over 70 kinds of protozoa. After my first bloody bout, I played host to salmonella twice more and to aggressive amoebas and parasites several times, probably much more than I am aware.

Ascaris roundworm parasites are so common they can be found inside the large intestines of one-quarter of the world's population and up to 90% of the infantile population of certain countries. Contracted mostly from contaminated water and uncooked vegetables fertilized with human shit, Ascaris invade the large intestine where they reproduce like mad. When their population reaches critical mass, they can jam up the large intestine, blocking the flow of shit until the intestine bursts. They can also gang up on the epiglottis in the throat, causing suffocation or asphyxia, or besiege the respiratory tract, provoking hemorrhage or inflammation of the lungs. These worms can lead to stunted growth in babies, and in children they often invade the liver, the peritoneal cavity and the appendix. Infected adults carry as many as 27 million worm eggs, and with up to 200,000 eggs excreted daily these humans can be seen as factories designed to spread parasites to friends and family.

Giardia is the most common parasite, flourishing within 9 million bodies in Mexico, with perhaps a 40% infection rate in Mexico City. Traveling within particles of human shit, Giardi survives in undercooked meat, in lettuce or canned salmon, and once inside the human body its eggs descend into the stomach and then worm their way to the small intestine where they hook themselves onto the wall provoking diarrhea and stomach pain. When mature, these protozoa migrate into the large intestine where they reproduce, giving rise to alternating bouts of diarrhea and constipation, as well as stomach pains and dysentery (painful diarrhea mixed with blood and mucus). Giardi can also penetrate into the bloodstream, causing anemia and damaging the liver, lungs and brain, and they can even disfigure a person's face with ulcers.

When pigs eat human shit (which they do surprisingly often) they can be contaminated with tapeworms, and when humans eat the infected pig meat they can contract cysticercoids. It is calculated that one in every three dishes of pork served in Mexico City contains this tapeworm (probably even higher for *tacos al pastor*, the meat coming from a huge slab of roasting pig meat). Over 3% of corpses examined in Mexico City showed signs of cysticercoids, and 2.5% of doctor consultations within the city were because of infections of this parasite. Once inside the human body, the adult tapeworm can reach up to seven feet long and with the small hooks on its head it can latch onto skin and muscles, as well as eyes, spinal column and brain. The presence of these worms usually provokes only mild discomfort, but their death can set off violent reactions that can cause muscle pain, weakness, fever, convulsions and brain inflammation. It is believed that tapeworms are responsible for half of all the cases of epilepsy in Mexico.

Trichinella usually enters humans who eat undercooked or poorly packaged pork, although it can also be acquired by eating meat from sea mammals, horses, bears and wild boars (the last two sold in several pre-Hispanic and Yucatan restaurants in Mexico City). After entering a human body, the female worms lay eggs that give rise to 1,000 larva which are transported to the large intestine by way of the lymph nodes and the bloodstream. Once mature, these parasites eat their way out of the intestines and travel throughout the body, penetrating muscles, especially those of the tongue, the eyes and between ribs, where they cause inflammation and aches and pain. When larvae reach the heart muscle, inflammation can occur and lead to heart attacks. The majority of the symptoms (thirst, fever, profuse sweating, bleeding beneath the fingernails, muscle aches or inflammation of the eyelids) present themselves only after the first week or two, making early detection difficult.

Other microorganisms that survive within the meat of animals and cause food poisoning in humans, including the very popular E. coli and my own personal favorite salmonella, can lead to mucus and blood in the feces, Down syndrome, peritonitis and in some cases death (usually from dehydration). Most Mexicans carry amoebas within them, and even those who don't suffer symptoms can share their amoebas with others. Often amoebas lie dormant until awakened by the presence of other amoebas, protozoa or even viruses, and gut parasites co-exist and often work better as a team, benefiting from the attacks of the others on the host's immune system. Like the united front of pigs, cows and sheep, a variety of aggressive microorganisms allows for greater penetration and dominance of human beings.

Gastrointestinal problems caused by parasites represent the most common diseases in the history of the Mexico City Valley. At the start of the 20th century, more than one out of every hundred people in the city died of gastrointestinal disorders. Antibiotics now offer the quickest, most effective short-term treatment for microorganisms but treatments that don't completely exterminate parasites only make them stronger. In the long run, antibiotics can do more damage to human hosts than to their parasites, not only giving rise to antibiotic-resistant and more virulent strains, but also killing off much of the beneficial gut flora, thus opening the body's defenses to other harmful parasites.

Aztecs understood that the best way to deal with parasites was to prevent their propagation and dispersion. Aztec cities had strict sanitary codes, with all human waste deposited in communal dumps, and thus Aztecs didn't suffer much from parasite infestation. When they were attacked by parasites, Aztecs used the natural defenses of plants to help fight off parasites. Local edible plants not only have antibiotic properties, they also act as probiotics. Papaya extract, pumpkin seeds, *ajenjo* (the plant absinthe is made from) and chiles all coexist with complex bacterial communities that have developed defenses against parasite invasions and which they share with their human consumers, which is why these plants have always been an essential part of the local diet.

The Spice Of Life   Despite the trendy food creations whipped up daily in Condesa restaurants, the least important thing about food, in terms of human evolution and survival, is that it looks enticing and stimulates one's tastes buds. The traditional Mexican diet is what it is because it has helped humans survive under harsh conditions, especially the existence of potentially lethal parasites. In other words, Mexican food doesn't exist because it tastes good but because it does good, and taste buds have evolved to perceive certain foods as tasty because they are nutritious and have properties that help ensure the survival of mankind.

This is especially true with chiles. Chiles were among the first plants ever cultivated in Mesoamerica. There are more varieties in Mexico than anywhere else and Mexicans are among the largest consumers of chile. Most Mexican dishes are cooked with chiles and those that aren't have chile added to them at the table with an endless variety of salsas.

Besides the immediate explosion of heat and taste, chiles contain natural chemicals that can kill off certain parasites, cure the common cold, prevent heart attack, get rid of phlegm and pus, help stop coughing up blood, treat blood in feces and piss, aid indigestion, treat both constipation and diarrhea, stimulate appetite, induce birth and shrink hemorrhoids. Chiles are believed to help combat cancer, especially in the prostate gland, by provoking cancer cells to self-destruct.

Chiles also stimulate the blood flow to sexual organs and thus act as an aphrodisiac (Aztec women were prohibited from eating chile during religious ceremonies to avoid getting sexually excited). The shape of many chiles is similar to that of the male sex organ, and thus is a favorite in *albures* (sexual wordplay), such as the Mexican macho's boastful apology: "Small but spicy." Due to all benefits above and beyond their taste, Aztecs considered chile as holy.

Chiles, however, are not perfect. They have been shown to scar intestines, irritate organs, and cause swelling and eruptions in undesirable parts of the body, especially in the digestive tract and in the anus. Chiles have been proven to promote the existence of carcinogens that lead to duodenal, liver and stomach cancer, and the probability of developing gastric cancer is five times greater among heavy consumers.

The United States recently claimed that jalapeño chiles imported from Mexico were responsible for an outbreak of salmonella, and chiles have also been implicated in cases of lead poisoning. A high lead content exists in food grown in urban fields where there is lead in the air, ground or the water, or in rural areas irrigated with sewage (which includes some of Mexico City's largest produce providers). Even if chiles leave the fields clean, they can become contaminated with lead from the earth in the bags in which they're transported, from the scales on which they're weighed or in the process of being dried out and ground into powder.

There is a big difference between chiles that have been grown without pesticides and chemical fertilizers and those that are industrially grown and processed. The majority of chile products sold in supermarkets and consumed in the Condesa are industrially-produced chile powders, canned chiles and bottled salsas, a far cry from the incredible variety of natural chiles that can still be found in the large neighborhood markets.

Junkfood Junkies

Like chile, the fruits used in dozens of Mexican candies can also become contaminated with lead if they are stored or sold in glazed ceramic pots. Traditional lead-glazed pottery is hardened at low temperatures, and therefore the lead remains in the glaze and can be released into foods and beverages, especially acidic foods, such as chiles, citric fruits, tomatoes, and lemon juice. Mexico is the number one consumer of lollipops in the world, approximately 90 pops per person a year. One of the leading candy companies exports 300 products to 27 countries (including their popular corn-shaped lollipops dipped in chile powder).

The States of California, Texas and Washington have all banned brands of chile and fruit sweets, as well as lollipops with chile dipping powder, due to the high levels of lead they claim to have found in these popular products. It is ironic that laws are passed in the United States to protect its citizens from the dangers of lead, while sugar, the main ingredient in lollipops and candies, has proven to be a much more lethal ingredient. Almost no one dies from lead poisoning in their food these days, but millions have their health seriously affected and their lifespan drastically reduced by sugar.

In Mexico, honey from bees and the syrup from the maguey plant were originally used as sweeteners. When sugarcane was brought over by the Spanish it quickly became a basic part of the local culture and economy (Cortés was the first landholder to cultivate sugarcane and produce sugar). In the Caribbean, the bulk of the sugar crop was exported to the US and Europe, but the sugar harvested in Mexico was mostly consumed locally.

Processing sugar cane into white sugar powder has changed a nutritional, traditional sweetener into a health hazard. Although sugar was originally merely crystallized cane juice (called *azucar mascabado* in Mexico) and thus retained most of the plant's vitamins and minerals, white sugar, by far the most common form of sugar consumed in North America today, is the byproduct of a chemical process that eliminates all natural fiber and protein. The liquid obtained from sugar cane, or from vegetables such as beets and corn, is washed with phosphoric acid and lime (the chemical, not the citric fruit) and carbon dioxide is added to speed up the chemical process. Sugar is whitened with sulfuric acid, boiled until thick, passed through more chemical processes, including a filtration process using animal bones, and then cooked until it crystallizes. In the end, white sugar is anything but natural and supplies only empty calories.

White sugar is present in almost all sweets, processed foods and soft drinks, and even in medicine, that is, in the majority of products Mexicans most consume these days. Excessive consumption of sugar can lead to health problems. Sugar depletes calcium in the body, which can lead to osteoporosis, and is involved in hypoglycemia. High blood sugar, in turn, can cause nervous system damage and is the leading cause of blindness among adults. When tissues and organs are over-loaded with excess sugar they become inflamed and age more rapidly. Cholesterol builds up on blood vessel walls damaged by excess blood sugar in an attempt to seal the many connective tissue cracks and leaks, and thus around three out of four adults with high blood sugar have high blood pressure. Sugar is also linked to the build-up of deadly body fats, and adults with high blood sugar have heart dis-ease death rates up to 4 times higher.

Mexico now has the world's highest rate of obesity, beating out even the United States. Seventy percent of all Mexicans, men and women, are overweight, while one third are obese. The concentration of obesity in Mexico City is even higher, as city-dwellers tend to consume energy-dense diets, high in saturated fat and sugar, and lead sedentary lifestyles (around 80 percent of adults do no exercise at all, while about one out of every three policemen in Mexico City is obese).

Obesity has been tied directly to the consumption of excessive amounts of sug-ar. Obesity is bad enough by itself, putting added pressure on organs and bones, but it can also lead to arthritis, hypertension, high levels of cholesterol and, more than anything else, diabetes. Over ten percent of all Mexicans adults have diabetes, which is now one of the leading causes of death among Mexican adults (a little more than twenty years ago it was number 35 on the death list), a rate more than 50% higher than in the United States. Severe forms of diabetic nerve disease are a major contributing cause of lower-extremity amputations, and more than half of non-traumatic lower-limb amputations occur among people with high blood sugar.

Childhood obesity, a phenomenon that barely existed a mere 20 years ago, has reached epidemic proportions within Mexico, and around one-third of all elemen-tary school children and almost half of all adolescents are overweight. In addition, almost one-fifth of the children under age five in Mexico are below normal height while one quarter suffer from anemia, both related to nutritional deficiencies caused when sugar-based products displace fruits and vegetables. Besides obesity and diabetes, asthma, arterial hypertension, arterial sclerosis, osteoporosis and cancer, all diseases in which diet plays a major role, are on the rise.

As in most of the developed world, the contemporary diet of the majority of Mexicans now relies heavily on the four basic modern food groups: sugar, fat, alcohol and nicotine. Modern-day industrial processes and chemicals used to produce greater quantities of food products in less time for less money to reach more consumers inevitably lead to health problems. As these products tend to be cheaper than natural food, the lower classes are their biggest consumers, and thus they are the ones who tend to be the most undernourished and overweight, victims of what is now called "poverty obesity."

The rise in fatal diseases that most affect Mexicans (diabetes, heart problems and cancer) can be attributed in large part to the industrialization of the food industry and the junk food it produces. Non-traditional food stuffs, such as processed wheat-based products, canned goods, salty snacks, fat-saturated foods and instant meals, have radically changed the millennial local diet and have created millions of Mexican junk-food junkies. Snack foods, a relatively new food genre in Mexico, are among the most important products within the manufacturing industry, with a market value of 750 million dollars. Stores in Mexico sell more potato chips, industrialized muffins and pastries (most of them imported) than beans, grains or canned foods.

Until a just few years ago, the breakfast distributed in Mexico City public schools consisted of milk, cookies and pastries. The sale of junk food in public schools, a huge business, was recently prohibited, although the local government doesn't have the authority to actually enter into the schools to enforce the law and thus its sale continues. One recent government health campaign aimed to fight obesity, called the Healthy Life and Well-being Movement, carried out in public schools throughout Mexico City, was promoted by both Coca-Cola and Pepsi.

High fructose corn syrup (HFCS) is a newer and sweeter sugar substitute made from (usually genetically modified) corn. Over the last couple of decades, HFCS consumption increased by more than 1,000%, largely because Mexico's soft drink manufacturers (both local brands, such as Boing, as well as imported ones such as Coca-Cola) switched from sugar to HFCS.

HFCS in beverages stimulates appetite which, when coupled with its caloric content, is in large part responsible for packing extra pounds onto people. Many soft drinks also contain caffeine, which can lead to addiction, affect blood pressure, increase heart rate, provoke cerebral stimulation, insomnia, headaches, gastric ulcers and anxiety. When consumed cold, the effects of caffeine increase. Artificial coloring, such as E-150, which gives colas their color, have been related to a deficiency of vitamin B-6 and hyperactivity.

Soft drinks represent almost one percent of the Mexican Gross National Product. In 2004, over 15 billion liters of soft drinks were distributed in Mexico. The average per capita consumption of soft drinks in Mexico is second only to the United States, and Mexicans tend to spend more on soft drinks than they do on the 10 basic foodstuffs, including milk, bread and eggs, together. Many of the lower-working class, especially construction workers, receive a significant amount of their calories from Coke.

Coca-Cola currently represents 70% of all soft drinks sold in Mexico, but to increase its market position the company plans to invest more than one billion dollars in Mexico in 2012. Coca-Cola not only spends millions of dollars on advertising and promotions it also uses strong-arm marketing activities to ensure its near monopoly. A 2005 ruling in Mexico levied a fine of 68 million dollars on the company, the largest fine in the history of the Anti-Trust Law, as the result of a lawsuit brought by a Mexican store owner who accused the company of trying to prevent the sale in his store of Big Cola, a soft drink imported from Peru that costs even less than Coke.

After the North American Free Trade Agreement went into effect, Mexico was flooded by high fructose corn syrup while at the same time it was forbidden to export cane sugar to the United States. This situation crippled the national sugar industry, led several plants to close down and forced hundreds of workers out of their jobs. During his years in office, ex-President Fox nationalized 27 of the 60 sugar plants in the country. When the Mexican Congress, in an attempt to protect the local sugar industry, voted to levy a tax on soft drinks containing high fructose corn syrup, ex-President Fox, who had been the director of Coca-Cola in Mexico before becoming president, vetoed the bill (a move which was later deemed unconstitutional and overturned).

Drinking imported soft drinks sweetened with high fructose corn syrup made from genetically-modified corn grown in industrial farms in mid-America might make Mexicans feel like they're participating in a trendy global phenomena, but it also has real and immediate effects on their inner organs and on Mexico's struggling sugar industry. The multi-billion dollar industry of imported US junk food and soft drinks in Mexico threatens Mexico's traditional diet and food production, is in large part responsible for the devastation of agriculture in the countryside, and is a major contributor to the massive emigration from the Mexican countryside that has led to overpopulation and widespread poverty in Mexico City.

Imported Tastes It might be hard to believe but half of all food consumed in Mexico these days comes from the United States. Mexico has gone from being a producer and exporter to becoming an importer of even its most traditional products. In the last decade, Mexico has doubled its imports of wheat and milk and tripled its imports of corn and rice.

Mexico spent almost 50 billion dollars on imported food in the last five years (equivalent to over half of its petroleum profits during the same period) and, not surprisingly, over the last decade Mexican food production has dropped over 30%. Mexico began to lose its alimentary self-sufficiency in the early 1970s, and by the 1980s it was cheaper to import food into Mexico than produce it. Over the last few decades the Mexican government support for local farmers, including guaranteed prices, distribution and commercialization centers, as well as credits and subsidies, has largely evaporated, victim of international trade agreements, thus severely undercutting the industry's competitiveness, at home and abroad, especially since many of these basic foods receive subsidies in the US.

In 1990, after the signing of the North American Free Trade Agreement, the government opened up certain sectors of the economy (previously restricted to Mexican nationals or to the Mexican government) allowing for up to 100 percent foreign ownership. Mexico now ranks third, after Canada and the UK, in US foreign direct investment. Foreign direct investment, that is, multinationals that own and operate companies within Mexico, disrupts national food production even more than imports. The more than $6 billion in sales of processed food from US foreign direct investment represent almost five times the value of US food exports. Nearly three-fourths of the U.S. foreign investment in Mexico is from companies that produce processed foods, such as snack foods, while about 15 percent is from beer and soft drink companies (U.S. global foreign direct investment in beverages has more than doubled since 2000, with Coca-Cola reaping the largest profits).

One-quarter of all money earned from the sale of US products in Mexico goes to one single company, Wal-Mart, which controls nearly 30% of the market. One in five Wal-Mart stores are located in Mexico, and a new store opens within the country every 5 days (there are currently over 700 in Mexico). Wal-Mart has acquired several chains of previously Mexican-owned supermarkets and department stores that sell food (Aurrera, Superama, Sam's Club, Suburbia) and several chains of restaurants (Vips, El Porton, Ragazzi).

The incredibly rapid expansion of Wal-Mart within Mexico was carefully calculated to put its competition out of business. In order to carry out this business blitzkrieg, executives at Wal-Mart in Mexico spent over 24 million dollars over the past couple of years bribing government officials (everyone from bureaucrats and neighborhood leaders all the way up to mayors) in order to circumvent environmental and community restrictions (such as the mega-store next door to the Teotihuacan pyramids).

Wal-Mart currently employs over 200,000 workers in Mexico, the single largest private employer in the country, yet it is estimated that for every two jobs that Wal-Mart creates, three jobs are lost in the area where a store is located. In addition, by importing most of the food sold in its stores, Wal-Mart has put out of business thousand and thousands of Mexican farmers and food producers. When workers in Mexico lose their jobs they often migrate illegally to the United States, and because they represent cheap labor, Wal-Mart was recently forced to pay a $13 million fine for employing illegal aliens in its stores.

Frankenfood To keep costs as low as possible, industrial food companies have begun to process food from genetically modified crops. Up to 70% of all processed food (such as soft drinks, ketchup, potato chips, cookies and cereals) in Wal-Mart-owned businesses throughout Mexico now contain genetically modified ingredients.

Genetically modified food is a whole new field. While it is true that conventional breeding methods have over the years created a wide variety of plants and animals that did not exist previously, genetic engineering is now capable of taking genes from one species, such as a fish or a virus, and placing them into an entirely different species, such as a tomato or a pig, thus creating new food species and sources (which is why many refer to it as Frankenfood).

The most common genetic modifications have been targeted at pest control, either by incorporating genes that create their own pesticides within plants or by creating plant strains that are more resistant to pesticides (the genes and pesticides are sold by the same company, Monsanto). Pigs have been modified to produce healthy fatty acids (like the ones in fish) to help reduce risk of heart attacks, and human vaccines are being developed from genetic modifications of tobacco and other plants. Although some of these new species are ostensibly being created to help human beings, once set free in nature these genetically modified organisms might very well grow, reproduce, mutate, migrate and evolve beyond the control of their creators.

The first large-scale commercial plantings of transgenic crops went into the ground in 1996, and in just two years genetically modified crops covered nearly 70 million acres in eight countries. The most common genetically modified foods are soy (over 50%), corn (30%), canola oil, potatoes, tomatoes and cotton. Genetically-modified corn and soy are also used as sweeteners, oils, texturizers and filler in dozens of processed products, such as chocolates, jams, bread, margarine, vegetable oils, milk, ice cream, flour, mayonnaise and even baby food. Mexican consumers are completely unaware of the quantities of modified food they are feeding themselves or their children since these products carry no labels to indicate their origin.

Although Mexico is one of the world's largest corn producers in the world, roughly a quarter of the corn consumed in Mexico today is imported from the United States. Since the Free Trade Agreement took effect, imports of corn to Mexico from the United States have increased nearly eighteen fold, and in 2008 US companies no longer had to pay any taxes or duties in Mexico for these exports. Mexico now imports over 13 million tons of basic grains from the US and Canada, half of which is corn and up to two-thirds of which are genetically modified.

It is unclear exactly how much genetically manipulated corn is spilling into the Mexican marketplace. Some estimate that up to 60 per cent of all shipments of corn to Mexico from US agro-business giants (most of which are barred from selling transgenic grains to the European Union and Japan) contain genetically modified corn. Although these imports are supposedly destined for animal consumption, a substantial portion of the 6 million tons imported is diverted for human consumption.

Corn has always been sacred in Mexico, where it was first cultivated some 5,000 years ago and where almost 60 different races of corn, each with a large number of sub-varieties, evolved. Unlike the limited number of varieties of corn available in the US or Europe, Mexican maize, grown all over the country in very different climates and conditions, comes in a wide variety of colors, sizes, shapes, textures and flavors.

US-imported genetically modified corn seed now dominates the local market and fields. Transgenic contamination could lead to the homogenization of Mexico's rich germ plasma, threatening the crops' genetic memory and leading to genetic erosion. Once corn is contaminated with sequences of genetically modified genes, all the descendants of this plant will also be genetically modified. Not only are the native and crossbred corn strains in danger of being contaminated but so are the wild varieties, including *teocintle*, the grandmother of Mexico's corn diversity.

The long-term health effects associated with consuming genetically modified food are unknown, although problems have already arisen. Kraft Foods was forced to recall millions of genetically modified corn tortillas sold to Taco Bell due to the complaints of consumers who had allergic reactions to the product. Nonetheless, genetically modified corn is now used by all the major Mexican tortilla companies, and it is also used in locally produced tostadas and cereal.

A secret study conducted by agro-business giant Monsanto (later suppressed by the company) revealed that rats fed corn modified to protect itself against root-worm developed smaller kidneys, experienced immune system damage or developed tumors, rats fed genetically modified soy showed significant changes in liver cells and rat offspring had a six time higher mortality rate. Another study showed that Monarch butterflies, which migrate between Canada and Mexico each year, were killed in the United States by eating the pollen from corn genetically modified to produce its own insecticide.

Although no one knows what Frankenfood will do to human genetics and thus to the evolution of the species, it is safe to say that when humans dick around with Mother Nature they usually get screwed in the end.

Last Bite The food consumed in a city shapes its inhabitants both physically and culturally. In the Condesa, as throughout Mexico City, completely different food cultures coexist, though not necessarily peacefully. Given that profit, not nutrition, health or tradition, determines diet these days, it is increasingly difficult to eat a meal that not only tastes good but is also good for one's body, neighborhood and culture.

The Aztecs consumed food grown locally, importing only certain delicacies for the ruling class. During the Colonial period, the Spaniards' introduction of meat into the diet in Mexico City not only beefed up the local cuisine it also radically transformed the physical landscape and ecosystem of the whole country. Over the last two decades, imported food from the US, especially processed food, has devastated the country's indigenous subsistence agriculture and radically transformed the local diet.

Although the industrialization of food has created an apparently endless variety of things to eat, today *chilangos* actually consume less than 60 different plants and animal species, while hunters and gathers in the same region thousands of years ago ingested up to 200 different species. In addition, what Mexicans eat these days isn't necessarily what their digestive system has evolved to digest best, as fresh corn, beans and other local plants that co-evolved with their human consumers no longer form the basis of the local diet.

Natural food provides more than just the vitamins and minerals, protein and carbohydrates listed on the side of processed food packages. Plants, for instance, contain both antibiotic and probiotic substances that strengthen human gut flora and help fight off parasites. When humans eat mostly imported products or processed food, however, these healthful properties are lost. In addition, industrial-grown plants, due to the prolonged use of pesticides and other toxic chemicals, lose their communities of microorganisms and thus no longer fortify human gut flora, a situation which has contributed to the alarming rise in immune-deficient illnesses.

It is selfish to think only of one's own stomach when preparing or ordering food. Human taste buds are designed to choose food that best nourishes the trillions of consumers within their digestive system. Bacteria rule our world and we are here to serve them. Local food provides the best diet for local bacteria, and local bacteria are best equipped to digest local foods. Because humans are colonized by local bacteria from the place where they grew up, local plants are optimally digested, which is why what we ate at home as children tastes so special.

The long process of co-evolution between man, plants and microorganisms in the Mexico City Valley has been broken, and *chilangos* now mostly crave food merely for the thrill of exciting their taste buds. While tongues these days might crave *bechamel* or teriyaki sauce, the large amounts of dairy products, fat and processed sugar in the dishes offered on fancy menus don't provide the correct nourishment for the millions of micro-mouths within the large intestine. Industrial food that titillates our tongue not only doesn't provide benefits to the local gut bacteria but it actually favors foreign parasites not integrated into the local ecosystem and which thrive on white sugar and gluten. Mexicans and their gut flora are unprepared to assimilate all the fat and processed food they are wolfing down, which is why they suffer even more from obesity, diabetes and other chronic illness than gringos.

Microbes are essential in helping to maintain our equilibrium with the world around us, yet their own equilibrium is at risk today. With climate shifts brought about by global warming, the destruction of huge areas of forests and nature reserves, widespread migration, millions of tons of toxic substances dumped into the water supply and the atmosphere, a radical shift in the food and alcohol consumed, and the widespread use of antibiotics and other microorganism-antagonistic medicine, the equilibrium of the microbe populations in Mexico City has been seriously disrupted.

These man-made changes put great environmental pressure on these microorganisms to evolve and adapt in order to survive, and thus bacteria, viruses and all other microscopic life forms are seen to be mutating ever more rapidly. For example, the microorganisms responsible for sexually transmitted diseases and respiratory system infections have evolved to the point where they are now resistant to almost all antibiotics, and these and other strains will continue to mutate and evolve much faster than any products developed by the medical-industrial complex. In addition, the radical changes within human micro-biota in Mexico City have led to an unprecedented increase in chronic, immune system-related diseases (asthma, allergies, diabetes, obesity, etc), and thus to a shift in the way people here die.

Because they are my greatest defense against disease and premature death, I try to keep my bacteria healthy and happy. I exercise almost every day, say no to stimulants and take my homeopathic medicine and probiotics every day. I avoid chile, dairy products, animal fat and white sugar and rarely eat out (never in the Condesa). I eat almost all my meals at home, feeding my local strains of bacteria with lots of tortillas, freshly-cooked beans, grilled nopales, avocados, homemade soups with local vegetables, beans or pumpkin-flower, and dishes made with *huitlacoche, quelites, huazontle* or *chapulines*. (To be honest, I also aggravate my little friends from time to time by shopping at foreign-owned supermarkets, consuming processed foods, and eating out at Japanese or Argentine restaurants, but they always get their revenge in the end.)

In general, these days there are so many health risks related to food sold on the street, in restaurants, markets and supermarkets in my neighborhood, and so many ways to get sick, everything from next-day parasite infections to terminal cancer, that my paranoia of disease often overpowers the pleasure of eating. Eating, which should be one of the joys of life and the basis of a long, healthy existence, often scares the shit out of me, and I often fear that my next meal might very well be my last. ✝

PHOTOS

ERVICIO　FORENS

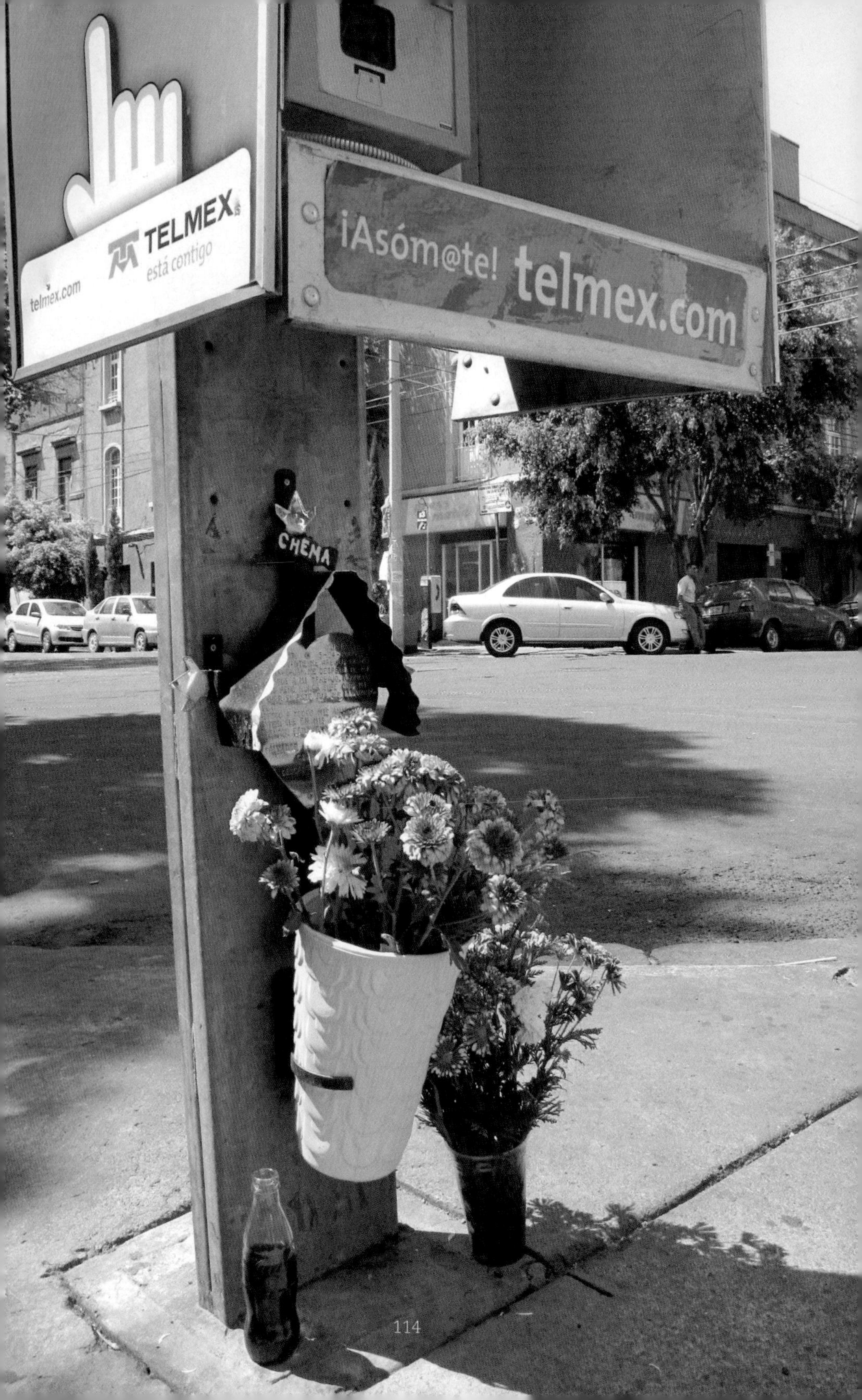
TELMEX
está contigo
telmex.com
¡Asóm@te! telmex.com
CHENA

CIRCUITO BICENTENARIO
CUERNAVACA
AV UNIVERSIDAD
2 GABRIEL MANCERA
CIRCUITO BICENTENARIO
DIV DEL NORTE
LAZARO CARDENAS
En esTe lugar
El dia sdeJunio
del 2003. Fallecio el Joven
Aaron David casTro Garcia
a la edad de 17 aRos y 3 meses por
obra y gracia del Señor. habiendo
nacido el 22 de Febrero de 1986
Quien siempre lo recordaremos
con amor y cariño su padre,
su madre, su hermano
y sus amigos.

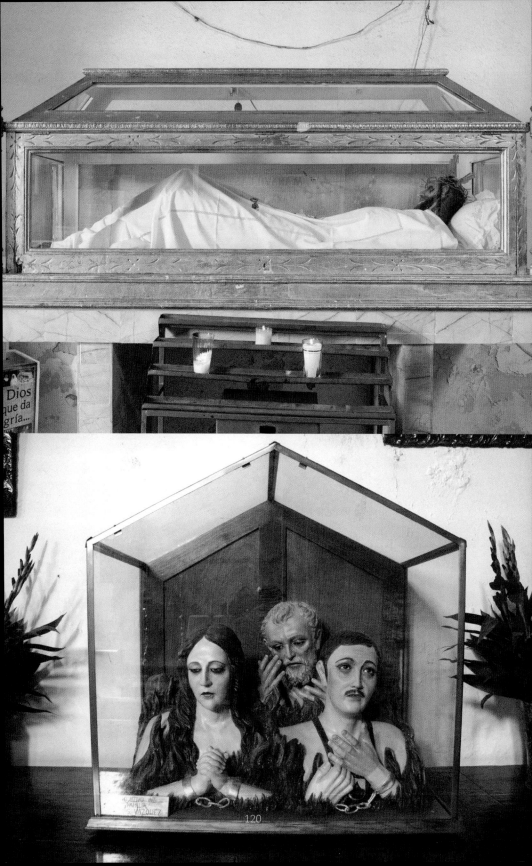

142

Photos

113 Old Mexico City Morgue with a statue of Coatlicue (Aztec goddess of death)

114-117 Crosses for those who died violently in the street

118-121 Religious figures in Catholic churches

122-125 Panoramic views of Mexico City air

126-129 Public toilets

130-133 Street food in the Condesa

134-137 Pulque and *pulquerías*

139-141 *La Santa Muerte* in Tepito

142-144 Graves in the Panteón de Dolores cemetery in Chapultepec Park

ALCOHOL

I Serve Alcohol I started drinking alcohol when I was thirteen. By the time I was fifteen I was tall enough to order drinks in bars and did so more or less every night for the next fifteen years. I occasionally went out with friends, or hung out with regulars, but mostly I drank alone, chugging down four or five shots of vodka in Polish or Ukrainian bars in the Lower East Side.

On my first night in Mexico City I wound up at an art opening a couple of blocks from where I was staying. I was surprised to see that there was an endless supply of free tequila served by fancy waiters in the gallery. With the help of the tequila and the giddiness of being in a new city and culture, I managed to meet more than a dozen artists and denizens from the local culture scene that night. Over the next few weeks I went to several more art openings where free wine, beer or tequila flowed freely, and met even more artists who liked drinking as much as I did. Although I had avoided going to art galleries and openings in NYC because of the loathsome art snob atmosphere, here in Mexico City, with the help of a few drinks, it was a lot of fun.

Alcohol is an important element within the contemporary art scene in Mexico City. Select brands of alcohol, both national and imported, sponsor art exhibitions in galleries and museums, and the quality and quantity of free booze determine the size and class of art lovers at the events. Journalists and critics are constantly plied with drinks at openings (the more they drink, the better the art looks) and the reporters and photographers who cover the art events mostly come just for the free booze. Mexican artists have designed the labels of bottles of alcohol and often appear drinking drinks in hip magazines, proud to promote companies that often sponsor their shows (Absolut Vodka commissioned public installations in the Condesa in which artists incorporated the bottle into the work). Being that they tend to work within the European tradition, a large number of Mexican artists are alcoholic, as are the poets and writers who praise the artists' work in catalogs.

After just a couple of weeks in Mexico City, a Mexican painter invited me to a weekly salon he hosted. The house in Roma he inherited from his father, a Mexican muralist, was old and teetering, a thick, dirty old rug covering the holes in the floor and the walls full of dusty paintings and the tables full of old books. The only surface not covered with old books, a large table in the middle of the room around which a dozen or so artists and writers sat, was instead covered with a motley collection of Mexican beer bottles brought by young foreigners and fancy bottles of wine or whiskey from the elder locals.

For our host, this weekly gathering was a great way to network with foreigners who had connections to galleries in the US and Europe, but for the rest of us it was a great weekly social gathering in which to get drunk (except when the host turned into an evil drunk). The salon ended when our host moved to Europe. After that I drank mostly in friend's houses or in cantinas surrounded by drunken men in suits.

When I opened Barracuda, the first 'bar' bar in Mexico City, it was a place where young women and men could go out at night by themselves, and it changed the way people drank in the city. The US-Mexico Free Trade Agreement had gone into effect a few years before I opened the bar, and imported liquor had already flooded the local market, promoted by multinational companies with large advertising budgets. In my bar, tequila was mostly shunned in favor of rum, vodka and gin mixed into exotic, fruity drinks that were a big hit with all the Mexicans who wanted to considered themselves international.

I made a lot of money, pimping for the multinational spirit industry's and serving alcohol to the thirsty hordes of Muppets (my term for Mexican yuppies but also a local drink made from Sprite and tequila). My bar enjoyed all the benefits alcohol companies lavish on their faithful customers: huge loans paid off in purchases, free awnings, glasses, mixers and shakers, and attractive models for special promotions. Alcohol companies paid for the fliers for all the live music and Dj events every weekend, paid for my huge photomurals, and they trained my bartenders and even sent my managers to Scotland for a course on whiskey.

Although I was constantly surrounded by bottles of all varieties of alcohol, I took not a drop to drink. This wasn't due to any professional code, but rather to the fact that I had gone to Peru and got sick the week before I started to renovate the bar. My doctor had told me I had to give up alcohol, so the last drink I had was the sixth martini at the inauguration of my bar. Everyone commented on how healthy, physically and economically, it was for me to not consume my own product, but alcohol was precisely what I needed to disconnect from my business concerns and to help me forget about my health problems.

Agua Viva Alcohol has existed almost as long as human settlements in the Mexico City Valley, and has permeated almost all human activities since then. In Mexico City, spirits are consumed during almost all religious celebrations and rituals and business deals are more often sealed with a glass of whiskey in a cantina than with a contract in an office. Even though most athletes are forbidden from consuming alcohol, all sports events, especially soccer, boxing, lucha libre, cock fights and horse and car racing are all sponsored by beer and alcohol companies, and the fans do their part in supporting their team by consuming as much beer as they can and yelling as much as possible.

Music and alcohol have always been a succesful mix. Mariachi music, along with *norteño*, *ranchero* and other traditional musical genres in Mexico, are full of songs of men celebrating their love for a woman with a few shots or purging the pain of being dumped or ignored by a woman by drinking until they drop. One of the ways Mexican men hope to make woman regret that they've betrayed or left them is by drinking themselves to death. These songs, like the alcohol they often sing about, are designed to help men drink to remember or to forget.

Although alcohol abuse, especially in the name of love, is a cultural activity promoted in all artistic mediums, it is most present in film, especially those that feature musical acts (during the Golden Age of Mexican Cinema, and even through the 80s, the majority of Mexican films had at least one scene in a club where a band or singer performs while the audience sits at tables drinking). The Mexican film industry has always worked in conjunction with the Mexican alcohol industry, especially tequila and beer companies, with many films receiving funding in exchange for product placement.

Due to the national cultural industry that has long promoted it, Mexican beer and tequila are consumed all around the world. Yet, up until recently, beer and tequila were not at all the most popular drinks in Mexico. Instead, the most popular, most sacred alcohol in Mexico is a little known and often slimy liquid called pulque. Pulque is an ancient alcohol, and its continued production and consumption are among the few surviving pre-Hispanic cultural practices today. To understand the history of pulque is to understand the history of Mexico.

During the Aztec empire pulque was the drink of emperors and warriors, utilized by the high priests to communicate with the gods. During the Colonial period it was the most popular drink and one of the biggest industries of the region. Today, however, it is considered the bottom-of-the-barrel alcohol and the few *pulquerías* that still exist in Mexico City are located in the poorest neighborhoods and are frequented by the lowest social strata.

As an illustration of the current status of pulque, the freshest, most delicious pulque I ever drank was on the curb of a concrete traffic island frequented by stray dogs and *teporochos* (homeless alcoholics), under a highway overpass rattled by heavy truck thru-traffic, one block from a minimum security prison, smack in the middle of one of the most heavily industrialized zones of Mexico City, at an improvised bar with plastic buckets functioning as stools and jars serving as glasses. This sad setting is increasingly common within the city, as pulque has never been so marginalized as it is today.

Pulque is a foamy beverage produced by the natural fermentation of the milky sap of the agave plant, with an alcohol content that ranges from 2% to 7% depending on whether it is served straight or cured. Known as *agua viva* (living water) due to the fact that it is composed of three bacterial cultures (Saccharomyces, Zymomonas and Lactobacillus) that continue to ferment the liquid even outside the plant and even within one's stomach, pulque introduces earth's beneficial bacteria into human gut flora, providing a healthy equilibrium with the microscopic world. (In comparison, the distillation of the agave sap is designed to kill off all microorganisms and thus neither tequila nor mezcal provide the health benefits of pulque.)

Agave plants are native to Central and North America, found everywhere from Canada to Columbia, though they tend to grow best at 4000–8000 feet above sea level, such as in and around the mountain city of Mexico City. Beginning almost two thousand years ago, all cultures throughout Mexico created their own pulque from a wide variety of local agaves. Some agave species flower after only three to four years while larger species may take 40–50 years. The cultivation of agaves and the production of pulque was most likely the basis for the first settled communities in Mexico. Latin for admirable or noble, agave was considered a miracle plant, its fibers used to make clothing, rope and textiles, its sap a source of water, medicine, soap, glue, paper and thread, its leaves used in thatch roofs or create fences and its spines turned into tools and sewing needles.

The *aguamiel* (honey water) is sucked out of the agave cactus by an elongated gourd twice a day, yielding as much as 8 liters per plant per day. A splash of fermented pulque is added to the fresh *aguamiel* to kick-start the fermentation process. (It is said that only men can make pulque or even be close to it while it is fermenting, for it is so delicate that women, with their acidic Ph, turn pulque bitter.)

After four to six months the plant will have yielded many hundreds of liters of *aguamiel* until, sucked dry, it finally dies.

The collected juice is stored in barrels and carried from the field to the fermentation sacks. During the Colonial period, these sacks were made of uncured cowhides stretched between wooden frames, while today most are made of oak or plastic and hold about 1,000 liters. The fermentation process takes from 7-14 days, and just before the peak of fermentation the pulque is transported to market. The areas of consumption have always been relatively near major agave areas as the rocking motion of mules, wagons, trucks or trains accelerates the fermentation and the pulque quickly rots. (Pulque in nahuatl actually means rancid or decomposed and refers to the pulque the Aztecs often sold to unwitting Spaniards, with *octli* being the true Aztec name of the drink.)

Its freshness and natural goodness make it a truly delicious, healthy drink, but pulque is definitely an acquired taste. To disguise its often slimy texture and yeasty taste, *pulquerías* 'cut' pulque with fruits, nuts, grains or greens, as well as with eggs, brown sugar or chiles. In the state of Tlaxcala, where it is known as *charagua*, the drink is served mixed with red chile and corn leaf, while in Guerrero *chiocle* is pulque mixed with chiles, the *epazote* herb, salt and garlic. Although it is older than tequila, tastier than mezcal, thicker than wine and healthier than beer, pulque remains virtually unknown outside of central Mexico.

A Heavenly High During the Aztec empire, and even centuries before, pulque was considered nectar of the gods and a panacea for mortals. Senior citizens over 50 were allowed to drink pulque to warm their blood and help them sleep, and women drank it after giving birth to help them recover their strength and to produce milk. Sick people were administered pulque, mixed with herbs and seeds, to help ease their pain, heal wounds and treat venereal diseases, and it was also used as an anti-inflammatory. Pulque served as an excellent source of nutrition, containing vitamins C, B-complex, D, E, and amino acids and minerals. During times of scarcity, it served as a food substitute due to its high level of proteins and carbohydrates, and substituted for water during droughts. In addition, pulque served as a ritual intoxicant to help steady the priest's hands during sacrifice and to ease the victim's fear and suffering. The ball players sacrificed after a game were messengers sent to implore the gods to keep the pulque flowing.

Precisely because it was such a potent quaff, commoners were prohibited from drinking except during special celebrations, such as at the end of the harvest, during rain ceremonies, for marriages, births, funerals and feasts to honor specific gods. Pulque was also administered to stimulate procreation, with drunken revelries designed especially for this purpose (in one festival pre-teens were made to drink pulque and dry hump each other). The celebrations of the dead were five-day binges in which everyone was encouraged to drink 'til they dropped, and it was prohibited from insulting or beating drunks during these ceremonies as they were under the protection of the pulque gods. During the festivals dedicated specifically to pulque, a giant stone rabbit representing a pulque god was filled with the liquid and everyone drank from straws stuck in its head.

The pulque gods, representing life and death and the celebration of the harvest, wore a half moon-shaped bone in their nose and painted their faces black and red. The goddess Mayahuel, depicted with 400 breasts as a symbol of fertility but also of the thorns of the cactus and the milky white liquid produced by the plant, lived in the heart of the maguey and pulque was her blood. Each of four hundred rabbit gods represented a different state of pulque intoxication, such as the head-opener, the hanger and the drowner.

Besides drinking it, indigenous people would often consume pulque through enemas. Besides the fact that alcohol is absorbed quicker and more efficiently through the large intestine, thus increasing its effects, it also leaves no trace of alcohol on one's breath and detection could be more easily avoided (there's also a pleasurable element to the administration of warm, milky liquid through the anal cavity, especially when inserted by a loved one).

Aztecs used enemas to introduce medicine, to treat hemorrhoids, diarrhea and venereal diseases, as well as for religious and ritual practices, such as to increase fertility and to increase rain (expelling liquids through the asshole was associated with rainfall). Tree bark (called pulque wood by the Aztecs and devil root by the Spaniards), seeds, flowers, fruits, tobacco and hallucinogenic mushrooms, peyote or even toads could be added to increase the drink's potency. This spiked pulque brought priests closer to the gods and helped them divine the future, interpret visions, make prophecies, and intuit the illness and encounter the cures for the ill.

The earliest Mexican enema, dating back three thousand years, is a ceramic figure in the shape of a smiling man with a hole in his head through which one would blow out the pulque, but they were also made from gourds, animal guts or rubber. Enemas have been discovered in caves surrounding the city, indicating that Aztecs held orgies where they could drink, dance and fornicate to their heart's content, far from the watchful eye of the authorities.

Pulque Resists Although it was impossible to keep everyone from enjoying this delicious, intoxicating liquid in between festivals and ceremonies, severe punishments for recreational drinking helped control the abuse of pulque in indigenous societies. Those caught drunk in public places had their heads shaved and received a beating, while repeat offenders had their houses destroyed and were prohibited from holding public office. Young people and nobles caught drunk were stoned, hung or beaten to death with sticks.

With the fall of the Aztec empire, pulque was abandoned by its gods and its consumption and production was left in the hands of mere mortals. As everyone could now freely consume what had previously been strictly regulated, widespread alcohol abuse quickly spread throughout the country. In addition, the Spanish began to import stronger alcohol for which the locals were biologically unprepared.

Wine, often prescribed as a medicine and seen as a source of nutrition, energy and courage, flowed at all meals of the Spaniards. Cortés brought several barrels with him on his voyage to Mexico, introduced the very first European grape vines into the country and, once established as the governor of New Spain, ordered the large-scale planting of vineyards. The first monks to arrive in Mexico in the 16th century brought grape vines to ensure a steady supply of wine for the mass, later setting up vineyards in their missions throughout the center and north of the country, thus making Mexico the first wine-producing country in the New World.

Cortés and other enterprising Spaniards tried to convert wine into a national industry but as the local production of wine, even on a very modest scale, competed with Spanish imports, the Spanish Crown eventually prohibited the planting of new vineyards (leaving the existing ones in operation) and continued to do so throughout the 300 years of Spanish rule in Mexico (the only exceptions being the Catholic missions).

Indigenous workers in the vineyards and elsewhere were originally paid in wine, ensuring a steady supply of alcoholics and alcohol-related deaths among the natives. To prevent this, a law in 1606 prohibited Spaniards from selling or paying for work with alcoholic beverages to natives or Africans, and those caught doing so would lose half of their earthly possession and could be ostracized permanently from New Spain. Like almost all other prohibitive proclamations relating to alcohol production and consumption, this law was widely ignored.

When the Spaniards realized that wine would never displace native alcohol, they seized control of pulque production and distribution, which soon became a very profitable business and a lucrative source of tax revenue for the Spanish crown. Taxes levied on pulque provided the fourth most important source of revenue for the Mexican government throughout the Colonial period and for centuries to come. (Even as late as the early 1950s, the two largest pulque producing states, Hidalgo and Tlaxcala, still received up to half of their total revenues from pulque.)

Economic interests, though, often conflicted with religious and moral ones. At the beginning of the 17th century, at the behest of the Church, there was an unsuccessful attempt to prohibit the sale and consumption of all local alcoholic beverages. Pulque, however, was an especially thorny issue for the Catholic Church in Mexico, a conflict of spiritual and material interests. At the same time the Church condemned the evils of drinking pulque (*pulquerías* were viewed as the Church's main competition for souls), the missionaries were the ones who owned the plantations of agave used for pulque production, or they rented their lands for such purpose, and the profit from the sale of pulque built the churches, convents and helped the Church maintain its power in Mexico.

When social problems associated with the consumption of alcohol got out of hand, spilling onto the streets where decent citizens circulated, the Spanish Viceroy in Mexico City passed a series of regulations meant to control and reduce its consumption. Pulque, however, was accused of instigating more than just barroom brawls and public indecency. Resistance against the Spanish, the aristocrats and the government, and against progress and order in general, was played out in large part in the *pulquerías*

In 1672, during a holiday when the city's inhabitants tended to get totally wasted, natives, Africans, mulattos and other mixed races went on a drunken rampage, protesting the lack of tortillas in the local markets while tons of corn was being sent to Spain. The royal palace was burnt to the ground and Spaniards caught on the street were attacked. The authorities blamed these so-called Corn Riots not on the profiteering of food during hard times but on the over-consumption of pulque, and decided to run all non-Europeans out from the center of the city and to prohibit the production of pulque and suspend its sale within the city. When they realized how much tax revenue was being lost, the pulque flowed once again.

Much of the laws and most of the police activity during Colonial times were directed at containing the damage caused by drunk and disorderly people. Punishment for being drunk in public depended upon your race and class. In 1760, non-European first-time offenders got fifty lashes in public and had their heads shaved, while second-time offenders got one hundred lashes over several days. Spaniards caught drunk for the first time spent fifteen days in jail and received twenty-five lashes with a whip. Second-time offenders, or first-time Spaniards from the lower classes, received a month in jail and two sets of twenty-five lashes, while third-time offenders got four years in the slammer.

Regardless of all the official efforts, alcohol and its effects on the lower classes continued to be a highly visible problem within the city. One of the biggest headaches of the authorities at that time was how to bury the anonymous, naked corpses that tended to accumulate around *pulquerías* and other drinking establishments.

Drinking Establishments

In 1784, there were 194 taverns in Mexico City dedicated to serving hard liquor to Europeans. Most taverns operated within the center of the city, while *pulquerías* were located mostly outside the city center, within the indigenous and lower class neighborhoods. Taverns were smaller than *pulquerías*, had less clientele, and were much less regulated. Taverns could open at 7am and close at 9pm, while *pulquerías* had to close by 6pm and on holidays couldn't open until after 1pm so as to not interfere with church mass. In the second half of the 17th century, the Viceroy limited the number of pulque establishments in Mexico City to 36, with 24 for men and 12 for women only. Later, when this law didn't achieve the desired effect, especially since it wasn't enforced very strictly, men and women were allowed to drink together again, although food, music and dancing in *pulquerías* were prohibited in order to dissuade people from staying a long time.

Although pulque was initially the drink of indigenous *campesinos* it eventually caught on amongst the Spaniards and mixed-races within Mexico City, extending all the way up to the wealthy classes. After the independence from Spain at the beginning of the 19th century, the number of *pulquerías* in Mexico City greatly increased and the pulque industry was transformed from small-scale production to large industrial factories. When the Jesuits were run out of the country in the 18th century, nobles, businessmen and wealthy landowners bought up their agave plantations. Pulque haciendas located just outside of the Mexico City Valley became huge, lucrative operations, employing up to one thousand workers, 500 mules and with up to half a million agaves. Often the pulque produced there was sold within *pulquerías* in Mexico City owned by the *hacendados* themselves. Modern transportation, especially the railroad, connected the pulque producing towns to Mexico City, increasing the area of distribution.

In their heyday in the 19th century, *pulquerías* were large drinking establishments staffed with administrators, barmen, bouncers, waitresses and children in charge of collecting the used *cajetes* (ceramic cups) and enticing passersby to enter. Many *pulquerías* were elegant establishments, with murals adorning the facades, bars made from mahogany, the inner walls covered with large mirrors and erotic paintings and decorated with colorful cut-out paper decorations. The *pulquerías* always had dirt floors, and one of the rituals of drinking pulque was to spill a bit of the drink onto the floor as an offering to the gods. Because so many pulque drinkers got lost in the sauce, *pulquerías* often had nihilistic names: My Life Ain't Worth Nothing, Last Stop, Memories of the Future, Loneliness, Little Hell and The Worries of Bacchus.

By law, *pulquerías* had to be located in plazas at a respectable distance from houses, open on only one side so as to allow for police observation. Credit was forbidden, as was accepting clothes for alcohol, and owners that didn't abide by these laws received fifty lashes. In 1833, the government established a fine of 10 pesos for every drunk found lying on the ground outside a drinking establishment.

In the mid-19th century, an outbreak of toxemia struck the area in and around Mexico City, and many blamed the disease on pulque. Porfirio Diaz once again ordered all *pulquerías* out of the center of the city and demanded that they install spittoons and offer porcelain urinals (at a time when there was hardly any plumbing or sewers in the city) to replace the communal hole-in-the-floors that also served as a site for prostitution and other sexual relations.

At the beginning of the 20th century, Mexico City residents consumed around one liter of pulque a day. During the Mexican Revolution, pulque production and distribution were disrupted, and with Agrarian Reform the large pulque haciendas were expropriated, the land subdivided, and the deeds handed over to *campesino* cooperatives. *Pulquerías* were shut down at the request of Revolutionaries, or forced to sell pulque to-go (signs outside read Come In, Order, Pay, Leave) and loitering around *pulquerías* became illegal. The lurid paintings that had graced the walls of these drinking establishments were banned, and the cheeky names of the *pulquerías* were replaced with the generic slogan "Pulque Sold Here." Some in power, such as the revolutionary leader Pancho Villa, who had outlawed the use of alcohol and marijuana amongst his troops, sought to prohibit pulque altogether. At the behest of moral, religious and government leaders, many *pulquerías* were shut down, and as a result pulque consumption dropped drastically, continuing in a downward spiral from that time on.

As *pulquerías* started to go under, a new kind of drinking establishment took their place. After the US invasion in the mid-19th century (which led to the annexation of California, Texas and Arizona), cantinas were established in Mexico City to service the US occupying troops. The locally produced drinks (pulque, mezcal, tequila and rum) were not very popular among gringos who preferred whiskey and beer. After the occupying troops were shipped back to the US, cantinas catered to the Mexican middle and upper classes. In 1886, fifteen cantinas operated in Mexico City but by 1915 there were around 250. Cantinas have long served as the traditional social center for Mexico City politicians and businessmen, and up until the early 1980s women were not allowed in cantinas

In 1870, there were more than 800 *pulquerías* in Mexico City, but by the end of the 20th century fewer than 50 existed. Today, within the Delegación Cuauhtemoc (which includes the Condesa, Roma and the Historic Center), there are several thousand bars, clubs, cantinas and other drinking establishments that serve alcohol, but less than a dozen of these are *pulquerías*.

Spanish Spirits

The Conquistadores brought with them to the New World the technique of distilling alcohol through the use of an alembic, originally invented by the Arabs and assimilated by the Spanish during the seven-hundred-year Moorish occupation of Spain. Distillation was immediately employed in the New World, with European alcohols such as brandy, rum and *aguardiente* fortifying the Conquistadores for the dirty work of nation-conquering still to be done. Tequila and mezcal were born from the mix of local plants and imported technology, and became the first mixed-race alcohols in the New World.

Mezcal is generally thought of as a single drink, but in fact it is a whole array of alcohols, including its most popular incarnation, tequila. Mezcal enjoys control of denomination, with only alcohol made from agaves in Oaxaca, Guerrero, Guanajuato, San Luis Potosi, Zacatecas, Durango and Tamaulipas being legally considered mezcal. Although distilled from agave plants, there are important regional differences in the agaves, the production, the ingredients added, and most importantly, in the taste. Mezcal is made mostly from the fermentation and distillation of the cooked core of the *espadín* and *tobablá* agaves, while tequila is distilled from *Weber azul* agave. To make any variety of mezcal or tequila, the agave must be cut down (unlike the agave that continues to produce pulque for months).

Around one hundred factories produce about 200 registered brands of mezcal, but there are thousands of other, smaller producers (*palenques*) that make their own unregistered, unnamed mezcals, usually sold in large glass, ceramic or plastic jugs. Although some in Mexico City drink mezcal, especially those who appreciate its purity, it has never been very popular in the city.

Tequila's name of origin is internationally recognized and controlled, and it designates the alcohol distilled from the *Weber azul* agave produced in certain towns of the state of Jalisco (where 99.7% of all tequila is produced) and in other nearby states. In the 1970s, before its place of origin was controlled, Japan, Spain and other countries began producing what they called tequila, made mostly from

157

corn syrup. Mexico established an agreement with the United States whereby Mexico would prevent the use of the term Bourbon by producers within its territory and the US would only recognize tequila as being authentic when produced in Mexico. Tequila is distilled twice and contains at least 51% agave (the other 49% is usually corn syrup or cane sugar), although the best tequilas are 100% agave (mezcal is almost always 100% agave).

The fact that almost everyone in the world knows about tequila, far fewer people outside of Mexico have an idea what mezcal really is, and almost no one outside of central Mexico has ever actually tasted pulque, is more a reflection of international marketing techniques than of the importance each drink has had within Mexico. Tequila and mezcal played a very minor role in the drinking habits in Mexico City until the last decade or so, when the major tequila manufacturers were incorporated into large multinational companies that, due to their success in the United States, began to aggressively advertise these drinks within the city. Before that, pulque, rum, aguardiente, brandy and, of course, beer were the main alcohols consumed in Mexico City.

Beer Here Even before the arrival of Spaniards, there existed within Mexico brews very similar to beer. When Cortés and Moctezuma first met they toasted their future friendship with *tesgüino,* a thick, foamy, amber drink resembling beer but made from corn. A mere two decades after the conquest of Mexico-Tenochtitlan, the first beer brewery was established with equipment imported from Belgium. Dark beer, its colored derived from the addition of sugarloaf, was the beer first produced in Mexico, followed later by ale and lager. Some beer was in fact made from barley, but others were cobbled together from wheat, lemon or pineapple rinds, tamarind, cloves, pepper, cilantro and sugar.

During the first years after Mexican Independence from Spain, seven breweries were functioning in Mexico City, owned by English, Spanish, German, Swiss and French businessmen. At the time, beer was an expensive luxury indulged in only by Europeans (mostly German or English) or Americans living in Mexico, costing up to 30 times more than pulque. With the advent of railroads, especially the line that ran from El Paso, Texas to Mexico City, beer from the United States began to flood into Mexico. It was not until Mexican breweries were modernized and ice machines imported, and when prices dropped enough for beer to begin to compete with pulque and other national drinks, that local beer began to be consumed widely within the country.

Several Mexican regimes, especially that of the dictator Porfirio Díaz, dedicated their efforts to helping Mexican businessmen import technology and culture from Europe in order to modernize Mexico. The beer industry began to assert itself in ways that pulque, without modern production, distribution and marketing, and without brand names, could not. (In ads that emphasized the nutritional, hygienic and modern nature of beer, pulque was portrayed as a drink fermented with dung that only attracted flies.)

Three million liters of beer were imported in 1890, mostly from the United States, England and Germany, but by 1910 only a half a million liters of foreign beer was being brought into Mexico. In 1919, Prohibition in the United States gave the Mexican alcohol industry an even greater window of opportunity. Mexico not only benefited by serving its alcohol to all the gringos who crossed the border where they could drink without breaking the law, but it also benefited from the absence of all the big brand competition coming from its northern neighbor. By 1920, with over 36 factories in operation, the Mexican beer industry was considered the second most important source of revenue in the country, and by 1925 more than one out of four Mexican workers were employed in the beer industry or its related businesses. Still and all, beer consumers represented only one tenth of the number of pulque drinkers.

In 1922, a group of Spanish businessmen created Cerveceria Modelo in Mexico City, introducing the brands of Modelo and Corona. With the onset of WWII, and while other beer companies were busy selling beer to the US army, Modelo expanded within Mexico, strengthening its distribution and sales with a large fleet of trucks, and modernizing its factories to be able to compete with foreign brands.

Soon after it began to operate, Modelo began to use the streets and locales of Mexico City as a backdrop for its image. Huge banners and neon signs were hung on important buildings (the first neon in Mexico was an ad for Modelo Beer installed atop a building in the Zócalo in 1928), hand-painted logos were blazoned across the facades of sports stadiums and bull-fight rings, beer commercials were projected before all films (many of which were funded by the beer industry), ads rode on trams and trains, paid-for articles appeared in magazines and newspapers, and calendars, trays, glasses and other promotional objects with images of traditional Mexican and Spanish women were given away to customers. One promotional campaign used a half-naked woman, the same one who graced the first labels of the bottles of Modelo, who was driven around Mexico City in a car without a visible driver.

Modelo also sponsored local soccer, baseball and basketball teams, lucha libre and bullfighting, as well as national holiday celebrations. In 1949, Modelo inaugurated its Corona Beer Garden, the site of mass balls, shows, television programs and celebrations, and it also created the Corona Caravan, a traveling show that for two decades promoted some of the most famous musicians, dancers and stars of stage and screen across the country. Radio became one of the greatest means of promotion for beer, with Modelo sponsoring concerts broadcast by the major stations.

Eventually, the various beer companies merged and since 1985 the beer industry in Mexico is a duopoly of Modelo and Cuauhtémoc Moctezuma (originally formed in Monterrey by a Mexican businessmen and a German brewer who had worked at Anheuser-Busch). Since 1999, Mexico is the third largest exporter of beer in the world (behind only Holland and Germany), the Mexican beer industry is the 8th largest in the world (with Corona the fourth best selling beer in the world) and beer represents over 75% of all alcohol consumed in Mexico City. Mexican beer companies have paid a high price for global expansion. Both of these Mexican beer giants are now mostly owned by foreign corporations (Cuauhtémoc Moctezuma by Heineken and Modelo by Anheuser-Busch).

Spiked Liquor Since pre-Hispanic times, pulque has been spiked with different fruits, herbs, seeds, roots, insects and hallucinogens. It was only when alcohol began to be commercialized and distributed far from the place of origin that other substances were added not to heighten the effects and improve the taste but rather to water down the liquor and lower the cost of its production.

Imported wine from Spain was often adulterated in Mexico, for which a law was passed in 1526 stating that those caught tampering with wine would have all their goods confiscated and receive 100 lashes of the whip. In 1886, Mexican medical authorities recommended prohibiting the adulteration of alcohol and imposing harsh penalties for those responsible, but little was done about it even with all the negative health effects. At the beginning of the 20th century, distributors of tequila, especially along the US border, began to extend their product with additives, usually alcohol derived from sugar cane or corn syrup, although more toxic additives were commonly used. In 1905, over 50 factories were shut down by the Mexican authorities for adulterating alcohol, but just one year later 26 new brands appeared, most from companies that didn't produce alcohol but instead only changed its composition. During the Mexican Revolution authorities prohibited the use of scarce foodstuffs (such as corn) for the production of alcohol, and consequently much of the alcohol was extended with chemical derivatives, often leading to poisoning amongst the ranks of the soldiers.

In 1964, the government allowed up to 30% of additives, and in 1970 the maximum was raised to 49%, a standard that continues today in the tequila industry. This measure was designed not only to allow producers to extend their precious, limited product but also offered a means to standardize and regulate the adulteration process. Methyl alcohol is legally allowed in tequila and mezcal in very small doses, although it is potentially a dangerous substance. Alcohol made from corn syrup, often used for industrial purposes and now as bio-diesel car fuel, contains many toxic substances that, in high quantities, can lead to blindness, insanity and even death.

In the 1990s, several brands of tequila appeared on the market, mostly in US cities with large Mexican populations, with such brand names as Black Death and Marijuana, that didn't heed the legal limits and most likely used additives other than those legally permitted. The Mexican government responded by discontinuing 40 brands and closing dozens of factories. In 2006, 65 brands of alcohol, most of them claiming to be tequila, were retired from the shelves.

In Mexico City, it's possible to buy alcohol on almost every block, whether at a corner store, cantina, liquor store, nightclub, hotel or restaurant (96% grain alcohol is one of the best sellers in drug stores). Many brands of alcohol sold are not legally registered, while bottles with registered brand names are often refilled with alcohol of dubious origin. Large criminal organizations are involved in adulterating or pirating alcohol in Mexico City. The pirates forge government stickers and seals and have machines designed to refill recycled bottles of legitimate brands. Within bars, adulterated alcohol can be served straight from a pirated bottled, exhibiting legal bottles but serving from pirated ones (which is why waiters often present the unopened bottles of liquor as if they were fine wine), or preparing pre-mixed drinks with adulterated alcohol.

It is estimated that 40% of all alcohol sold in Mexico is pirated. Adulterated alcohol is sold mainly in neighborhood markets, in grocery stores, and in all-you-can-drink bars and clubs that cater to young adults and minors. Each year, nine million liters of adulterated alcohol are consumed in Mexico, usually tequila, rum and more upscale liquors such as cognac and whisky. Depending on how it is adulterated, pirate alcohol can lead to dizziness, weakness, nausea, headaches, vomiting, blindness, lung collapse, comas and death.

Dead Drunk Alcohol is without doubt the greatest social drug ever invented, conquering timidity, loosening the tongue, increasing libido and making others seem more interesting and attractive. When consumed, alcohol slows down brain activity and relaxes muscles, thus inducing feelings of happiness and euphoria. It also gets rid of, at least momentarily, many unpleasant sensations, such as anxiety, obsessive thoughts, shyness and even bad memories. Any substance that produces a sense of pleasure or well-being will be sought out and consumed by human beings, despite any negative effects it might have.

Alcohol actually has quite a few negative effects. Although it is one of the best social lubricants, alcohol is not always a performance enhancer. Chronic alcohol consumption leads to impotence and erectile dysfunction known as drinker's droop. Long-term alcohol abuse affects the nervous system and impairs the impulses between the brain's pituitary gland and the genitals responsible for dilating the blood vessels in the penis needed to achieve an erection. Prolonged alcohol abuse can cause irreversible damage to the nerves in the penis leading to alcohol impotence in men even when they are sober.

Excessive drinking can decrease sperm production, lower testosterone levels and diminish sexual drive and function. Male alcoholics tend to lose facial hair, their voice becomes more high-pitched, their tits grow and their testicles shrink. Both men and women alcoholics wind up with distended, mushy bellies and flaccid skin, and the breasts of women alcoholics tend to shrink, and loss of physical beauty leads to decreased sexual activity. Among chronic female drinkers, alcohol may cause menstrual irregularities and infertility, and can contribute to the premature births of babies that suffer from physical and mental defects.

Alcohol irritates the gastrointestinal system and causes the secretion of gastric juices, both of which can lead to ulcers, and it leads to poor digestion of food, weight loss and bowel irregularities, as well as decreased resistance to infections, thus making alcoholics vulnerable to chronic parasites. Alcohol abuse can also affect the nervous system, creating serious mental diseases, loss of memory, a break with reality caused by vitamin deficiencies and malnutrition, as well as irreversible brain lesions. Alcohol gives rise to hypertension, heart attacks and stroke and has been associated with several types of cancer. Prolonged alcohol consumption depletes the chemicals in the liver that break down fats, and thus the liver can itself become enveloped in fat. Cirrhosis, a condition in which a massive formation of fat and dead tissues prevent it from filtering toxins from the blood, leads to comas and death. (In Mexico City, up to 30% of heavy drinkers develop cirrhosis, a very high percentage compared to other major cities.)

For the millions of *chilangos* who live below the poverty level and suffer from malnutrition, alcohol abuse is especially unhealthy since it impedes the body's absorption of nutrients and leads to vitamin deficiencies. The cost of supporting an alcohol habit, which is often greater than that spent on food, contributes to the poverty of the drinker, and without money many use alcohol as a food substitute. As the poor also tend to consume poor quality alcohol, health risks are multiplied. If you add up its role in diseases, accidents, suicides and homicides, alcohol is one of Mexico City's greatest serial killers.

Mexican Style

Mexicans have a reputation for not being able to handle their alcohol. To give just one personal example, in my first month in Mexico City I needed to get my sneakers fixed and so I went to a shoe repair stand a block from my apartment. The owner was about my age and a decent looking guy. When he heard that I was from New York City he got all excited since he had lived one year in North Carolina and he said he just loved gringos. Although it was only two in the afternoon, he went and bought a pint of local rotgut vodka to celebrate. As we drank shots straight from the bottle he admitted that he had a hard time on the other side of the border, and halfway through the bottle he said, slurring his speech, that he hated the US and gringos. By the time we had finished the bottle I had a good buzz but he was ugly drunk, crying and offering me his wife, a pretty woman who stood there watching us the whole time without saying anything.

Even though I've seen many perfectly normal looking Mexican men reduced to sniveling, incoherent, aggressive louts after just a drink or two, I find it hard to generalize about Mexicans and alcohol. Cultural differences are often identified by their distinct drinking habits (Russians are renowned for their ability to drink any quantity and quality alcohol, Irish can recite poetry after drinking themselves under the table, Asians and Jews are teetotalers) but these are all generalizations. All cultural stereotypes and even genetic profiling fall short of what is in fact a much more complex reality, for they tend to ignore significant differences between men and women, large and small, rich and poor, and between different religions and levels of education. (As a general rule of thumb, when talking about cultures, especially foreign ones, it's important to remember that there is always less of a difference between any two cultures than within any single culture.) With such a long history, and within an urban center as large and multicultural as Mexico City, alcohol consumption is a complex concoction.

Certain cultures possess certain genes that determine the metabolism of alcohol, which in turn affects reactions to alcohol and proclivity to alcoholism (13% of all Mexican men are alcoholic), and thus the way Mexicans react to alcohol is in part biologically based. On the other hand, as most native Mexicans were forbidden to drink regularly until five hundred years ago, their livers have not yet completely adapted to assimilate high-proof alcohol.

In one study, scientists discovered a predisposition to cirrhosis amongst the Otomí (the original settlers in the Mexico City Valley and the original producers of pulque) four times above the national average. Yet, drawing any conclusions from the relation between alcohol, indigenous genes and certain health problems is complicated by the fact that most indigenous cultures live in poverty, suffer from high levels of malnourishment and reside in highly contaminated environments, all contributing factors to cirrhosis.

More than any genetic predisposition, cultural and social factors seem to determine the effect alcohol has on health and social issues. Aztec drinking took place on certain social and religious occasions, when locals were encouraged to drink to excess. In this way, drinking brought communities together to provide a regular catharsis of internal tensions, suppressed aggression and sexuality. Drinking along with one's neighbors and under the guidance of religious leaders was a healthy act free from feelings of shame and bad conscience. As a result, Aztecs had very low rates of alcoholism before the Conquest.

After the fall of Mexico-Tenochtitlan, the social, religious and even health benefits of heavy drinking on holidays disappeared and in their place Catholic guilt and sin became associated with alcohol consumption. Aztecs watched horrified as their whole culture (religion, language, economy and social standing) crumbled before their eyes and was violently replaced by a foreign, aggressive culture, casting the locals adrift in a sea of uncertainty in which alcohol surely helped them numb themselves to this cataclysm. The shift after the Spanish Conquest from a temperate Aztec society to one of widespread alcohol use and abuse shows how this is not a genetically programmed trait but rather a cultural artifact of colonialism.

Alcohol forced upon the natives by the Spaniards generated profits, kept them in debt, and weakened them physically and culturally, all of which paved the way for easy domination. Yet some contend that all the negative stereotypes of natives during the Spanish Colony, including self-destructiveness, laziness, lying, cheating and especially alcohol abuse, actually represent forms of resistance to colonialism.

In Mexico, alcohol was never equally distributed amongst the population. From pre-Hispanic times up until very recently, men have had much greater access to alcohol. Throughout Colonial times, male priests cultivated the grapes and agave and distilled the wine and tequila, and they were the ones who performed communion with the aid of wine. At baptism and marriages men exchanged and consumed bottles of liquor as part of the ritual while women merely looked on.

Today, however, having gained in social standing and equality, women in Mexico City are drinking almost as often as men, although they tend to drink less (the average alcohol intake for males is five to seven drinks a night as compared to one to two drinks for females). Most women don't drink as much simply because their liver is smaller and thus can't absorb as much alcohol, while the fluctuation of hormone levels due to menstruation, pregnancy and menopause, as well as the fact of having less water in their body, make women more vulnerable to higher intoxication rates.

As far as religious differences are concerned, 80% of Mexican Protestants are abstinent as compared to 38% among Catholics, while indigenous communities, at least those that are not Protestant, tend to suffer higher rates of alcoholism than the national average. AA, which in Mexico has a strong religious element to it, is one of the only rehab programs available to the majority of the population.

Many of those currently living in Mexico City originally came from other parts of the country, mostly rural areas, a situation that can produce a sense of isolation and a feeling of being cut off from one's roots. Most of these new arrivals live in poverty, have no job security and no access to decent health care. In addition, besides economic problems, there are also high levels of social, sexual, gender and racial stress that comes from the difficulty of adapting to life in the big city. The excessive drinking by immigrants in Mexico City can be seen as a form of self-medication for all the stress and social problems they experience.

Gringos and Europeans tend to consume alcohol daily, while Mexicans drink less often but tend to drink more when they do drink. This pattern of binge drinking causes severe social problems, including domestic violence, abuse of minors, gang violence, suicides and homicides (about half of all suicides and one-third of homicides are committed under the effects of alcohol). Acts of violence against women and children occur in homes, while the street is the scene of violence between men. Alcohol is involved in at least half of the reported cases of domestic violence (in Mexico City the husband is the main aggressor while in the countryside it's the father). Domestic violence and alcohol abuse tend to lead to sexual violence and rape, the spread of venereal disease and undesired pregnancies.

Due to the high elevation of Mexico City, drinkers here get drunk quicker, suffer more drunken symptoms and have worse hangovers than those who drink at sea level. Drinking and driving at high elevations can be a deadly mix. The increase of reaction time while driving drunk is augmented by the lack of oxygen in the atmosphere and the diminished oxygen uptake by the brain, leading to higher numbers of traffic fatalities within the city. Binge drinking and driving has made alcohol a much more lethal weapon now than ever before. Traffic accidents (pedestrians run over by cars, passengers killed in crashes, drivers who ram their cars into cement walls, trees or poles, flipped cars and passengers who fall from speeding vehicles, in that order) are the number one cause of violent death in Mexico City, more than homicides or suicides. More than half of all deaths related to traffic accidents occur between Thursday and Saturday, mostly after midnight, when teenagers and young adults return from bars and discos. The greatest number of traffic deaths occur in the district that encompasses the Condesa, Roma and the Historic Center.

For me, the risk of dying as a result of my alcohol consumption is minimal. I rarely drink 'til I drop, and I have been poisoned by alcohol only a few times in over twenty years (although I recently vomited my guts out and hallucinated wildly after drinking too many shots of a cheap mezcal). Getting hit by a drunk driver while out walking, riding my bike or driving, or getting into a fight with and shot by a drunk driver, however, are among the most likely ways I will die in Mexico City.

Even if my death isn't caused directly or indirectly by it, alcohol has already done serious damage to my life. The strain caused by the thousands of yuppies, secretaries and businessmen driving in and out of my neighborhood almost every night to get stupid drunk is more than me or my neighborhood can bear. The huge billboards advertising alcohol all throughout the neighborhood, the level of noise coming from the bars and restaurants, the insane traffic and honking that goes on late into the night, and the broken beer bottles and vomit on the street are merely the ugly symptoms of a much more serious disease, namely, the widespread corruption of the local government. The juicy kickbacks obtained from allowing dozens of bars and restaurants serving liquor to open without the proper permits, in buildings and locales that aren't legally licensed for such businesses, has led directly to the mass nightly invasion.

Just as consumers in the US who snort cocaine and smoke pot are directly responsible for the narco-violence in Mexico, so too the vomiting multitudes are responsible for the decimation of the Condesa. Being that alcohol has become its single-crop economy, my neighborhood is no longer a self-sufficient *barrio*, one with its own culture and an economy that serves its own residents, but instead an alcoholic theme park for the lowest level of global lifestyle consumers, the harbingers of the death of Mexico City culture. ✝

SICK CITY

Stressed and Depressed

I worked at many different jobs in New York City (selling nuts on the street, scooping ice cream, as a shortorder cook, busboy, waiter, bartender, freelance proofreading, adjunct professor, magazine editor), but I never made much money. Money, though, has never been the driving force of my life. I was fine so long as I had enough to pay the rent, eat out in diners, drink cheap beer, shoot pool, go to the movies and buy books and records.

In Mexico City, I got a job right away writing introductions for a series of forty 'great works' of literature printed as cheap paperbacks with cartoon images on the covers, and I started translating articles for magazines and art catalogs. I made enough *pesos* to keep me in tacos and tequila, to play pool and go to the movies as much as I wanted. One day, years later, an opportunity presented itself to buy out the owners of a pool hall in the Condesa that had been around for seventy years. My first business venture turned out to be a success, and for the first time in my life money poured in. A couple of years later, I started up a restaurant/bar, and my income doubled. I invested my earnings in a film I wrote and directed and shot within my pool hall. The promotional line for the film was: "In order to win, you have to know how to lose."

While I was making my film, my pool hall was stolen from me behind my back by a minor partner and my bar was shut down for six months by the government (I refused to pay bribes). After selling off the bar to cover debts that had accumulated while closed, the only thing I was left with after so many years of being a high-powered businessman were angry partners, debt and lawsuits being handled by incompetent lawyers.

During the time all this bad business was going down I was very sick. I had lost twenty pounds that I couldn't really afford to lose and I was shitting my guts out more than a dozen times a day. Being weak, skinny and sick made it much easier for me to get even sicker. My colitis and the high dose of cortisone I took lowered my body's immune system, converting me into an open wound. What didn't kill me made me bleed out of my ass.

My economic and health problems overlapped and made each other worse. I was constantly worrying, moody, irritable, agitated. I felt lonely, isolated and depressed, and I withdrew socially. I couldn't sleep, I couldn't enjoy sex, I couldn't even have fun playing with my kids. One more problem (divorce or a death in the family) would have buried me. I dreamt about going home to NYC, regressing to a time when I was young and carefree, before all the bad shit had happened.

During this period I experienced greater amounts of stress than ever before. Stress is an intense experience. The constant injection of adrenaline and other stress-related chemicals into my body made my heart beat faster, my lungs work harder, worried my digestion and released large quantities of fat and sugar into my blood system, all of which put an extra strain on my inner organs. My large intestine took the brunt of the stress, but my lungs and liver also suffered.

Throughout those long years, stress also wrecked havoc on my immune system, making me chronically tired and weak, always running a high fever and catching every virus that passed through the city. Besides weakening me physically, stress hormones assaulted my central nervous system, clouding my memory of what life was like before everything had turned to shit and limiting my thoughts of the future to nightmare scenarios and suicide. I had trouble sitting still long enough to read a book, I was unable to maintain an intelligent conversation and constantly on the verge of tears or violent rage.

Even before I went into business and got sick I was high-strung and nervous, like a typical New Yorker. Cities create stress and the bigger and more chaotic the city, the more stress its inhabitants must endure. Yet NYC stress had been my drug of preference, for it kept me wide awake and in survival mode. Stress is a physiological reaction designed to help humans cope with immediate, physical danger by priming their system for a flight or fight response, something I needed when confronted with gangs or psychos.

My legal battles, debts and chronic illness in Mexico City, however, were not threats that could be dealt with by increased sensorial acuity or a burst of physical force. The high levels of adrenaline in my bloodstream only served to make me panic, to yell at those around me (mostly my family) or to keep me pacing back and forth like a caged rat. Over time, I could feel how all this stress was wearing down my muscles, weakening my body and paving the way for serious mental problems.

High levels of stress over long periods of time can push the neurosis of city living over the edge and into psychosis. The perceived degree of control (or lack thereof) that city dwellers have over their daily lives affects their mental health. A city is always out of control, or at least, out of the control of its inhabitants, since it is much more complex than human consciousness. Noise, overcrowding, alienation, social inequities, economic hardship, street violence and racism all increase stress and decrease the amount of control a person feels. As a result, city dwellers have a 21% increased risk of anxiety disorders and a 39% increased risk of mood disorders, while the incidence of schizophrenia is twice as high in those born and brought up in cities.

I eventually closed down my restaurant/bar and settled out of court with most of those suing me. Instead of gaining peace of mind I now had nothing to do but worry. I felt I had lost all ability to make a living writing or to do anything else creative, and I could see no hope for the future. I entered a period of deep depression that lasted for years. I rarely left my house, avoided everyone I knew and those I didn't know, as well, overdosed on television and was continually sighing, crying or cursing my fate.

Although they involve different chemicals and are the opposite in terms of nervous activity, both stress and depression did pretty much the same thing to me, namely, they ground down my body and soul, depleted my vital energy and helped make me a pathetic victim of a chronic illness. My life was out of control and if I wanted to live much longer I needed help.

Hope Peddlers

I made an appointment to see the foremost specialist in chronic ulcerative colitis in New York City and flew there for the consultation. In the waiting room I watched patients, the majority of them reduced to mere flesh and bones, shuffle in and out of the office. They looked like they were on the verge of death. When I saw myself in the reflection of a window I realized I wasn't doing any better.

Inside his office, the doctor and I watched the video recording of the fiber optic journey through my large intestine. His jovial mood of minutes before quickly became serious. Doctors, however, are never without hope, otherwise they'd be out of a job. Sitting in his comfy, air-conditioned, quiet Upper East Side office, this dignified doctor looked me in my eye and, without blinking, suggested removing a foot of my anal tract and reconnecting what was left of my large intestine to my anus, assuring me I'd only have to use a colostomy bag for three months. When I turned pale and sunk further into my seat, he offered me an alternative. He was currently conducting some cutting-edge research and could prescribe a drug to me that was still in the experimental stage. The drug was designed to lower T-cells to help prevent the body's immune system from viewing the large intestine as an alien and attacking it. When I inquired if there were any side effects, he mentioned, as if it were just a minor detail, that with so few T-cells I would be vulnerable to countless other diseases. The important thing, he quickly emphasized, was that I wouldn't have to worry about colitis any more.

I said nothing, just clenched my jaw and forked over 700 dollars in cash. At the door he offered up some parting words of comfort: "Don't worry, colitis won't kill you... (dramatic pause) though it won't let you live well, either." It turns out that isn't really true. Colitis in itself might not kill people but it tends to lay the groundwork, as four out of ten colitis sufferers develop colon cancer. Even if colitis doesn't lead to cancer it can debilitate people so much they become prey to aggressive parasites or viruses that can finish them off. What's more, the stress of a chronic, humiliating illness such as colitis often leads to suicide, an alternative that didn't seem all that more extreme than being disemboweled.

I walked a few blocks over to Central Park and sat on the edge of a baseball field. It was a nice spring day and several fathers were out playing ball with their sons. As I sat there I realized that, as things were going, that kind of carefree, happy life was no longer a possibility for me, and that sickness unto death was all that was left for me.

When I got back to Mexico City I was so pissed off at that smug Upper East Side doctor and his desire to play god with my large intestine (not to mention the insulting amount of money he charged) that I considered alternative medicine. I sought out treatment from a Japanese acupuncturist (covered from head to toe with needles connected by wires to a battery) and a Chinese holistic healer (who had people drink their own urine). I consulted a French natural healer who put me on a carbohydrate-free diet (I lost ten more pounds in one month). I went to see a longhaired Jewish Mexican from a wealthy family who dispensed indigenous herbal cures, and at his bidding I drank several horribly tasting teas made from bark and roots (including the natural form of cortisone). I swallowed vitamins and supplemented my diet with minerals. I stuffed garlic and potato suppositories up my ass. I mixed volcanic ash into my morning glass of orange juice. I purged myself with coffee and vinegar enemas.

I listened carefully to the stories of hope each of these sincere healers offered me, I appreciated the logic of their treatments and on my way back home from every consultation I did my best to believe I was finally about to get better. Regardless of how extreme the treatment, regardless of whether it drew on indigenous,

European or Asian knowledge, nothing worked. As the options began to run out, I became convinced that neither science nor traditional healing could help me. What I needed was a miracle.

I Put A Spell On You

Even in these modern times, even with all its yuppies and malls, skyscrapers and highways, cell phones and cable TV, magic and miracles still play an important part of everyday life in Mexico City. Most Mexicans turn to the Catholic Church for miracles. Church-sanctioned miracles, however, are only for good Catholics, and being that I am a Jewish atheist I must look elsewhere.

In Mexico City, the greatest number of miracles outside the Catholic Church occur in local markets. I take the Metro to the Sonora market on the outskirts of the Historic Center, home to dozens of *brujas* and *brujos* (female and male witches) and *chamanes* (shamans) who work out of stalls in which they perform *limpias* (spiritual cleansings), healing rituals, initiations and predictions. A *brujo* from Veracruz, wrists and neck covered in gold chains, welcomes me into a tiny space underneath a stairway surrounded by shelves stocked with magic products. He grips a white and a brown egg in one hand and passes them around my body, starting at the top of my head and working his way down. He tells me that money and health problems often come from those around us, and that the eggs will suck up the evil spirits possessing my body. I pay the equivalent of less than twenty dollars and take the Metro back home, waiting for the magic to kick in.

No miracle occurs and my problems continue. Still, I respect the work of these traditional healers and the magic products sold in the market. I had gone to the market years before as a tourist and, like everyone who goes there, was fascinated with all the colorful, crazy magic products on sales. This time, however, sitting on line waiting for my *limpia*, observing those in need of help, I came to understand a bit more how economic and health problems are related, and what exactly healers do when they rub eggs and blow smoke on people.

Spiritual healers have been in great demand since the days of Mexico-Tenochtitlan. Given that the Aztecs believed the world had already been destroyed four times by cataclysms and that the fifth and final time was soon to come (in which all of mankind was be destroyed by earthquakes), added to the constant threat of floods, hailstorms or droughts that could destroy harvests and lead to widespread hunger, not to mention the human sacrifices and executions performed in public, and given the presence of dozens of vengeful gods who were easily angered by humans who failed to feed and worship them sufficiently, as well as evil spells that envious neighbors or lovers often cast upon unsuspecting people, life was very stressful back then, too.

Unlike the large number of healers who worked in the Aztec empire, and unlike traditional rural healers today, the urban spiritual healer these days isn't supported financially by the community and thus must make a buck like anyone else. Competition is steep and so healers tend to borrow techniques and talismans from other spiritual practices (such as crystals, Buddha figures, Navajo dream catchers and Feng Shui) in an effort to keep up with the latest trends and to attract the widest public possible.

The Sonora Market is non-denominational and thus open to all spiritual paths, with saints and baby Jesus dolls on sale alongside figures of *santería* and voodoo. Catholic crosses, Jewish stars, Asian icons, Hindu incense, Egyptian hieroglyphics and African *orishas* are all given equal opportunity on the stands in the stalls. Unlike official Catholic dogma that treats all other religions and spiritual practices as the work of the devil, the Sonora Market isn't exclusionary and is in fact one of the few places in all of Mexico where all religions and spiritual practices peacefully coexist.

Although only a few of the neighborhood markets have traditional spiritual healers who attend those in need, almost all have *botánicas* or stalls that sell a wide range of do-it-yourself cures. The owners of the *botánicas* mix their own powders, sprays, perfumes, candles and soaps, though they usually purchase pre-printed packages and labels with which to sell them. Many of the magic products sold in the Sonora Market contain exotic ingredients, such as rattlesnake sperm, and most are made in Mexico, while others are imported from Cuba, Haiti, Venezuela, Miami and even Japan (that is, if you believe what the label says).

The witchcraft and *candomblé* markets in Sao Paulo, Rio and Bahia are not nearly as large or as international as the Sonora Market. In Cuba, the *santería* shops located in back yards are part animal farm and part hardware store for the island's *babalaos*, and they provide only the most basic ritual needs (eggs, chickens, pigs, necklaces and rum) and few pre-packaged products. The *botánicas* in the Puerto Rican communities in New York City and the rest of the US sell some of the same magic products but lack the wide selection of herbs, or the services of so many shamans and *santeros*, and they don't stock so many colorful packaged products from so many countries and for so many problems.

Although they represent the largest group of consumers, it is not just working class men and women who come to Sonora in need of help. The culture class, tourists and even desperate suburban housewives all pass through the aisles of the market, and there are magic products designed for most every socially marginalized group. Several powders attract same-sex lovers or offer to make sure your gay lover remains with you. Many powders offer to help attract 'clients,' although these clients are not those who work for corporations (as the design might imply), but are those that seek the services of professional sex workers The criminal population receives help from a long list of products sanctioned by La Santa Muerte and Jesus Malverde (a bandit hung by the government in 1909 who has become the patron saint to *narcos*). Since crime is a crap shoot with the odds firmly stacked against them, criminals can use all the spiritual help they can get, and this is where many of them come for miracles.

Men who want to dominate the beautiful women who give them the cold shoulder, the unemployed who need to find a job or get some cash quick, workers fed up from not having been paid (one of the biggest complaints in Mexico City), wives whose husbands chase after any woman they can lay their hands on, those who are the victims of a curse or the evil eye or who have had their soul stolen, all come to the Sonora Market in search of help. Those with enough money consult healers but even the poorest can afford cheap miracle products that serve as spiritual self-medication.

The Don Juan of Money instructs the user to place three coins into the package of miracle powder and spread some of the powder around their business while chanting: "Just as I step on this powder so my steps will lead me to money." Another powder, You Won't be Able to With Anyone Else, instructs women to add this powder to the water with which they wash their lover's private parts before and after making love in order to gain control over their man and make him physically unable to have sex with anyone else. To carry out the instructions for the I Have You Tied Up and Nailed Down powder, a photograph of the person you want to control must be placed on a rag doll, and the doll must be baptized with holy water, then tied up and nailed down, and the powder along with thirteen drops of perfume must be sprinkled over it on Tuesdays, Saturdays and Sundays. By sprinkling powder on your hands and neck at night before going to bed, the Humiliating Hunchback will help you defeat all enemies.

The fantasy images on the packages and the colorful ingredients within help increase faith in these magic products and thus help these products perform the required miracle. This is in fact identical to the relation between pharmaceuticals and their consumers. For instance, Prozac has been shown to have no clinical value for those suffering from mild depression, yet millions of mildly depressed people take it and experience an improvement in their mental health. The fact that a doctor or pharmacist recommends a medicine, and that the medicine is sold in serious, scientific packages branded with an exotic Latin or Greek name, and that consumers are completely ignorant of the chemicals contained in and the medical value of the product, all help to increase the effectiveness of the drug. The same holds true for Mexican magic products.

Placebos are some of the most powerful products sold in the medical and alternative markets. It is the faith that one places in a product, a faith reinforced by the professional who recommends it, by its presentation, by the rituals that must accompany its use, that determines in large part its efficacy. The positive effects of pharmaceutical medicine in general is much more dependent upon of the consumer than the medical industry would like to admit. Mexicans, like human beings all around the world, need a bit of magic to help them survive. The magic, however, isn't in the products they consume, nor in the religions they subscribe to, but rather it is what they will themselves to believe in their desperate minds.

Mexican Beauty

Although men all over the world love, lust for, have sex and make babies with women of every color, size, shape and features, beauty has recently become globalized and standardized. As can be seen in most Hollywood films, television shows and advertisements, beauty these days tends toward thin, tall, white and blond. The gulf that exists between global ideals of beauty and the majority of local Mexican women (who tend to be shorter, squatter and darker) creates a sense of desperation in them that often drives them to products or medical practitioners that offer them miraculous, extreme makeovers. Working class Mexican women invest a sizable chunk of their income in beauty treatments and products designed especially to hide their indigenous roots and features, including soaps that whiten skin, chemicals that lighten hair and contacts lenses that brighten eyes. There is even a cheap plastic device that promises to transform prominent Aztec noses into sleek European ones.

The Aztec word for beauty is a combination of the words jade and feathers, referring to beauty accessories rather than any natural look. Jewels, gold and colorful feathers were the height of fashion in Mexico-Tenochtitlan, and the more women glittered the more beautiful they were considered. To get attention, Aztec women wore piercings of jewels and shiny metals, had dental decorations that included gold-capped teeth or teeth filed down into exotic shapes, or received dental encrustations of jade, hematite, pyrite or turquoise, most by the time they were 15 years old. Aztec prostitutes painted their faces with colored powders, washed their feet with incense and dye, dyed their hair with black mud or indigo, whitened their teeth with cochineal, and painted their hands and necks with non-permanent tattoos, and only they were allowed to wind their hair into two plaits that jutted up like horns above their eyebrows.

Aztec aesthetics still survive today, as many women in Mexico City dye their hair, wear it feathered and arched above their faces like the crests of exotic birds, and paint their eyes and cheeks with bright colors. Although teeth grills and encrustations are accepted accessories only within the *bling-bling* crowd, and piercings within the younger generation, conservative Mexican women often accessorize their finger nails with fake diamonds or other flashy encrustations, some with chains dangling off of them.

In Mexico City, the expression "looks that kill" actually applies less to natural features or curves and more to the health costs related to looking good. The daily use of cheap perfume, hair dye, lipstick, mascara, rouge and foundation, sold in subways stalls or on the street, leads to the absorbtion through the skin of high levels of lead (often compounded by harmful chemicals present in popular, unlicensed diet drugs). Bleach is still a common ingredient in Mexican beauty products designed to lighten human skin (it is banned in the US and Europe), as are toxic chemicals such as mercury, corticosteroids or hydroquinone which can actually darken and harden skin and is tied to blood cancer. In addition to ruining their own health, and that of the babies they give birth to and carry around with them, the hundreds of thousands of dyed blondes and painted beauties in Mexico City are responsible for dumping thousands of gallons of toxic chemicals into the environment, thus making the city even uglier.

Beauty, however, is not just skin-deep. Mexican women are second only to gringas in the use of cosmetic surgery. Like magic products and religion, cosmetic surgery offers to help women find a lover, solve their marital problems, cure depression and help get a better job. The most common surgical interventions in Mexico City are nose jobs and breast and butt implants. To help women achieve their dreams, banks in Mexico City now offer loans to desperate housewives and aspiring models for up to $25,000 at 24% interest. As wealthy women in Mexico City often fly to the United States for cosmetic surgery, Mexicana Airlines (before it went bankrupt) offered all-inclusive health tourism packages. One such deal included a round-trip flight from Mexico City to San Antonio, hotel, and medical examinations at the Methodist Healthcare System at the hands of bilingual doctors. Basic packages cost $1,400 per person, while more specialized cosmetic services went for $4,300, including an extra couple of days to relax and shop at local malls until the bandages came off.

The beauty industry in Mexico City is an equal-opportunity provider, and women who can't afford to pay for costly surgeons can choose among thousands of unlicensed, untrained doctors who gravitate to cosmetic surgery and weight loss. To lower costs, these unlicensed practitioners often use pirated products, including breast implants imported illegally from China, that add increased risks of infection and can give rise to acute and chronic diseases, as well as the probability of the body rejecting the foreign matter.

Adding curves to women's bodies by injecting liquids such as paraffin and silicon, as well as baby, vegetable and even car oil, is a common practice in Mexico City, and many of those who inject these chemicals into women's bodies are housewives or neighbors who are merely supplementing their income. The buttocks represent around half of all of these interventions, followed by breasts, legs, thighs and hips, with cheeks and lips, both facial and vaginal, receiving their share of injections. Side effects from these injections can include pain, lumps, skin thickening, hyper-pigmentation, vein and arterial malformations and inflammation, as well as arthritis. Beauty clinics in Mexico are prohibited by law from injecting subcutaneously any substance, prescribing diets or weight-loss treatments, carrying out dermal abrasions or peelings or prescribing medicine, but these are precisely the kind of treatments offered in most beauty salons.

This same dangerous disregard for women's bodies can be found in the drug smuggling industry, where women are coerced into swallowing or stuffing bags of coke into various bodily cavities, or using their breasts and butts as virtual suitcases, at times even with zippers sewn into their flesh for future shipments.

Unlike beauty, there is nothing natural about ugliness. The media and advertising mania that inspires women to change the way they look, coercing them to hide their own culture or race, is ugly, as is the parasitic profit from women's insecurities and dreams. In the end, the cosmetic and aesthetic procedures, the toxic beauty products and unhealthy diets, all contribute to the city's prevailing unhealthiness and ugliness. In Mexico City, beauty can get ugly, health care can often be a scary business and getting sick is a real health risk.

Health Hysteria The obsession of so many Mexican women (and men, as well) to completely transform their face, hair and body reveals the sad fact that many human beings are more than willing to radically transform their own body and culture in order to get a shot at happiness. Given the fact that the first aesthetic interventions or extreme makeovers almost always lead to more medical procedures and products, neither control nor happiness is actually achieved in this way. And if a person can't even control their own looks, how can they control something as complicated as their own life?

Lack of control is one of the basic causes of illness in Mexico City. Mexicans seek help not only to treat their health problems but also to deal with all the problems beyond their control. Emotional problems, such as those related to a sense of ugliness, a lack of love, the loss of a spouse, infidelity, marital conflicts, the loss of a job, business failure, and tax, legal or moral conflicts, can often lead to physical symptoms, including headaches, vertigo, fatigue, weakness, high or low blood pressure, stomach problems and depression, which in turn can, over time and under enough stress, become serious illnesses.

Chilangos also complain about suffering from spiritual problems, such as the loss of their soul. Medical doctors don't recognize these problems as legitimate medical conditions, and they tend to classify the symptoms, everything from stomach aches to mental instability, as hysteric and blame the sufferers for inventing these complaints merely to gain their attention. Instead of dismissing these symptoms as hysteric reactions, traditional Mexican healers are trained to deal with this situation. Spiritual healers in Mexico City seek a balance between the physical, mental and spiritual aspects of a person, and they understand that a person must be in harmony with their physical and social environment in order to be spiritually healthy.

Harmony and well-being are not easy to achieve in Mexico City. The high levels of microorganisms and toxic substances in the air, water and food, and the intense traffic and urban density cause serious stress and can unbalance even the healthiest person. In Mexico City, where millions of people are crushed together daily in the Metro and on the streets, panic and aggressive reactions must be repressed. Over time this repression wears down a person's immune system and eventually manifests itself in physical symptoms and illness. Economic difficulties, widespread throughout the population, also directly affect health, for without the basic goods and services to survive physical and mental health are impossible.

According to traditional healers, mental illness is merely an imbalance between a human being and the world around them. Newly arrived, poor immigrants from the countryside, especially those from indigenous communities, often have trouble adapting to the rhythm and cultural differences of the big city and thus suffer from a range of symptoms and illnesses caused by their stress. Traditional Mexican healers are trained to help bridge the gap between these two different cultures, rural and urban, the traditional and the modern, indigenous and European. The herbs and rituals these traditional healers use ease anxiety and stress, the major underlying causes of most of these illnesses. By undergoing *limpias* or by using miracle products, along with the required rituals and prayers, a person feels like they are no longer just a victim but instead are actively participating in improving their own lives and solving their own problems.

Black Magic Although most everyone assumes that superstitious beliefs and practices come from 'primitive' indigenous cultures, it is in fact the 'enlightened' Europeans who are responsible for many of the superstitions to be found within Mexico. Spaniards believed, for example, that a closed fist with the thumb sticking out between the index finer and the middle finger warded off *mal de ojo* (evil eye), crystals kept illness away, and that bells scared off evil spirits. In addition to indigenous and European beliefs, Africa brought its own brand of spiritual beliefs, magical practices and miracle cures to the New World.

When Cortés first sailed to Mexico in 1519, six African male slaves and one female mulatto were on board. Twenty years later, Cortés placed an order for 500 slaves to help make up for the loss of indigenous workers killed by the sword, disease or incapacitated by alcoholism. When the Catholic Church declared that the natives in Mexico did in fact possess a soul and therefore could not be turned into slaves, the demand for African slaves increased dramatically.

Africans were brought to Mexico to work the mines, sugar plantations and textile factories, as well as to carry out public works and to provide domestic help to the landed gentry in Mexico City and other major urban areas. During the three hundred years of the slave trade, up to half a million Africans were brought to Mexico (in addition to the one-hundred thousand slaves from the Philippines, Borneo, New Guinea, Malaysia and China), and those of African descent quickly outnumbered the Europeans in Colonial Mexico.

Most African slaves in Mexico publicly accepted Catholicism, but the Catholic saints they worshipped were chosen because they resembled African *orishas*. Spanish slave masters invented the term *santería* (way of the saints) to make fun of the Africans' obsession with Catholic saints at the expense of the Holy Trinity, but it accurately indicated the objects of their worship. Like saints, *orishas* are asked for help with very practical matters (love, money, the law), and are offered food, drink, cigars and other gifts in return. *Sánteria* practices often include blood sacrifices of animals, ritual possession, the use of magic powders and charms, candles, plants, *limpias*, beads, necklaces, amulets, rocks and voodoo cloth figures. Like the indigenous *curanderos*, the Africans in Mexico also had their own shamans who could cure illnesses with powders made from plants and animals.

In Colonial Mexico, traditional indigenous medicine and *sánteria* were branded as pagan practices and prohibited and punished by the Church. The Spanish Inquisition in Mexico ruled that indigenous peoples could not be tried for heresy but that those of African descent could, and thus many were accused of such crimes as denying Christianity, blasphemy, bigamy and witchcraft and sentenced to torture or death.

The African presence in Mexico, the legacy of the forced displacement of hundreds of thousands of Africans, deeply influenced indigenous and *mestizo* social, cultural and medicinal practices. Although slavery ended in the 19th century, *sánteria* and traditional African healing continued, spreading and combining with local practices in Mexico and throughout the Caribbean, especially in Cuba. The constant flow between Cuban and Mexico, even today, has helped keep *sánteria* alive and well in the Sonora Market and elsewhere throughout Mexico City.

Got That Herb

In addition to the magic products sold there, the Sonora Market has been the largest distribution center of natural remedies for over fifty years. Over one thousand tons of dried herbs, roots, branches, bark, seeds, leaves and flowers are sold in Mexico each year, one hundred and fifty tons in the Sonora Market.

In Africa, around 80% of the population treat their problems with traditional medicine, in China around 40%, and in Mexico more than 50% are diagnosed and treated with traditional medicine, mainly for chronic illnesses such as arthritis, gastrointestinal problems, skin disease, multiple sclerosis and even cancer. Traditional healing with plants, consumed mostly as teas, has been a constant cultural practice in Mexico for thousands of years, and Mexico possesses the second largest number of medicinal plants in the world (after China).

In the 15th century, Moctezuma I, the Aztec's founding emperor, established the first botanical garden in Mexico City, and as the Aztecs conquered new lands specimens were brought back and planted there. These gardens were used for medical research but plants were also given away to citizens suffering from illnesses with the condition that they report back on the results.

The Aztecs used plants to remove excess fluids, reduce swelling, staunch bleeding and to treat infections. One common plant, *cempoalxochitl* (marigolds), the orange Day of the Dead flower, treated 'cold' diseases such as fever, dropsy and phlegm-related illnesses, as well as edemas, arthritis and spasms. (These same plants remain popular today amongst *curanderos* and are generally used in the treatment of gastrointestinal ailments and respiratory diseases, two of the most common complaints in Mexico City.)

The Aztecs also utilized certain plants to cause harm or to manipulate the emotions or libido of others by mixing powders into the intended victim's food or drink (especially *cacao* which hid their taste or smell). Known as *toloache* in Mexico, *datura* species have hallucinogenic qualities (their active alkaloids include atropine and scopolamine) and were used by Aztecs as medicine, for divination and for evil purposes, such as causing a person to become paralyzed and mute or to make them go mad. One powder made from a species of plant supposedly made people grow so fat they burst and die. Powders made from insects or animals were also used by the Aztecs to harm or gain control over others. One concoction made from butterfly wings could kill a person weeks after being consumed, a powder made from a bird's beak prevented erections, while a potion made from a certain species of snake caused frenetic sexual or masturbatory activity that eventually resulted in death (a lethal indigenous version of Spanish Fly).

The use of lethal plants or animal substances, especially those with delayed action, provided a possibility of eliminating competition without being caught at the scene of the crime. While all murder was punishable by death, killing another through poisoning or sorcery was considered such a heinous crime in Aztec society that the offender was bludgeoned to death with a truncheon. Although abortion was a common practice among the Aztecs, and plants were used to cause miscarriages, *curanderos* or midwifes were at times paid to make a woman abort against her will, an act considered evil and severely punished when discovered. *Curanderos* were also adept at defending against the ill effects of malevolent practices induced by others, using purgatives and sweat-inducing plants to expel evil spirits and substances.

Although spiritual healers and herb doctors are the best known of the pre-Hispanic medical practitioners, there was actually a very well developed medical establishment in Mexico-Tenochtitlan, with many Aztec health practitioners way ahead of their European colleagues. Aztec doctors who specialized in internal medicine, surgery and obstetrics possessed an extensive knowledge of human anatomy thanks to all the human sacrifices and wars, and they performed surgery with a wide variety of surgical instruments and were efficient at cauterizing wounds, setting bones in place with splints and draining abscesses. The Aztecs had several specialized hospitals, including those for the elderly, war veterans, pregnant women, children, the poor, those with congenital malformations, albinos, lepers, mental retards and even for the terminally ill.

The *temezcal*, the pre-Hispanic version of a steam bath, was an important element of medical care. Each neighborhood in Mexico-Tenochtitlan had its own *temezcal*, most located in ceremonial centers. Built inside domes of clay, adobe or stone and often constructed underground, high temperature and steam were created by heated rocks, ceramic shards or whole walls that were doused with water. Branches, oils and herbs were used as astringents to not only cleanse the body but also as cures. Through the open pores, natural medicine were introduced into the body to treat respiratory illnesses, the flu, muscle cramps, circulatory diseases, skin diseases, nervous disorders, insomnia and stress. Aztec women, aided by midwives, usually gave birth in *temezcales*. Midwives would help women give birth by massaging their bellies and would give teas to cause contractions, and they were also responsible for cutting the umbilical cord and for killing all deformed children and abandoning the children whose mothers died in childbirth. Sweating, both in the *temezcales* and by use of plants and herbs was encouraged during births and for several illnesses.

There were over forty different kinds of healers, both male and female, including doctors, surgeons, midwives, chiropractors, eye doctors, dentists and dream interpreters. Some healers would diagnose patients by looking at their reflection in a bowl of water, others by ingesting psychoactive drugs or during spiritual trances. Temple priests cured with prayer, fasting and self-flagellation. Shamans or witch-doctors were often cripples or epileptics. Depending on the illness, treatment could include praying, spells, natural medicine, singing, the laying on of hands, incisions in the patient's arms, legs, tongues, ears, nose or penis, the use of magic objects such as rocks or jade, blowing smoke into the patient's mouth or nose, or the administration of psychoactive plants.

There was an Aztec god of pharmaceuticals, another for medicinal plants, others for doctors, surgeons, midwives and prophets, and one for fertility. Quetzacoatl, the plumed serpent, was believed to be able to cure all illnesses. Gods not only cured, they could also spread disease. The god of plants provoked illnesses that appeared during springtime, including problems with vision, skin and ulcers, while the wind god caused rheumatism and shivering. The god of witches was responsible for leprosy, gout, plagues and insanity.

Even will all their medical institutions and healers, Aztec medicine was based mostly on the prevention of disease. Eating and drinking plants, insects and animals adapted to their surroundings boosted human defenses and gave humans an advantage in the war against microorganisms, essential in order to survive in such a hostile environment.

Charlatans And Quacks

Although the Catholic Church's persecution of traditional healing and *sánteria* began with the arrival of the first priests in the New World, their persecutory practices were strenghtened by the emergence of Mexico's medical institutions. (Mexico City's first Medical School was located in the same building that had housed the Inquisition.) To ensure a complete break with the past, all indigenous religious and spiritual practices were excluded from modern Mexican medical institutions. As one early law stated: "He who commits fraud, exploiting to their advantage the worries, superstitions or the ignorance of people, by means of a supposed evocation of spirits, or promising to discover treasures, or to make cures, or to predict the future, or by means of other similar frauds, will suffer a heavy sentence and a second-class fine." To make sure the medical world remained free from primitive superstitions, all doctors had to prove that their Spanish heritage was free of any and all mixed blood in order to obtain their license

During the reign of Porfirio Díaz, when all things European were regarded as superior to local ones, medical associations multiplied and the National Medical Institute was founded in 1888 as an attempt to monopolize the practice of medicine. Today, several different medical associations try to corner the market by certifying doctors, charging high fees and requiring specialized exams. The only thing that brings all these competing medical associations together is a shared intolerance of and disdain for health practitioners who lack academic and professional credentials.

Medical practitioners who base their treatments on miraculous elixirs or perform miracle cures, however, have always been common in Mexico. Many of these hucksters came from Europe, bringing with them a charlatan tradition that stretches back centuries. One foreigner called the Holy Doctor claimed to heal all kinds of illnesses (including broken bones and blindness) with spit, while other quacks claimed to heal with the laying on of hands, in the style of the medieval French and English kings. The most famous of these charlatans, a Polish man named something like Meraulyock, with long blond hair, a hefty moustache and a pointy beard, walked off a French ship anchored in Veracruz around 1865 dressed in a long Turkish robe. He claimed he was a doctor, a dentist and a pharmacist, and carried a suitcase full of San Jacob oil, an elixir that cured "flatulence, pain, colic, bad moods, rough and dry skin and even the removal of corns and calluses."

Over time his name was transformed into *merolico*, a term used in Mexico that has come to describe all charlatans and street vendors of miraculous remedies. (Up until only a few years ago, *merolicos* still put on shows with snakes and other live animals in Mexico City parks, outside Metro stations and along the main avenues, hawking their cures to the curious and needy.) Since the 19th century, miraculous elixirs and cures have been advertised in Mexican magazines and newspapers, and there are dozens of health manuals and books on domestic cures and remedies, with cartoon covers and illustrations to capture the attention of the masses. Magic products and books are sold, and unlicensed doctors tend to advertise, where the masses will most see them. Often, long lists of diseases treated are advertised on hand-painted street signs, on the sides and windows of buildings, in flyers, magazines, within the Metro and on the Internet.

Pirate Rx The *curanderos* and healers who have been practicing health care in Mexico City for thousands of years are considered charlatans and quacks by the medical authorities, but medical doctors in Mexico City are not necessarily more trustworty. Mexico has very lax laws for those who practice medicine. No license or certificate is required (in the US, doctors need a license and must be recertified every five years). In any case, being certified in Mexico, not a requirement, is merely a monetary transaction, one in which a person need only sign up with a professional association and pay a fee. Even so, thousands of practitioners in Mexico lack the necessary diplomas or experience, especially in the world of cosmetic and plastic surgery, weight loss and cancer treatment.

Even licensed doctors, though, those who proudly hang their diplomas on the wall of their offices, might very well have bought the answers to their professional exams, a common practice, or visited Plaza Santo Domingo in the Historic Center where for a small fee diplomas from any university and licenses from the association of your choice are printed up in a matter of minutes at affordable prices. It's hard to tell who's a quack and who's not, and for the majority of people in Mexico City health care ultimately boils down to what a consumer can afford.

Unlike those who work for the medical-industrial complex, homeopathic doctors make their own affordable, all-natural, toxic-free medicine. Instead of conceiving of medicine as weapons, homeopathic doctors prescribe their treatments to increase a person's own defenses. Once as established in Mexico (and in the US and Europe) as medical doctors, homeopathic doctors have been marginalized and now service merely a small part of the city's population. Allopathic doctors sneer at homeopathic medicine and accuse its practitioners of being modern-day charlatans, while those who practice homeopathic medicine believe that the medical institutions have robbed them of their rightful place in society and have sold out medicine to corporate interests.

As much as the medical authorities despise homeopathic medicine, there is nothing that gets them so hysteric as pirated medicine. The sale of pirated medicine worldwide generates over one and a half billion dollars annually, somewhere around 20% of all pharmaceutical sales, and Internet pirate drug sales are a promising new market. Pirated medicine, which includes adulterated, falsified, expired or stolen drugs, and which might be the same chemical compound as the registered drug, the same but less, or something else entirely, including being just a harmless placebo, is always much cheaper than the pharmaceuticals they rip off.

The most common pirated drugs are antibiotics, analgesics, steroids, antihistamines, children cough syrup and Viagra. Pfizer claims losses of upwards of 10 million dollars due to pirated versions of their bestselling erectile dysfunction drug

Viagra. Pirated versions can either be sold as Viagra or some other brand with a similar name and similar claims, are often capsules and not pills, and the package is usually just a photocopy of the original design. Viagramax, a Mexican pirated version, "guarantees an erection three times longer than Viagra; is completely safe and has no side effects; increases sexual potency; offers harder erections; and is certified by doctors," not to mention that it only costs a fraction of the price.

The DEA has alerted US consumers to the risk of using pirated versions of Viagra sold in Mexico, while the FDA issued a similar warning in relation to the anticholesterol drug Lipitor and the drug Evista used to treat osteoporosis, claiming that these pirated products don't have the same amount of active ingredients and thus don't offer the same effects. Joint US/Mexico police raids have led to the closing of 19 clandestine laboratories in Mexico and the confiscation of over 100 tons of medicine.

In addition to drugs, pirate activities include a wide gamut of health-related accessories. In the hotels around La Merced, pirated condoms made in China, Malaysia, the US and locally that don't meet quality standards for the control of AIDS and venereal diseases and often don't even prevent pregnancy are sold to prostitutes. Besides having to worry about pirated doctors, drugs and other health-related products, thousands of the ambulances that roam the streets of Mexico City are unlicensed, while most of those who work in these ambulances and give emergency services are not even paramedics. Not even health insurance is sacred, as the sale of pirate insurance policies represents 10% of the insurance market.

Drug Wars With the aim of gaining control of the hearts and bodies of 100 million potential consumers in Mexico, drug wars are currently raging in Mexico. In 1987, almost one hundred Mexican companies produced around 250 pharmaceuticals covering 67% of the market, but since the North American Free Trade Agreement went into effect only one-quarter of these local companies have survived and multinational pharmaceutical companies now dominate the market, their sales accounting for 70% of the annual 120 billion dollar legal drug sales in Mexico.

In addition to patented medicine, both national and international companies manufacture generic drugs, a lucrative market in Mexico. Generics provide the same therapeutic benefits without any need to run costly laboratory trials to prove their effectiveness, and thus can be offered at a discount of up to 75% of brand-name pharmaceuticals. The main dealer of generics in Mexico is Dr. Simi and his chain of *Farmacias de Similares*, in operation since 1997. Dr. Simi owns two pharmaceutical plants, over 50 laboratories and boasts over 3,500 drug stores that peddle his products ("the same but cheaper") to 12 million drug users in Mexico alone (in Guatemala Dr. Simi has partnered up with Nobel-prize winner Rigoberta Menchu).

In addition to its aggressive ad campaign all over the city, in the Metro and on television (both commercials and its own television show about health), Dr. Simi drugstores attract customers by hiring people to dance inside an oversized Dr. Simi cartoon-like character in a white lab suit. A long-used advertisement for the Dr. Simi drugstores showed a benevolent grey-haired man dressed as a family doctor (Dr. Simi) standing up to *Raterín Raterón* (Little Big Rat), a fat man in a top hat carrying a huge sack of money on his shoulder (representing foreign pharmaceutical companies).

In 2006, Dr. Simi, aka Victor González Torres, ran for president (he lost). His nephew is the president of the Green Party (the green refers more to money than to the environment) which helped the PRI win the 2012 presidential election, and his brother owns another pharmacy chain. Due to its political connections, Dr. Simi has grown rapidly since the recent amendment to the Health Law which permits the inclusion of generics in over-the-counter healthcare. The government recently created *Seguro Popular*, a healthcare initiative designed to provide healthcare services and medicine, both brand name and generics, to 50 million people. With his political connections, Dr. Simi has been able to carve out 10% of the national sales of drugs, and with the new President he helped get elected sales will surely take off.

Dr. Simi has long been engaged in an all-out drug war with the established drug industry, including the multinationals operating within Mexico and with the governmental regulatory institutions. Both sides have taken each other to court, with charges of fraud, slander, corruption and traffic of influence, but there has been no clear winner and, meanwhile, business continues as usual. Most of the multinational and local manufacturers have repeatedly attacked the lack of quality controls and medical ethics of Dr. Simi, while the US government has sued the Mexican Health Department for providing local industries with confidential information about their products without permission to sell copies of their products. On the other hand, Dr. Simi accuses the Mexican government (the PAN party in power for the last two presidencies) of selling out to foreign companies. (Like much of the Mexican economy, the only ones who can stand up to the multinationals are local business mafias promoted by corrupt politicians, and in neither case does the country or its citizens benefit.)

Both the pharmaceuticals and the generic manufacturers have to compete with health products that are sold not as medicine but rather as dietary supplements, cosmetics, herbs or hygienic products. Some of the wealthiest Mexicans deal in these drugs. Genomma Lab is a new firm that produces over-the-counter health products (laxatives, treatments for wounds, and remedies for obesity and acne), and it is rumored that the company belongs to Carlos Slim since it distributes its products mainly through his chain of Sanborns. Omnilife, owned by Jorge Vergara (who also owns the Guadalajara Chivas soccer team), is a vitamin and health product manufacturer who makes millions by employing legions of door-to-door salespeople who receive commissions instead of a salary.

Sports medicine is also a huge market in Mexico. Initially, anabolic steroids were used to treat depression, osteoporosis, bone fractures, cancer and other chronic illnesses, but in the last few decades these steroids have been the drug of preference for the world of sports and physical fitness. Although they are forbidden in international competitions, within Mexico steroid use among soccer and baseball players, boxers, wrestlers and weightlifters is common. As there is no law against their production or consumption in Mexico, steroids are widely produced in Mexico for both local consumption and for export.

Steroid use is illegal in the US. Over 80% of all anabolic steroids confiscated by police in the US come from Mexico, and this illegal steroid market generates over 50 million dollars in profit each year, with eight Mexican companies dominating this market since the early 1990s. Steroids such as Omifin, Novaldex, Novegan, Stenox and Humatrop are sold out of Mexico through the Internet and in pharmacies located near the US/Mexico border.

Before WWII, sex hormones derived from slaughterhouse animals' brains were produced by German companies, but their production was suspended during the war, allowing the US to take the lead in the race to synthesize the hormones more inexpensively. US researchers began extracting steroids from wild poisonous yams (including one called *cabeza de negro* or black man's head) and other plants naturally abundant in Mexico, and from these were able to synthesize progesterone. After the war, steroidal sex hormones were produced in Mexico and exported around the world. (Research into sex hormones in Mexico led to the patent in the US of the contraceptive pill, first marketed in 1960 and one of the global pharmaceutical industry's all time best seller.) Corticosteroids, considered a wonder drug, was first used in the 1960s to treat metabolic diseases and arthritis.

Dianabol, an early brand of corticosteroids, first appeared in 1960 and quickly became the most used anabolic steroid in sports. Chemically, it is very similar to testosterone, producing side effects such as enlarged breasts, water retention, oily skin, acne, body hair and male pattern baldness. Long-term use can often lead to the atrophy of sexual glands and to impotence. Heart and circulatory problems, as well as leukemia, are common and its continued used can cause jaundice and liver dysfunction and increases aggression and mood swings. When it was taken off the shelves due to health risks, Dianabol became one of the most commonly bought black market oral steroids in the US, and varieties manufactured in Mexico still sell well in the US.

Drug Stores With all the diseases and health problems that come from living in the city, and having to deal with so many quacks and bogus treatments, it's a miracle anyone can remain healthy in Mexico City. A population free of illness, however, would prove quite unhealthy for a large part of the city's economy. In contrast to the Aztec's holistic view of the body, the modern medical-industrial complex has dismembered the human body into separate organs that need to be attended by specialists and treated with costly medicine. Instead of viewing sickness as an imbalance between the workings of the body and the world around it, diseases have been reduced to mere symptoms, and in turn symptoms (such as sneezing, coughing, phlegm, pus, fever) are no longer viewed as the body's natural defenses but have become evils that must be eliminated. The stress of battling traffic and urban congestion, the extremely high levels of pollution, and food and water laden with parasites and toxic chemicals are all godsends for a medical-industrial complex that offers medicine for every symptom.

Mexico is the 10th largest consumer of pharmaceuticals in the world. Even though medicine is cheaper in Mexico than in the rest of the Americas (with the exception of Ecuador and Venezuela), drug profits are still greater than in any country except for the US. Drug culture within Mexico is well entrenched. Multinational companies push their product through governmental initiatives and major media ads (pharmaceutical companies are not prohibited from advertising their products on television, as in most countries).

In Mexico City, where economic interests are never seen as a conflict but rather an opportunity, doctors not only act as willing stooges for pharmaceutical companies who lavish them with free samples, equipment and even kick-backs, many also own their own private drugstores. This all leads to a situation in which more than half of all medical consultations end with drugs being prescribed to a patient. As a direct result of the zealousness of pharmaceutical pushers, ten percent of all hospital deaths result from erroneous prescriptions or over-medication. Twenty-four-hour drugstores cluster around city hospitals, parasitic on the sick and ailing, their profits increasing with the rise in acute and chronic illnesses in the city.

The most abused drugs in Mexico City are antibiotics. The blunderbuss approach of antibiotics might cure symptoms rapidly but over time they provoke health problems that convert people into chronic users (a pharmaceutical company's best customer). As a result of the abuse of antibiotics, E. Coli and the microorganisms responsible for urinary infections have developed antibiotic resistance of up to 90% in more than half of the population in Mexico City. Although antibiotics are not an effective treatment for viral infections, which represents the main cause of the common cold, doctors, especially pediatricians, have no qualms about prescribing them to their sniffling patients even before receiving the results of laboratory studies and sometimes without even conducting a check-up (phone consultations with doctors usually end with drug prescriptions).

Even so, around 95% of *chilangos* don't even bother to call their doctor and instead self-medicate. When Mexicans have doubts about what medication they need, and when they are unwilling to wait for a doctor's appointment or to pay a doctor's fee, they just head over to their neighborhood drugstore for advice. Unfortunately, Mexico is the country in the Americas with the fewest pharmacists actually working in pharmacies. Being that trained pharmacists are expensive employees, owners of drug stores instead hire unskilled workers, whose recommendations for medications are often just shots in the dark or verbatim advice from drug companies. Many times, though, people don't even ask pharmacy employees and just go right ahead and order their favorite brand of antibiotics or other prescription medicine by phone from a drug store and have them brought to their home by bicycle delivery boys.

Due to their easy availability and low cost (medicine is subsidized by the Mexican government), drug abuse is widespread in Mexico. Up to 40% of all prescription drugs are sold over-the-counter without a prescription in most drug stores, or in pharmacies located in department stores or supermarkets.

Mexican drugstores, whether inside larger stores or alone, are among the fastest growing sector in terms of profit and in the number of units being inaugurated each year. In addition to free medical advice, drugstores offer injections into peoples' butts for a small fee right behind the pharmacy counter. Besides the pharmacies, there are hundreds of non-licensed, non-trained individuals (many of them housewives) working out of their own homes all over the city who offer injections for a nominal fee, as well.

Around 70% of all consultations made in the past years by Mexicans who possess government insurance were in clinics attached to pharmacies (such as Dr. Simi), and these clinics represent the privatization of medical attention in Mexico. To open up one of these clinics an entrepreneur need only fill out the usual paperwork for any business, without any special knowledge or authorization. By law, pharmacies and clinics must be separate entities, but a thin wall is enough to divide them, and patients often pay for the consultation (around $3 dollars a visit) and the medicine in the same window. Unlike government hospitals, no appointments are needed, and unlike hospitals that tend to be located far away from patients, pharmacy clinics are available in every neighborhood and, in some neighborhoods, on almost every corner. Since 2010, you now need a prescription to buy antibiotics in most drugstores in Mexico City, but the only real result of this measure has been to funnel more business into these clinic/pharmacies where consultations that lead to prescriptions can be had in minutes.

Medicine of Mass Destruction

The relatively recent discovery of microscopic creatures has proven to be a miraculous shot in the arm for the medical world. By immediately branding these invisible creatures as hostile aliens, the medical-industrial complex was given total liberty to declare war against all microorganisms. Doctors and pharmacists were licensed to hunt down and kill all illegal aliens in our mouths, armpits, crotches, large intestines or wherever else they roamed. With an interspecies war in full swing, it was easy for medical authorities to convince us that our own defenses were actually illnesses that could only be cured with industrial-strength medicine.

Huge healthcare and hygiene industries emerged that sold a whole range of products of mass destruction, including mouthwash, antiperspirants, deodorizers, detergents, anti-flu medicine and antibiotics. Almost overnight, the bacterial communities that had co-evolved with human beings for hundreds of thousands of years became our enemies and interspecies symbiosis was unilaterally abandoned.

This paranoia, however, wasn't completely unjustified. Throughout the history of mankind, and up until just a few decades ago, parasites were responsible for the greatest number of human fatalities. With the invention of antibiotics, parasite-related deaths dropped spectacularly and it seemed that man had finally liberated itself from the ravages of Nature. The problem is that not all microorganisms are parasites, and in fact the great majority of microorganisms actually help us to fend off aggressive parasites. Antibiotics, however, aren't designed to differentiate between beneficial bacteria and aggressive invaders.

In the long run, and when viewed in terms of the whole species, antibiotics do more damage than good to humans. As deaths caused by parasite-based diseases plummeted with the advent of antibiotics, extreme overpopulation exploded all over the planet, especially in the developing world. Too many human beings living together in densely populated urban spaces for longer lifespans tend to overwhelm developing economies and cause widespread poverty, disease and death.

In addition, parasites are the embodiment of natural selection, killing off the weakest organisms while allowing the fittest to survive, and thus they help strenghten the human race. Parasites also help maintain harmony by not allowing only one species to dominate all others, thus preventing the human race from expanding so much that we completely deplete the environment and cause our own demise (and that of other organisms). Modern medicine, however, has interrupted this natural process and now benefits from the overpopulation and the epidemic of chronic illness that affect mega-cities like Mexico City.

On a macro-economic level, the global medical-industrial complex is part of a united front of predatorial colonizers that make developing countries dependent upon imported products and technology, thus redirecting the flow of their capital and resources and weakening the local communities and traditional culture that had maintained their own self-sufficient economies. Throughout our history, we humans have had to rely on our own body to defend against parasite infections, but with the pandemic spread of modern medicine we are no longer capable of fighting our own battles. By making the human race dependent on medicine and health and hygiene products, the global medical-industrial complex has reordered biological systems around the world, positioning itself as the sole intermediary between the human species and microorganisms (exactly as the Catholic Church positioned itself as the sole intermediary between man and God)

By treating all microorganisms within us as our enemies, the medical-industrial complex completely misunderstands health. Health is not the absence of organisms that cause illnesses. In fact, most of us live most of our lives with potentially lethal parasites and even cancer cells in our bodies. The fact that they are not triggered and do not multiply is due to our immune system, that is, to the billions of beneficial bacteria that keep potentially lethal invaders in their place. Only when our defenses are compromised by poverty, malnourishment or stress, by the buildup of toxic substances within our organs or by an indiscriminate use of antibiotics, do these parasites and cancer cells multiply and expand.

It's time we realize that we are only as healthy as the beneficial communities of microorganisms within our large intestine and throughout our body. By casting microorganisms as our enemies, by bombarding our bodies with unneeded health, hygiene and beauty products, we are exterminating our greatest allies. When microorganisms in our body come under attack and can no longer fulfill their role of maintaining equilibrium, things start to fall apart for all species.

To take just one example of how much humans depend upon microorganisms for their survival, and how any disruption of the micro-cities within us affect the cities around us, the total destruction of the Aztec civilization by the Spanish also represented a genocide of the complex communities within the large intestines of those living in Mexico-Tenochtitlan. The parasites that provoked the plagues that decimated the indigenous cultures in Mexico were able to kill so many millions of natives precisely because their local gut flora had been thoroughly weakened by stress, poverty, slavery and malnutrition, thus leaving the Aztecs defenseless on a biological level against foreign invasion.

The radical transformation of the local diet over the last few decades, along with the indiscriminate use of antibiotics and other products designed to kill alien invaders has decimated local communities of microorganisms, especially in our gut flora, making people vulnerable to a whole slew of chronic, degenerative diseases. Because human beings now rarely die from parasite infections, they rarely die from natural causes (natural deaths in Mexico City have decreased over the last decade by 30%). Instead, human beings now suffer and die mostly from chronic, degenerative diseases caused by an inability to defend against man-made threats within the environment. ✝

Death, God and Bacteria

I am an atheist. I never believed in God, although as a young kid I used to pray to a Martin Luther King poster I had in my room just after he had been assassinated, and once as a teenager I asked God for help when I got my hand stuck in an elevator door. Atheists are not entirely free of superstitious behavior and thoughts, but we deny them any transcendent nature and see them only as obsessions. However, when pushed far enough by particularly adverse circumstances, atheists will sometimes give up their scientific notions of causality and ask for help from the great beyond. Having exhausted all medical and even some magical solutions, and still suffering from chronic money and health problems, I am ready to turn to even more extreme measures. With no doctor or lawyer able to remedy my situation, I consider other options.

I am invited to the Havana Film Festival to show my film, finally finished with post-production money from the Mexican Film Institute. While I'm here I decide to get some spiritual help for my mundane problems of health and finances. I accompany a *babalao* named Leandro to a local market in Buena Vista where we buy two pigeons and a chicken and bring them back to his apartment. He rips the head off of one of the pigeons, spilling the blood onto an altar with handmade figures and objects caked with thick dried blood in his bedroom. Then, in the living room, Leandro slits the throat of the other pigeon and the chicken and spills their blood onto three funky metal figures of the *orishas* Ellegua, Ogun and Oshun that he made especially for me. I wipe the blood off the floor using feathers I pluck off the dead chicken, clean the figures and wrap them up in newspaper.

Back in Mexico City, every Monday morning in my bedroom I knock three times on the floor, place tortillas and fruit in a bowl and tequila in a glass, light two candles and pray (it sounds more like begging) for help. After a year or so of carrying out my weekly rituals, and seeing how my health hasn't improved and that I am still drowning in debt and without any job prospects, I give up talking to my *orishas*. I always felt somewhat skeptical asking for economic help from a religion that came from and serviced some of the poorest people and countries in the world, especially since I come from a culture and religion (Judaism) that does quite well financially for its followers. (Perhaps it was my Jewish scepticism that kept me from reaping the benefits of *santería*.)

We all want to believe that our behavior and faith somehow affect our fate, and that if we could only find the right combination of thoughts, words and actions things would get better. Organized religion has gained the faith of billions of people worldwide precisely by ordering, or at least standardizing, these ritualistic behaviors. In Mexico, Catholic ritualistic behavior is very common and very public. Soccer players, boxers and other professional athletes cross themselves before entering the ring or field, vendors kiss the first pesos they receive each day, and taxi drivers are condemned to cross themselves every time they drive by a church. More extreme ritualistic behaviors accrue even greater benefits upon the believer. On certain religious holidays, Catholics crawl on their knees along the main avenues for miles, carrying large crosses or flagellating themselves, either to ask for a miracle or to give thanks for favors received.

More than anything else, death brings humans to religion. The fear of death, the grief associated with the death of loved ones or the realization of the inevitability of one's own future death has long inspired human beings to believe in forces beyond their control. For most of our history, death came mostly from the handiwork of invisible parasites, although their existence was unknown up until just a few decades ago. Thus, for most of history, human beings had no clue as to why their loved ones got sick and passed away, and this lack of knowledge inspired all kinds of flights of imagination. Elaborate beliefs that attempted to make sense of senseless death emerged, as did superstitious behaviors, and over time these evolved into complex religions. It is no coincidence that the greatest outbreaks of religious activity occurred during the greatest outbreaks of parasite-based plagues and it seems logical to assume that the most extreme religious cultures exist in cities with the greatest parasite activity.

Until microscopes were invented, humans searched for the meaning of life and death in non-natural realms, eventually giving rise to the creation of gods. If, however, anything on earth resembles a god it is bacteria. Bacteria is the great architect of life, for not only was it the very first life form on earth but it has been intimately involved in the creation and evolution of all species. Like a god, bacteria are invisible and omnipresent, and being that they can replicate asexually ad infinitum they are eternal and indestructible. Due to their role in human death, bacteria can also be seen as the Holy Ghost or the Grim Reaper.

Although I can't actually see them, I believe in bacteria as others believe in their one, true God. I believe that bacteria directly influence my life and will play a major role in my death, and that they will be waiting for me when I die to usher me into the great beyond. Being that I am probably the only human who worships and prays to bacteria, a faith with a following of one, my beliefs are not recognized as a religion by the Mexican government.

Church and State According to its Constitution, Mexico has no official religion. By law, the Mexican government can't support or favor any religious institution nor can religion exist in public education or in any other public institution. Nonetheless, almost 97% of all Mexicans are religious, Mexico is one of the most Catholic countries in the world (second only to Brazil in the total number of believers), and Catholicism has played a major role in almost all aspects of Mexican culture since its arrival in Mexico.

In order to monopolize man's relation to the spiritual realm and the hereafter, the Catholic Church established the first printing presses in the New World and banned the sale and possession of all other books, and although it founded the first universities it kept the vast majority of the country illiterate (98% illiteracy as late as 1821). To retain its power, the Church fought against Independence from Spain, supported the invasion of Mexico by US marines and by France, signed a treaty with Porfirio Díaz to support him during his 40-year dictatorship, fought against the Mexican Revolution and battled against the ruling political party (PRI) for 70 years.

Up until the Mexican Revolution instituted its land reform, the Catholic Church owned 65% of the real estate in the country. The PRI, the political party born out of the Revolution, abolished the legal and property rights of all religious institutions, prohibited priests from voting and banned worship in public places. Nonetheless, Mexico has remained a Catholic country, the Church dominates civil society, many political leaders are active members of the Church, and many of the most important businessmen and cultural figures are products of religious educational institutions and maintain close ties to the ecclesiastic elite.

In the last decade or so, especially with the last two presidents, both members of the PAN (the religious right party), religious institutions have regained their legal status, men of the cloth are once again able to vote, Mexico reestablished diplomatic relations with the Vatican and Pope John Paul II visited Mexico several times. In the last couple of years new laws have made it more difficult for religious institutions not associated with the Catholic Church to operate and spread their beliefs in Mexico, allowing for an even greater monopolization of religious activity.

Despite the Constitutional ban on the Church from meddling in State affairs, the Church is engaged in a constant fight against Mexico City's left-wing government (PRD) and actively campaigns against abortion and gay marriage (both recently legalized in Mexico City, the only part of the country to do so). The *Opus Dei* and *Legión de Cristo*, two of the most powerful, most reactionary wings of the Church, own hundreds of churches and dozens of universities and schools throughout the country and are very influential within the PAN (the ruling party for the past 12 years). Marcial Maciel, the founder of the *Legión de Cristo*, an intimate friend of Pope Paul II (as well as a drug fiend, embezzler and pederast), wielded great power within Mexican politics up until his death in 2008.

Although the separation between Church and the military is also part of the Constitution, one church in front of the main military base in Mexico City caters to soldiers and officers. This church greets followers with a huge sculpture in front of the church in which Christ gives succor to a wounded soldier armed with a semi-automatic weapon. Inside the church, a large stained glass window presents the archangel Michael, dressed as a paratrooper, battling devils. Being that it tends to cater to the rich and powerful, the Catholic Church also has ties to wealthy *narcos*, who often foot the bill for the construction or improvement of churches across the country.

Deaths of the Saints

Unlike Cuba, most Mexicans pray not in their own homes but rather in official houses of worship. Thousands of Catholic churches dot the Mexico City landscape, from churches founded in the days of Conquistadores to futuristic ones built just recently, from tiny one-room affairs to huge cathedrals, and all are centrally organized.

The Condesa has three churches (as well as two synagogues and over a dozen yoga studios where Eastern spirituality is practiced). In Tepito, however, a neighborhood with a strong sense of community and a history that stretches back to pre-Hispanic times, located in the Historic Center just a few blocks from the Metropolitan Cathedral, there are even fewer houses of worship than in the Condesa.

This doesn't mean, however, that *tepiteños* are any less religious. In fact, they are so religious they create their own centers of worship. On almost every street corner and in the patio of every apartment building, locals have erected elaborate glass display cases, some as large as small two-story houses, with sufficient fluorescent lighting to illuminate their saints (and half the block) at night. Fancifully dressed baby Jesuses, crucified Christs, Virgins of Guadalupe, San Judas and several other Catholic saints and religious figures reside in these glass altars.

Although Catholics in Mexico believe in God and pay their respects to the Virgin Mary and Jesus, when a miracle is most needed they tend to direct their prayers to saints. The Catholic saints brought to the New World were often better assimilated by natives than Jesus or the Almighty due to the fact that many of these figures resembled indigenous gods (just like *santería*). The similarities between imported and local religious icons at first was seen as an opportunity to smuggle in earlier, pagan figures of worship under the guise of church-approved saints, but the Aztec gods disappeared completely after a generation or two.

Even though the Church is prohibited from engaging in commercial activity within their houses of prayer (especially in the Colonial churches that are property of the nation), the major churches in Mexico have stalls that sell framed images, necklaces and Catholic saint trading cards listing the prayers that must be said to obtain miracles.

San Judas Tadeo, a green-faced saint with a flame coming out from atop his head, often pictured martyred by a club or sword, is the saint of difficult or desperate causes, and has recently become especially popular among adolescents and young adults in Mexico City, especially those involved in gangs or drugs. The Church uses miracle saints such as San Judas to hook young Mexicans on religion.

A man of the cloth must suffer a gruesome death in the line of duty to become a Catholic saint, and the more hideous the death the more power this saint has to confer miracles. Catholic saints have been crucified, stoned to death, decapitated, run through by spears, dragged to their death, hung from trees, thrown into a vat of boiling oil, burned at the stake, torn to bits by lions and had their brains bashed in by clubs.

The first Mexican to become a saint, San Felipe de Jesús, was born in 1572 in Mexico City and as a young man was sent to the Philippines to carry out his religious service. On the trip back, his ship ran into a storm and was swept to Japan, where Felipe lived and worked with Franciscan monks for many years. When the Japanese took up arms against the Catholic missionaries, they cut off one of Felipe's ears, hung him on a cross and impaled him on two lances. Felipe was beatified thirty years later and ordained a saint 65 years after his death, and he is now considered the patron saint of Mexico City, protector against natural disasters.

During the first five hundred years after Mexico became a nation only a few locals were ordained as saints. In 2000, however, on one of his visits to Mexico,

Pope John Paul II canonized 25 martyred priests and laymen killed in the *Guerras Cristeros*, the Church's two-year war waged against the anti-religious Mexican authorities who took power after the Mexican Revolution. Even though Mexico now possesses many of its own, Mexicans still tend to prefer European saints.

Holy Death Most of the altars in Tepito contain Catholic saints and holy figures, but there are also some that feature a new Mexican saint, one feared and despised by the Catholic Church. This local saint holds an even more prominent place within the religious activity of the neighborhood and boasts the most elaborate altar of all. Given the fact that almost no one in Tepito pays income tax (the vast majority work in the informal sector of the economy), the only thing *tepiteños* can be sure of is death. Not surprisingly, this saint is depicted as death herself and is called *La Santa Muerte* (Saint Death).

As befits the representation of death on earth, no one knows exactly where or when *La Santa Muerte* was born. In Mexico City, *La Santa Muerte* appeared on the streets of the tougher neighborhoods in the early 1990s (making her the newest saint in town). Whatever her origin, the cult of *La Santa Muerte* now exists in every state in Mexico, in southwestern United States (there are fifteen parishes in Los Angeles alone), and throughout Central America (the *mara salvatrucha*, the gangs that spread from East L.A. to Central America, are devoted followers).

Many believe *La Santa Muerte* is a direct descendant of the Aztec gods of death, gods who not only decided the destiny of the dead but also granted wishes to the living. During the Aztec days of the dead, the period of mourning when a family member died and celebrated once a year from then on, the bereaved family would adorn the deceased's grave with food, liquor and tobacco, offerings the dead had to bring to the lords of the afterlife to gain admission. Cuatlicue, the Aztec goddess of the earth, life and death, depicted with a skull strapped to her bellybutton, might very well be a precursor to *La Santa Muerte*, although any direct link with Aztec traditions is unlikely as the indigenous gods and religious rituals were abruptly put to rest after the Conquest.

Others see *La Santa Muerte* as a new version of Saint Pascual Bailón, the saint of kitchens and desserts. During an extremely deadly plague in the mid-16th century in Mexico, this saint was publicly displayed in funeral pyres as a skeleton dressed in robes, covered in jewelry, wearing a crown and stretched out in a horse-drawn cart. Given that representing death is not a very saintly thing to do, the Catholic Church publicly burnt his image and statues and outlawed him as a saint. The persecution of Bailón didn't end there, for in 1914 the Mexican government sent in troops to destroy images of this saint who had spread throughout the State of Chiapas. Even so, Bailón still survives today and is worshipped by both Catholics and those devoted to witchcraft (much like *La Santa Muerte*).

Another early death figure was *La Buena Muerte* (The Good Death), depicted as a skull and crossbones or skeleton. Around the 13th century, the Church created *Buena Muerte* brotherhoods in Europe to help Catholics avoid a bad death, such as that caused by plagues, and to inspire them to cleanse their souls before they left this life and to die like a good Catholic. Unlike *La Santa Muerte*, *La Buena Muerte* was not a saint prayed to or of whom favors were asked, as the idea of worshipping death has always been heretical within the Church (official dogma states that Christ defeated death when he was resurrected after his crucifixion, but Christ, martyrs and saints tend to be glorified in their moment of demise).

Besides pre-Hispanic and European Catholic rites, the rituals associated with *La Santa Muerte* also share much in common with *santería* brought to Mexico by Africans. The offerings presented to the *orishas* are very similar to those given to *La Santa Muerte*, and Ellgua, like *La Santa Muerte*, specializes in helping people out of difficult legal situations.

To many people, *La Santa Muerte* has taken the place of the traditional Catholic saints as the one to turn to in time of need, offering not just spiritual but also economic and even sexual healing. In part due to her name, in part due to her representation as a skeleton carrying a scythe, in part because of all the criminal types who so faithfully worship her, *La Santa Muerte* is often accused of inflicting suffering and death upon people. Although this is not necessarily so, violence and even murder can actually be a way to liberate oneself from the abuse of others, and believers invoke *La Santa Muerte* to help ward off evil. Those who ask for favors are said to become indebted to her and must continue to offer her gifts for the rest of their lives (or else). Those who ask *La Santa Muerte* to harm others are said to assume a blood debt (much like Aztecs who were born with a blood debt to the gods, paid off by self-bloodletting or human sacrifice) which requires even more devotion and sacrifice.

Even more than any Catholic saint, *La Santa Muerte* has her own line of consumer products, including incense, candles, sprays, powders, laminated cards and statues (from tiny ones that fit on your dashboard to larger-than-human), and her face is emblazoned on tee-shirts, earrings, bracelets, necklaces and tattooed onto thick arms and wide backs. Besides epitomizing the aesthetic of the Mexico City death metal and gothic crowd, *La Santa Muerte* reigns supreme in the city jails, within the criminal class and in the informal work force, all strongly represented within the neighborhood of Tepito.

Followers dress their *Santa Muerte* figures with clothes of different colors depending on what they wish for: gold for money, business and power; ivory to find peace, harmony and success; red for love, passion and emotional stability; white to purify homes from envy and bad blood; green to sort out legal problems; amber to fight drug and alcohol addictions; violet to fend off sickness; and black to counteract the evil eye and other malevolent invocations. To gain her favor, *La Sante Muerte* is usually offered flowers, candy, chocolate, fruits, tequila, rum, sweet liquors, dark beer, cigarettes, cigars or joints.

Altars are essential for maintaining a good relation with *La Santa Muerte*, and neighbors in Tepito devote substantial amounts of time, money and imagination to create them. At the most elaborate of her altars in Tepito, on the first Monday of every week, just before mass is held, the woman in charge of the giant glass display completely reworks the installation. The largest *Santa Muerte* figure often appears in a white wedding dress with a veil partially covering her face, silver chains and crosses dangling down from her neck and from her boney fingers. Dozens of other smaller *Santa Muerte* figures, as well as tiny toy-like figures of death, are also dressed each week, constantly changing colors and outfits. Dazzling fluorescent lights illuminate the altar which is surrounded by plastic flowers and objects related to death, and a small room next to it accommodates all the lit candles her followers bring her.

Although on the very first of each month her followers come to pay her respects, *La Santa Muerte* celebrates her birthday every October 31st, serenaded by Mariachis and with a birthday cake. Each of her followers bring their own handmade *Santa Muerte* figure to the altar, some so large they must be carried by four strong men. Tepito has a reputation for crime and violence, as does *La Santa Muerte*, but during this night her followers freely exchange beaded necklaces, flowers, candies, magic sprays and marijuana, and it is one of the most respectful, supportive community gatherings that exist in Mexico City.

Pirate Territory

Tepito's next-door neighbor, Tlatelolco, was the commercial center of the Aztec empire, its market the largest in the Americas. *Pochtecas*, the merchants that controlled trade between Mexico-Tenochtitlan and the rest of the Aztec empire, resided mostly in this area. Members of an exclusive and powerful guild, the *pochtecas* didn't deal in basic goods but instead bartered for luxury items (gold, jewels, feathers) and stimulants (tobacco, cacao and psychoactive substances) in far-off lands in order to supply the Aztec elite. Being that *pochtecas* knew all the routes and back roads of all parts of the country, as well as the local customs and languages, they acted as spies and tax collectors for the Aztec rulers, for which they were hated by the outer colonies. Although they maintained a low profile and wore modest clothes, Aztecs generally despised them for hoarding wealth and for the distinctions they alone were granted.

The *pochetcas* obeyed their own laws, possessed their own security forces and represented a semi-independent force within the empire, the only commoners who enjoyed the benefits of royalty. When a *pochteca* died he went to the same afterlife as the warriors who died in battle. As these merchants were the only ones allowed to buy and sell slaves, they were also the only ones who could ascend socially by sacrificing others in their place.

Not only because they trafficked in intoxicants but also because they traveled in armed caravans, threw huge parties for the whole town, paid for temples and civic centers to be built and were sought out by politicians and religious leaders, they could be considered the first Mexican narcos. After the Conquest many of them became outlaws and continued to supply hallucinogens and narcotic substances to the local populace. Given that most *pochetcas* lived in or around the neighborhood, they represent the direct ancestors of the drug traffickers and outlaws that have long made Tepito such a notorious neighborhood.

Since the days of the Aztec empire, markets have always been the largest employers within the Mexican service sector and the city's largest markets have always been in and around Tepito. La Merced, located on the edge of the Tepito, was the largest market in Mexico City during most of the 20th century. During the last few decades, La Merced and other neighborhood markets have had their business undercut by the convenience stores (both national and international chains) that have popped up on almost every corner. Many who had previously worked in these markets have been forced to seek work within the informal economy, often selling pirated goods on the streets or driving pirate taxis. With the influx of cheap products illegally imported from China, many workers in local manufacturing also lost their jobs and have been forced into the informal economy. This fluctuating informal workforce also provides the labor base of the illegal drug industry and in the criminal underworld within Tepito.

In the last century, Tepito went from being the center of used clothes and second-hand goods to being the hub of *fayuca* (mostly illegally imported electrical appliances). By the early 20th century, Tepito and environs had become home to a large Jewish and Lebanese population that controlled most of the city's textile and clothing industry within the city. Most of the knock-off jeans and designer clothes of the 70s and early 80s in Mexico were manufactured by local entrepreneurs in Tepito sweatshops.

After the 1985 earthquake hit the neighborhood hard, the residential population of Tepito plummeted and commerce took over. Most of the sidewalks and streets are now overrun by stalls set up underneath colored tarps that extend for dozens of blocks in all directions, creating a cramped outdoor mall. Most of the rented space in the neighborhood was converted into commercial use, with many of the buildings hollowed out and joined to other buildings, converted into huge, clandestine warehouses for illegal goods and used as hideouts or escape routes during police raids.

Since the Free Trade Agreement removed restrictions and tariffs on electrical appliances, the *fayuca* business waned and Tepito has since evolved into pirate territory. The illegal reproduction and sale of DVDs, videos, CDs, computer programs and video games, as well as knock-offs of brand-name clothes, perfume and accessories, represents the most lucrative industry in Mexico. In the last few years, Koreans have taken over much of the pirate clothes and accessories business in Mexico City, shipping illegal merchandise from China into Los Angeles in huge containers and then smuggling it down across the border and into Tepito.

Mexico is second only to China and Russia in pirate profits, and sales from these illegal goods represent three times that of Pemex, the government-owned oil monopoly. Forty percent of all sales in Mexico are from pirated goods and up to seventy percent of all CDs and DVDs sold in Mexico City are pirated, most of them reproduced in and around Tepito.

Copies of Hollywood movies are sold on the street in Tepito before they are shown in movie theaters, months before they are released in DVD, and cost a mere a fraction of the price of a movie ticket or rental in any Blockbuster store around the city. At first, pirated copies were shot with digital video cameras during preview screenings in the US (the action in the movie accompanied by shadows of moviegoers getting up out of their seats to go the bathroom, or by the sounds of popcorn crunching or someone coughing) and due to the poor quality of sound and image, the millions of dollars Hollywood spent on special effects inevitably became lost in translation. These days, however, with all the peer-to-peer sharing sites on the Web, pirated copies are digitally identical to commercial DVDs. If it weren't for the existence of these popularly priced pirated goods, the majority of the inhabitants of Mexico City wouldn't have access to international film culture.

The biggest business in Tepito isn't selling pirated videos, DVDs or CDs, though. Instead, the big money is made here through the sale of the means of reproduction: master copies of feature films and music CDs, printed covers, plastic cases, as well as multiple digital recorders. Tepito offers one-stop shopping to entrepreneurs ready to set up their very own private pirate studios. Hollywood is amongst the most dominant global industries, accused of unfair competition against foreign film industries and of force feeding American values to local cultures around the world. Yet for all its global force, Hollywood is virtually powerless against the unlicensed reproduction and distribution of its own products sold at a fraction of the cost by local entrepreneurs in Tepito and elsewhere.

Recent neo-liberal economic policies, such as the North American Free Trade Agreement designed to usher in US products into Mexico, have led to massive lay-offs and the migration of millions from the countryside to Mexico City, swelling the ranks of the informally employed (up to 60% of the total work force) and forcing a large segment of the population into illegal activities, including *piratería*, drug dealing and prostitution.

Tepito is credited in history books as being the setting of the Aztec's final stand against the Spanish conquistadores. The neighborhood's reputation for resistance continues today, and Tepito remains mostly beyond the long arm of the law. Only when newly elected governments try to make good on election promises, when lawsuits by US software, music and film companies exert enough pressure on the Federal government, or when real estate speculators convince local politicians to act, do the police march into the neighborhood, always in large numbers and in full riot gear. Even if the police were more effective, the legislation is on the side of Tepito, as pirating goods is not an offense punishable by imprisonment. Intellectual property is somewhat of a foreign concept in Mexico, and enforcing it is deemed almost anti-patriotic. DVDs and CDs are regularly confiscated and burned, but almost no one is ever arrested and the next day the show goes on as usual.

Having a large tattoo of La Vigen de Guadalupe on your back used to protect you from being stabbed or shot, but today criminals and *narcos* tend to feel safer with *La Santa Muerte* covering their backs. Being that out of every ten prisoners in Mexico City jails at least three are from Tepito, and that *La Santa Muerte* specializes in helping those in precarious legal and economic situations, it is easy to see why this unholy saint has been so successful in cornering a significant segment of local spirituality.

Uncontrolled Substances

Indigenous cultures in the Mexico City Valley collected and consumed psychoactive substances, among them weeds, flowers, leaves, tree bark, cacti and mushrooms. Recreational use of these substances was strictly prohibited, although emperor Moctezuma was fond of serving magic mushrooms (known as "meat of the gods") to his dinner guests, and commoners would often sneak off into mountain caves to hold wild psychodelic orgies. As these natural substances were associated with pagan religious practices, the Spaniards outlawed their use immediately after the Conquest.

Marijuana was first introduced into Mexico by the Conquistadores, and it rapidly spread throughout indigenous communities for ritual (and eventually recreational) use. After the Mexican Revolution, and under the guise of combating opium trafficking, the government ran much of the Chinese population out of the country. Mexican traffickers quickly stepped in and took over the lucrative opium supply to the US, creating the first modern Mexican drug cartels.

Over time, and with imported technology, natural stimulants gave way to synthesized narcotics. When Saigon fell to the Communists at the end of the Vietnam War, Mexican 'mud' began to displace China 'white' in the US heroin market, that is, until a joint operation in 1978 of US and Mexican armed forces destroyed much of the Mexican poppy and marijuana production with the help of Agent Orange (a toxic herbicide manufactured by Monsanto).

Opium, laudanum, marijuana and morphine were readily available in Mexican drug stores at the end of the 19th century, and some of them were even available in local markets and in hardware stores, as well. Up until the first decades of the 20th century, opium and other poppy derivatives were still sold as miracle cures in local pharmacies, and even quite recently codeine and other narcotics could still be bought over the counter without a prescription. Marihuana, cocaine, opium, heroin and morphine, used regularly since the late 19th century, only became illegal in Mexico in the early decades of the 20th century, mostly due to pressure from the United States. Glue, especially popular among homeless kids, is sold in hardware and school-supply stores everywhere.

Methamphetamines are one of the newest drugs in town, synthesized in makeshift laboratories or even in kitchens using inexpensive ingredients, and often sold stamped with brand names like Mitsubishi, Rolls Royce and Walt Disney. Methamphetamines are mass-produced in Mexico for export to the lucrative US and European markets and successfully compete with the cocaine export industry.

The true scale of methamphetamine production in Mexico City was revealed with the arrest of Zhenli Ye Gon, a Mexican businessman of Chinese origin, a few years ago. Ye Gon is currently under arrest in the US, accused of trafficking methamphetamine precursors into Mexico from Asia after having almost 50,000 pounds of pseudoephedrine seized by Mexican customs in 2007. It is estimated that two-thirds of all pseudoephedrine, a substance used in anti-flu medicine, was bought from pharmacies in Mexico City to be used to manufacture methamphetamines, and Ye Gon's arrest forced authorities to retire all products in pharmacies that use pseudoephedrine as a main ingredient.

At the time of his arrest, two hundred million dollars in cash was found in Ye Gon's house in the upscale Lomas de Chapultepec neighborhood, the single largest drug-cash seizure in history. Ye Gon was preparing to build a huge factory to be equipped with eight state-of-the-art pill manufacturing machines capable of producing sufficient amphetamine to supply up to 80 per cent of the American market. The machines, made by a German company, each has the capacity to produce up to 50,000 pills per hour, and at full production these machines together could produce almost three million pills a day, worth an estimated fourteen million dollars on the wholesale black market. Of the eight machines that passed through Mexican customs, only one has been accounted for so far.

Although Ye Gon was caught with 60 tons of pseudoephedrine (as a comparison, only two and a half tons were confiscated in all of Europe in 2004), for some reason he has only been convicted of conspiracy to traffic 500 grams of methamphetamine from Mexico into the US, giving rise to several conspiracy theories. Ye Gon accuses the Mexican government of using him and his operation to launder money that was to be used to ensure President Calerdon's election, and two Mexican Federal agents involved in the arrests at the Ye Gon mansion were found dead soon afterwards.

Large-scale wars for the control of the drug market began as soon as drugs were made illegal and they continue up until today. None of this large-scale illegal drug manufacturing and trafficking would exist in Mexico if it were not for the insatiable habits of US drug consumers. The sound of sniffing and toking to be heard coming from north of the border is directly responsible for all the drug violence south of the border. Mexico is the number one supplier of marijuana and the number two of heroin to the US, and up to 70% of all methamphetamines consumed in the US are made in Mexico or in US labs controlled by Mexican cartels. Although Mexico used to be merely a transfer point to the US for drug shipments from Colombia and other Latin American countries, it has now consolidated itself as a illegal drug producer, distributor and, on a much smaller scale, consumer.

Although Mexican *narcos* do their best to satisfy the consuming needs of drug users in the US, many gringos prefer to cross the border in search of cheaper, better quality substances straight from the source. During Prohibition, Mexico became the official cantina and whorehouse for gringos, and artists and scientists have been traveling to Mexico for centuries to sample local psychoactive delicacies. Since the 1950s and 60s, Mexico has become a destination for narco-tourists (the Beats being the most famous) overjoyed to be able to purchase pills in the pharmacies and narcotics in the markets. Succeeding generations of narco-tourists have taken advantage of the fact that several substances controlled in the US, such as

Quaaludes, Percodans, Valiums, methadone and amphetamines were (and some are even still) available over-the-counter.

In Mexico City, where the army is not directly involved in the war against drugs, the local government has begun focusing its efforts to arrest the lowest-level drug dealers (*narcomenudistas*), a legacy of ex-NYC Mayor Giuliani's visit to Mexico City where he was paid one million dollars to give his opinion of crime control in the city. In Mexico City, drug consumption is nothing compared with that on the northern side of the border, and petty dealers, easy prey for the police due to their lack of political and law enforcement ties, represent a very low priority in a city that has much more serious crime problems (Mexican prisons are vastly overpopulated with small-time dealers and consumers of illegal drugs).

The police and local authorities themselves represent one of the bigger drug problems in Mexico City, as many of them supply the local dealers, or and often shake them and their customers down. Surprisingly enough, it was the PAN, the Catholic right-wing party, which promoted an initiative to decriminalize the possession of small quantities of drugs for consumers in order to combat police shakedowns (drug consumers caught would be registered as addicts and would have to seek counseling). After a phone call from then-President GW Bush a day before the vote in Congress, the PAN decided to vote against its own bill. In any case, Mexico City recently decriminalized pot and other consumer drugs although the quantities permitted are so small and the specifics of the law so unclear that police extortion continues.

Besides being the center of the pirate industry, Tepito is also one of the major supply points for illegal substances in Mexico City. About 10 percent of all the city's drugs are shipped into Tepito, cut (not always with the healthiest chemicals) and distributed to local dealers throughout the city. The drug trade within Tepito is well organized, indicating a high level of collaboration between drug traffickers and local authorities.

Police And Thieves

Although she is normally associated with criminals, police often look to *La Santa Muerte* for help, too, and can often be seen standing in front of the *Santa Muerte* altar in Tepito. Given the fact that they are paid so little, must constantly kick back money to higher-ranking officers in the precincts (who in turn pay off those further up the pyramid of power), and must pay for their own uniforms, pistols and patrol cars, police are highly motivated to actively pursue all those who infringe upon the law. Some police activity actually involves arresting criminals, but as the criminal justice system is completely corrupt (98% of all criminals walk, while 80% of all those in jail were arrested for crimes involving less than 50 dollars, that, is, those who couldn't buy their way out), police mostly serve as informal debts collectors for the government, demanding immediate payment for any infraction or crime committed. Although decent citizens never tire of complaining about police corruption, the fact that they can slip a cop a few bills and walk away from a traffic violation or other misdemeanor is one of the great advantages of living in Mexico City.

More than just letting criminals operate freely, police are actively involved in all aspects of criminal activity. During the 1970s and 80s, when *El Negro* Durazo was Mexico City's police chief, *la mordida* (the bite or payoff) became institutionalized and the underworld connections of the police became highly organized through *La Hermandad* (The Brotherhood). In Mexico, nothing is so well organized as crime, and police involvement contributes to the business-like nature with which it is conducted and for the lack of turf wars (like those plaguing much of the country).

Illegal activities such as drugs, prostituion, gambling, car theft and kidnapping represent a significant source of income for the local police, and even abortion, which was illegal in Mexico City up until the 21st century, was prey to police shakedowns. All pirate and informal sector activities must pay police protection, which make neighborhoods like Tepito partners in crime with their friendly neighborhood police, and with the local political party power structures, as well.

Up until recently, the criminal element in Tepito had a very special relationship with the PRI, the official party in power for 70 years. After the '85 earthquake, whose effects were felt most violently in the surrounding neighborhoods of the Historic Center and Tlatelolco, though also within Tepito, a profound political shift occurred. As the official party neglected the neighborhood in its moment of tragedy, community groups organized to rescue and restore order in the area. These groups were eventually co-opted by the PRD, the leftist oppositional party, which now benefits from the money and political force that Tepito represents (*golpeadores* or hitters from Tepito are often used to swell rallies and violently quash opposition). The PRD, in power in the district that includes my neighborhood as well as Tepito, controls the pirate taxis and the pirate markets, as well as the kickbacks and payoffs from all the bars, restaurants and strip joints.

The Mexico City government has launched major police incursions in Tepito in the last couple of years. Although no high level dealers have been caught, nor much product confiscated, the City bulldozed several housing projects in Tepito that were, according to the government, owned and operated by drug traffickers. This war against drugs within the area has less to do with drugs and more to do with gentrification of the Historic Center and the lucrative real estate speculation going on in the neighborhood.

Working Women

Like the drug trade, prostitution provides much-needed employment. There are currently upwards of 200,000 prostitutes in Mexico City, about half who work the street and of which 70 percent are women. Of these, more than fifteen thousand women work the main avenues around La Merced, located next door to Tepito, where sex takes place in hotels or in tiny shacks located in the patio of apartment buildings.

Prostitutes range from older veterans who can still hook clients well into their 60s to underage prostitutes (up to 5,000 working in the city), many of whom are homeless girls trapped into turning tricks, or Central American immigrants who have gotten stuck in Mexico City on their way to cross the US border. Around La Merced, the first shift begins early in the morning and services the truckers who bring merchandise to the market and those paid to shuttle the goods around on dollies, while the second shift works late into the night for sex consumers. Elite escort services in the city can charge up to $300 dollars an hour, spas and massage parlors can cost up to $70, while street hookers in La Merced, the lowest rung of the ladder, settle for around $15 a pop, part of which goes to pay for the hotel.

Prostitution goes way back in Mexico. The Aztecs had gentlemen's club where prostitutes, exotic dancers, and escorts worked. In-house orgies were often large, organized events, animated by alcohol and psychoactive substances. During wartime, many working women would travel with the troops, their services paid for in part by the consumers and in part by the State, which understood their usefulness in helping to keep warriors from raping women in the towns they passed through (leading to even more anti-imperial sentiment throughout the land). Prostitutes in Mexico-Tenochtitlan never married, although due to a lack of birth control they tended to have lots of babies. Registered prostitutes enjoyed certain legal benefits (such as being able to denounce those who had abused them) but freelancers were severely punished. Cortés' concubine Marina, known as La Malinche or la chingada (the fucked), was sold into prostitution as a young girl by her parents.

When the Spaniards conquered Mexico they eliminated all indigenous institutions of prostitution, thus giving rise to an illegal and uncontrolled market. Prostitution was regulated beginning in the late 1800s, with prostitutes obliged to register and undergo medical examinations, but in the 1930s it was once again de-regulated. Although illegal today, prostitution is tolerated in certain areas in certain neighborhoods in Mexico City, and prostitutes can be fined for working outside these tolerance zones. Prostitution is prohibited in brothels, bars, night-clubs or cabarets (all places where it is very common), a seemingly benevolent law that in fact forces women onto the street and leaves them open to extortion by the police and to violence from clients. Pimping is against the law, but police tend to fulfill the role in everything but the clothes, working both sides of the transaction (demanding money from the sex workers and shaking down johns after intercourse by threatening to arrest them or inform their wives of their activities).

In the Aztec empire, prostitutes worshipped the goddess Tlazolteotl, responsible for inciting sexual desire and devouring the spiritual filth produced by sex. Nowadays, many prostitutes seek help from *La Santa Muerte* in order to stay healthy, make more money and to have a steady supply of clients. Their clients, in turn, ask *La Santa Muerte* to help them make enough money to continue visiting the prostitutes and to avoid venereal disease and AIDS.

Many gay prostitutes work the streets and the public baths, while transvestites, usually unable to find formal employment, are often forced to sell their chemically-dependent bodies for a living. Next to prostitutes, the homosexual population in Mexico is the target of some of the Catholic Church's worst attacks, even despite the large numbers of gay priests. Gays and lesbians tend to feel excluded in large part from the Church, and many, especially those of the lower classes, look to *La Santa Muerte* for help in dealing with the aggressive, stressful situation they must deal with in such a homophobic society (after Brazil, Mexico has the highest rates of murders of gay men).

Cortés accused all Mexicans of being sodomites, but it is unclear what role homosexuality played in pre-Hispanic society. Some scholars have claimed that young men were often used as chicken boys for the priests, who in turn pimped them out to the wealthy and rulers during holidays and festivals, and there are accounts of transvestites being tolerated and even allowed to marry men. On the other hand, there are accounts of ultra-violent punishments handed out for being caught having sex with other men (the submissive man had his bowels ripped out his asshole).

Today, along with the thousands of imported porn films (both gay and straight), there are dozens of Mexican movies sold in Tepito that cater to all sexual preferences (some of the best sellers these days are films with local high school, junior high and elementary school girls). One of the newest genres is a homemade series of films shot with hidden cameras inside prostitute hotels in which the men who buy them on the streets of Tepito might very well have a walk-in role in them.

Just as magic products in the Sonora Market are designed for all marginalized and criminal groups, so too *La Santa Muerte* provides all-inclusive coverage of both good citizens and all others, regardless of race, religion or sexual preference (a sharp contrast to the door policies of the Catholic Church).

Mexorcism Although Mexico is still predominantly Catholic, the Church has been facing some stiff competition recently, its trump card of eternal salvation losing ground to other religions and practices that offer immediate help with problems in this world.

In the last decade or so there has been an impressive rise in the number of Protestants, both US Mormons and Brazilian evangelists of the Pare de Sufrir (Stop Suffering) church. Although the Mormons stick mostly to villages in the interior of the country, the Brazilians have concentrated their efforts within Mexico City. With thick accents, shiny dark suits and slicked back hair, Pare de Sufrir ministers have been buying up and renovating old, classic movie theaters in Mexico City, where every Friday afternoon mega-rallies are held in which people are cured through prayer and the laying on of hands. Pare de Sufrir also reaches out to Mexicans with a two-hour late night television program.

Although the Catholic Church is annoyed by the rise of Protestants in Mexico, their public enemy number one is *La Santa Muerte*. The Church considers anyone who worships *La Santa Muete* to be possessed by the devil, and to rid them of their satanic possession the Mexican Catholic Church has had recourse to one of its most controversial medieval practices, that is, exorcism.

According to Father Mendoza, in charge of the Cuajimalpa chuch and one of the eight Vatican-approved exorcists working in Mexico City, there has been an outbreak of diabolical possessions in Mexico over the last few years (400 alone in the small state of Queretaro). Father Mendoza blames this increase on the rise of hippies, rock and roll, drugs, Protestantism, New Age, and satanic cults and symbols (including *La Santa Muerte*). The hundreds of good Catholics or their family members who seek his help are sinners who have "opened the door to the Devil" by dabbling in *santería*, witchcraft, shamanism, Tarot cards, Ouija boards, palm readings, crystal balls or *limpias*. In fact, though, rather than their failure, it is the success that these other practices are enjoying, especially the cult surrounding *La Santa Muerte*, that has inspired the Church in Mexico to turn to such an extreme practice as exorcism.

The last few Popes have worked hard to convince people of the existence of the devil, claiming that the devil's greatest accomplishment was convincing people he didn't exist. Father Mendoza, and most other Mexican priests, do their best to warn their followers that they are surrounded by the devil and that they and their families are in imminent danger. According to the Church, disrespect of sacred Catholic symbols, such as images of God, the Holy Virgin, the saints and sacraments, reveal the devil's work, while all enemies of the Church (such as those in favor of abortion, birth control and gay marriage, or those infuriated by the church's protection of pederasts) are manipulated by the devil to do his bidding.

Exorcisms, which the Church prefers to refer to as liberation prayers, are designed to drive the devil out. In Cuajimalpa, the dozens of Catholics who come each weekend to be exorcized bring salt, oil and candles to Father Mendoza so that he can cleanse their or their family's personal objects that have been possessed by the devil. During marathon sessions that can last for hours, Father Mendoza implores the devil to leave the body of the victim in the name of the Father, the Son and the Holy Ghost, using his collection of Catholic saints to go *mano a mano* with unholy saints such as *La Santa Muerte*.

In most of the Catholic Church institutions outside of Mexico, exorcists tend to be regarded as fanatics and loonies. In Mexico City, though, exorcists are highly esteemed for they represent a healthy source of revenue for the church (hefty contributions are suggested for these private exorcism sessions). Although the Church accuses traditional spiritual healers, *santeros* and Protestant ministers of contributing to the source of diabolical possessions, they in fact perform services (*limpias*, the laying on of hands, the expulsion of the devil) that are almost identical to the Catholic Church's exorcisms (and with the exception of the Protestant ministers, they do so without making the sufferer feel like a vile sinner).

Despite the fact that exorcism is the church's oldest, most extreme weapon to expel evil influences in the spirits and minds of Mexicans, it has been unable to stop the rise of *La Santa Muerte* in Tepito and the rest of Mexico City. ✝

AFTER LIFE

Final Destination

I have no life insurance policy, no last will or testament. I'm in no rush to organize all the bureaucratic details of my departure since I still have plenty of time to put my life in order. Yet, as insurance companies know, it's a good bet I'll drop dead sooner than I expect. I know I'm going to die, I fully understand that all life ends in death, but that doesn't mean I accept or can really imagine the fact that one day I will be no longer. There is such a difference between the living and the dead that I just can't make the leap of imagination necessary to see myself crossing over to the other side.

Just in case I do die someday, I hereby declare that I would like my earthly remains to be cremated and that it is my wish to have half of my ashes scattered from atop the Williamsburg Bridge halfway between Brooklyn and the Lower East Side. I ask that the rest of my ashes be tossed inside the cave in Chapultepec Park's Audiorama, a public garden directly below the Chapultepec Castle where people sit and listen to loud classical music. It's not that I really love classical music (I don't) or that I really love Chapultepec Park (I do), but I choose this cave as the final resting place for half of my earthly remains because of the fact that the Aztecs believed it was an entrance into the afterlife.

The Aztecs had four possible destinations after death, the first and most common being Mictlan, the underworld where hunger, misery, plagues and suffering awaited those who had died in less than heroic ways (from disease, for example). Mictlantecuhti, the god of shadows (depicted as a human skeleton with his liver or a spurt of blood jutting out from his ribcage), ruled the nine rivers of the underworld and harvested the souls of the dead. The journey to Mictlan was difficult and dangerous, and the souls had to avoid rocks that crashed into each other, climb across deserts and mountains, withstand a wind of sharp obsidian shards and avoid being eaten by a crocodile, with only a *choloesquincle* dog as their guide. At the end of the journey, a person's heart, stripped of all individual characteristics, became converted into a divine seed from which another human life emerged. A second destination was reserved for young children, who after dying prematurely went to await their second opportunity of life on earth under the branches of a fruit tree.

The third destination, Sun Heaven, was reserved for warriors who died in battle and women who had died in childbirth. It took 80 days to ascend into Sun Heaven, during which time the surviving family members had to mourn them and were prohibited from bathing. Those who had been burned alive during a human sacrifice without cursing and screaming were also welcome, even if they were slaves or prisoners.

The final destination, Tlalocan, was a tropical paradise that awaited all those whose death was related to water (drowned, struck by lightning, or from diseases such as leprosy, gout or dropsy), and their corpses were buried in the earth, a gift to Tlaloc, the god of rain and agriculture.

The Aztecs believed that life and death were part of the same cycle. Human life existed thanks to energy that came from the earth and death was a way to return this life force back to the earth. In the same way, ancestors gave life to children and thus children were obliged to feed and maintain their dead ancestors with food and drink placed on their graves. Being that death was part of the blood debt every human owed the gods (a debt they were taught to respect and obey throughout their education), the Aztecs weren't as afraid of death as they were concerned about how they died, for this would determine their destination after life. Even those who had lived a life of crime or sin could regain their status in the eternal hereafter if they sacrificed themselves, figuratively or literally, for the gods.

Spirits of a human's soul, of their mental faculties and even of their family ties would be released from their body at the time of death. These spirits could become ghosts or diseases that haunted the living, but usually they were claimed by the gods responsible for their demise (for instance, those who died drunk had their spirits claimed by Ometochtli, the main pulque god). The final destination of an Aztec's soul wasn't conceived of as an eternity of punishment or salvation (as in the Catholic Church) but rather as a contract in which their spirit had to work for a god for four years and then would disintegrate.

Given that they were considered entrances into the afterlife, Aztecs buried the corpses or scattered the ashes of their loved ones inside caves. This cave in Audiorama could very well have been one of the entrances to Tlalocan, as the lush green woods of Chapultepec had long provided fresh, clean water for the whole city. If this is true, I'll be the first gringo to spend his afterlife in sunny Aztec paradise.

Underground Culture

In fact, though, I don't have to die to be transported into the Aztec world, all I need to do is to pick up a shovel and start digging. Digging down into the floor of this cave would uncover a history of life and death in Mexico City. Then again, all holes dug into the earth anywhere in the city create time tunnels into the remote past. Beneath the streets of modern Mexico City lies the ancient Aztec city of Mexico-Tenochtitlan, and nowhere is this more true than in the heart of the Historic Center of the city.

The New Houses of Moctezuma, the center of Aztec political and administrative activity, lie under the National Palace, the modern Mexican equivalent; the Aztec pyramid dedicated to Quetzacoatl (as large as the Sun pyramid) lies beneath the Metropolitan Cathedral; buried beneath the Archbishop's House is an intact Aztec temple devoted to the god Tezcatlipoca; the headquarters of the Inquisition squats on top of an Aztec school for the children of nobles; the Education Department's main offices cover the temples of Coateocalli and Cihualcoatl; while deep below the Palacio de Bellas Artes sits an Aztec boat dock and canal.

Every time a new subway line is dug, the foundation of a building is laid, land for a new mall is excavated, a well is dug or underground pipes installed, the city's past emerges. The deeper one digs the further back in time one travels, from contemporary, modern, colonial, Aztec, Toltec, Olmec all the way back to pre-historic times. The architecture of death, that is, burial sites and sacrificial temples built to last for all eternity, best withstand the ravages of time and are constantly being uncovered beneath the city's streets, as are the bones and urns containing the ashes of extinct cultures.

In ancient Mexico, nomadic hunter-gatherers customarily burned their dead, as did the warrior nations, for there was no point in creating long-lasting burial sites if the families wouldn't be around to pay their respects. Settled, agricultural societies, on the other hand, generally buried their dead as a natural part of the life cycle. The Aztec culture, originally nomadic then later sedentary, did both.

In Mexico-Tenochtitlan, commoners were usually cremated and their ashes buried beneath their house in a simple ceremony. Nobles and important dignitaries were wrapped from head to toe in blankets or thin fiber mats and then brought to a pyramid temple to be cremated on a pyre, and then cremated a second time four days later, their bones chopped up and ground down to ashes and placed in an urn. The ashes of the nobles would be buried inside pyramids, and large quantities of food and pulque, as well as eagles, jaguars, pumas and rattlesnakes sacrificed for the occasion, were buried with them. Their wife, servants and maids would be tricked into getting drunk on pulque and then hit over the head and buried with their masters, too.

An Aztec's final resting place played an important role in helping their spirit reach the best possible afterlife. For instance, having your bones or ashes buried underneath your own shack was not the same as receiving a burial chamber within a cave or pyramid, for the closer your bodily remains were to the entrance to the next life the quicker and easier the journey. Pyramids, the greatest example of indigenous architecture of the dead, were designed to help souls reach their final destinations just as the Spanish churches built in Mexico City served as stairways to heaven.

In 1524, just three years after the Spanish Conquest of Mexico, construction began on the Metropolitan Cathedral, Spain's first and greatest architectural wonder in the New World. The Cathedral was built directly on top of a large section of the Templo Mayor, the most important Aztec ceremonial center, not only to benefit from the attraction of the sacred site, but also to announce to natives far and wide the victory of their one, true god over all the false Aztec pagan deities. The Spanish were intent upon destroying all vestiges of the indigenous cultures, especially the pagan architecture, yet by burying Aztec ceremonial sites directly beneath their own houses of worship the Catholic Church unintentionally preserved deep within the earth some of the most important indigenous religious sites. Thus, the oldest churches in Mexico City can be seen as tombstones or crosses marking the sites where Aztec temples are still buried.

Although the Metropolitan Cathedral was to be a complete break with all earlier Aztec temples, the original building was made with *tezontle* (volcanic rock 'bathed in blood') from the parts of the Templo Mayor that had been destroyed and, just as in Aztec times, indigenous slave labor was used to construct this holy of sites. And like the Aztec pyramids and temples, this house of worship was also a house of death, the site of funeral ceremonies and a repository of the bones of the dead.

Churches served as the first cemeteries in Mexico, with corpses buried in the gardens, patios and even inside the walls, beneath the floorboards or underneath the altars of the church itself. The closer a Catholic was buried to the main altar, the less climbing they had to do after death, and the taller the church the shorter the walk along the stairway to heaven. If you managed to get yourself buried inside the Metropolitan Cathedral, the largest, tallest and most sacred church in Mexico, your entrance into heaven was practically assured.

The most sacred burial site within the Metropolitan Cathedral, the Archbishops Crypt, a circular chamber located in the basement directly beneath the rear altar, was built in 1937 and is reserved for the Church elite. To enter the Crypt you must pass through a door made from a huge tombstone. Inside, a semi-circular floor-to-ceiling wall of niches preserves the earthly remains of all the Mexican archbishops since the founding of Mexico (empty niches await the current and future archbishops). Although the crypt is located underground and has no windows, the words *Lux Perpetua Luceat Eis*, a Latin phrase from the Requiem funeral mass which means Let the Light Shine Forever Upon You, are inscribed in silver letters on an arch in the middle of the chamber.

The tomb of Juan Zumarraga lies in the very center of the Archbishop's Crypt. Besides being Mexico's first Archbishop, Zumarraga was also its first Inquisitor. For his first official act, he had natives build a giant bonfire in the Zócalo, the plaza in front of the Cathedral, into which he threw all the indigenous books, paintings and idols he could get his hands on. At the foot of this Inquisitor's white stone tomb sits an Aztec death head and behind Zumarraga's head, underneath an almost life-sized crucified Christ, lies the large volcanic rock that was used as a sacrificial stone in the Templo Mayor and upon which many a Spaniard had his heart carved out.

These hardcore Aztec death cult objects (along with dozens of Aztec funeral offerings, sacrificed babies, and human and animal bones) were discovered during recent excavations beneath the Cathedral. Due to the fact that they are considered pagan, no Catholic church in Mexico displays within its sacred walls any indigenous religious objects. The fact that two important Aztec death icons lie inside this most holy of Catholic sites is thus very strange. Perhaps the Church feels that these Aztec idols and objects have lost their pagan powers and are mere kitch decorations. Or perhaps the Church is no longer so sure that they are the Chosen Ones and, just in case, they want these pre-Hispanic death sculptures near to their tombs to help them get into a good Aztec afterlife.

Holy Bones

After the conquest of Mexico, the Catholic Church, which viewed all indigenous beliefs of life after death as superstition and blasphemy, prohibited Aztec burial ceremonies and quickly monopolized the afterlife, establishing itself as the indispensable intermediary between life and eternity. Just as it altered the way natives were to live, the Spanish Conquest radically transformed the way human beings in Mexico City died and the way in which their bodies were disposed.

A Catholic death in Colonial Mexico consisted of a funeral service presided over by a priest and with the corpse being buried in a grave. Before they were laid into the ground, however, the eyes and mouth of the deceased were shut, the body covered in a white sheet or cloth, placed in a wooden coffin and stretched out in the same way as Christ when taken down from the cross (on one's back, arms crossed over the chest, one foot on top of the other). The coffin was then carried from the deceased's home and mourners carrying torches (symbolizing the soul) accompanied the coffin into the church. The corpse and tomb were sprinkled with holy water to keep the deceased's soul safe from the devil and the priest prayed for their safe passage into heaven.

In Mexico, funerals were often national events of the highest order. Between 1559 and 1819, dozens of major funeral services were held in Mexico City for local archbishops and royalty (as well as funerals *in abstensia* for the kings, queens and popes in Spain). The funeral pyres that housed the noble corpses, usually erected inside the Metropolitan Cathedral, provided the centerpiece of the elaborate ceremonies. These funeral pyres, also called catafalques and commonly referred to as death machines, were multi-floor temples covered in black cloth and gold leaf and often constructed in the shape of a pyramid. Prominent architects, sculptors, painters, poets and artisans adorned these death machines with images, figures and texts depicting the life and death of the dearly departed (accompanied by skeletons and skulls).

More than just mourning a public figure, these funerals served to illustrate the divine status of certain human beings. According to the Catholic Church, death is punishment for one's sins. Sins, however, affect more than just a person's death and the final destination of their soul, they also affect their physical remains. As the state of a corpse revealed the spiritual purity and divinity of the departed, the preservation of the bodily remains of the ruling elite was an important affair. Perfume and anointing processes (a nice word for embalming) ensured that the mortal remains of these personages did not give rise to gossip or speculation. Either as the result of natural gases or from post-mortem procedures, the corpses of religious figures that eventually mummified instead of becoming worm meat stood a much better chance of attaining sainthood, and they also provided living proof that Catholics, if they live a righteous life, can attain immortality in their death.

When these grand funeral processions ended, certain of the personage's body parts (eyes, heart, liver, intestines, bones) would be donated to different churches or convents where each body part would receive its own elaborate funeral ceremony. Post-mortem organ and skeletal donations were warmly welcomed, although churches and royalty often bought body parts on the black market, as well.

The physical remains of saints have always been considered holy relics, believed to possess curative, even magical powers. No matter how small the fragment, each relic contains all of a saint's miraculous power. As the existence of holy relics within a church meant an increased influx of worshippers and alms, there was a great demand for such objects. The wealthy in Mexico would often pay large sums of money to obtain body parts or relics of saints, which conferred not only social distinction but also provided their owners with extra spiritual blessings. To meet the demand, priests began to hack up the corpses of Christian saints into increasingly smaller bits.

Relics are given Latin names depending upon their origin: *corpois* (from the body), *ex capillus* (hair), *ex carne* (muscle), *ex ossibus* (bones), *ex praercordis* (stomach or intestines), *ex pelle* (skin) and *ex cineribus* (ashes). Body parts of saints, including their bones, blood or cremated ashes, are considered first-class relics. Second-class relics are a saint's clothes or religious accessories, while items that have come in contact with the body or grave of a saint are referred to as representative relics.

Many exotic body parts or paraphernalia from saints and religious figures have been collected and are prominently displayed in the Vatican and other reputable houses of worship, including: mother's milk from the Virgin Mary; Christ's circumcision knife and foreskin (14 churches claim that theirs is the one, true foreskin); the tail of the donkey that Christ rode into Jerusalem; a sneeze from the Holy Spirit and a sigh from Saint Joseph. The holiest of all relics in Mexico, safeguarded within the Metropolitan Cathedral, is a splinter from the cross Christ was crucified upon.

After the Conquest, a large number of saints' body parts were sent by boat to Mexico to help convert souls in the New World. The arrival of these relics would often be accompanied by a large procession from the port town of Veracruz all the way to Mexico City. Relics are still very popular, and major collections travel from church to church around the world, bringing in the crowds of faithful who believe that proximity to the bones and other sacred scraps will provide them with miracle cures. (In order to receive blessings or pardon from the saints, the Church insists that worshippers must approach these relics without any morbid curiosity.) Pope John Paul II, who passed away in 2005, had somewhat of a revival in 2011 when a vial of his blood was flown to Mexico City and displayed in churches around the country.

The Chapel of Relics, located within the Metropolitan Cathedral, contains the skeletons, craniums, molars, hands, fingers, feet, intestines, hair and bones of 150 saints, including Maria Magdalena, Saint Gonzaga, Saint Francis, Saint Augustine, as well as a few of the legendary 10,000 Virgins. Within the exquisitely carved wooden floor-to-ceiling altar inside this chapel lie two wax figures of women encased in elaborate glass cubicles. These life-size figures are themselves merely display cases for the bits of bone that are set within their wax bodies, a window having been sewn into their clothes to permit them to be seen. Several bone fragments are also displayed within gold and silver hands and trophies and inside framed tapestries.

Like Catholic saints, Mexican political leaders also have a history of being brutally murdered. Depending on which history you believe, Moctezuma was killed either by an angry mob throwing rocks while he was paraded around on a roof by Cortés, or he was stabbed in the groin by Cuauhtémoc as punishment for allowing himself to become Cortés' chicken boy. The great warrior Cuauhtémoc became emperor of Mexico-Tenochtitlan after Moctezuma's successor Cuitlahuac died from small pox, but he was soon captured by the Conquistadores trying to escape the siege of the city in a canoe dressed as a woman, and was tortured and eventually murdered.

Miguel Hidalgo was shot by a firing squad in 1811, as was José Maria Morelos in 1815, both leaders of the Mexican Independence movement. Mexico's Emperor Agustin de Iturbide and President Vicente Guerrero were both shot and killed by a firing squad in 1831, and Emperor Maximilian and President Miguel Miramón were also both shot and killed by firing squad in 1867. President Manuel Robles Pezuela was assassinated in 1873, President Francisco I. Madero in 1913, Emiliano Zapata in 1919, President Venustiano Carranza in 1920, Pancho Villa in 1923, and President Álvaro Obregón in 1928. Colossio, the man who would have been president in 1994, was shot and killed (the mystery of his murder has never been cleared up although his predecessor, ex-President Carlos Salinas, is generally believed to have been behind the assassination).

Death is not always a leader's last act. Emperor Maximilian's corpse was embalmed in order to keep it from rotting on its way back to Mexico City, but during the trip the coffin fell out of the cart and his corpse was thrown into the mud. In Mexico City, his body was embalmed once more and black glass balls were placed in his eye sockets. His corpse was by then so degraded that even his own mother couldn't recognize him. The doctor who performed the second embalming and others who passed through the room he was kept in stole several items of his blood-stained clothes, the bullets extracted from his body, and even some hair off his head and chin.

The bronze cast of Emperor Maximilian's face, the table upon which the second embalming was performed, and the coffin he had been transported in are currently displayed in three different museums, while the face cast and the deathbed of Benito Juarez, the man who killed Maximilian, are exhibited in the National Palace. The bones of Emperor Iturbide are currently on display in the Metropolitan Cathedral, while Anastasio Bustamante, the man responsible for bringing Iturbide's bones back to Mexico City, requested his own heart be plucked from his body and placed in an urn to be buried alongside Iturbide.

Twelve of the leaders of the War of Independence were shot in a firing squad and four of them had their heads severed from their bodies and displayed in public. Their skulls and bones rested underneath the Metropolitan Cathedral for a century until they were transferred and put on exhibit in the Monument to Independence in 1925. In 2011, their remains were removed from the Monument and taken to a laboratory in the Chapultepec Castle where they were measured and examined (to see if any of them had in fact been shot in the back of the head rather than killed by a firing squad) and their identities officially established. After this forensic examination, their bones were displayed in the National Palace for one year as part of the Bicentennial celebration and then returned to the Independence Monument.

Certain body parts of certain Mexican presidents have become national symbols. Whilst still a general, President Alvaro Obregon had his arm blown off by a grenade in a battle against Pancho Villa during the Mexican Revolution. (As Obregon tells the story, neither he nor his men could find his arm until someone had the bright idea of holding up a gold coin, at which time his arm came crawling out by itself and grabbed the coin). After several previous attempts on his life, Obregon was finally assassinated by a caricaturist who shot him in the back after sketching his portrait. Obregon's lost arm was preserved in a monument dedicated to him located on the site of the restaurant where his assassination took place, although recently his family felt the public exhibition of this body part was undignified and had it cremated.

President Santa Anna, the man responsible for giving away half of the territory of Mexico (California, Arizona and Texas) to the gringos, had his leg amputated due to diabetes. The leg was buried in a cemetery in Mexico City with all the pomp and circumstance of an official funeral. When Santa Anna dissolved Congress in 1844 there were riots in the streets of the city. One mob made its way to the cemetery and dug up Santa Anna's leg and carried it through the streets chanting "Death to the one-legged thief." Santa Anna was eventually run out of office and fled to Cuba. Although his dismembered leg was never recovered, the wooden leg he used in the last years of his life is currently on display in the Chapultepec Castle.

A Fine and Quiet Place

From the day it opened its doors for business, the Catholic Church in Mexico City prompted everyone to go forth and procreate. As a result, the human population quickly overwhelmed the city and the churches could no longer accommodate the city's dead. Cemeteries began to be established outside church walls (although the Church still ran them and got to decide who would be admitted and at what cost).

In 1833, a cholera epidemic ravaged the city and killed thousands, and to accommodate so much death all cemeteries were forced to receive corpses, regardless of religion or race. In 1859, President Benito Juárez secularized the cemeteries, putting the local government in charge of their administration. New cemeteries had to be located outside of the city, at least 2,000 meters upwind from the last house, with separate sections for those who had died from common diseases and those who had died from contagious diseases.

The cemeteries that existed in the city at that time failed to meet the increasing population of the dead. To remedy the situation, Mrs. Dolores Murrieta de Galloso bought almost two and a half million square meters of land in the Chapultepec woods in 1870 in order to construct a public cemetery. Before it became a final resting place for the dead, the land had been a ranch, the site of Our Lady of Bethlehem (the city's most important mill for grinding wheat) and the first rag and paper factory in the Americas (owned by an Englishman). Dolores died before the cemetery was finished and was one of the first to be buried there around 1875 (in a simple tomb without any honors). Dolores' family finished the work on the cemetery and named it in her honor, Panteón Civil de Dolores.

The Panteón de Dolores is the largest and oldest site of eternal rest in Latin America, housing over 700,000 tombs and mausoleums and with a permanent population of around six million souls (more than any city in the country except Mexico City). The cemetery is so large and has so many roads crisscrossing it that street signs, exactly like those in the city around it, must be used to help families drive to their beloved's grave. Hundreds of thousands of miniature buildings dot the landscape, ranging in style from Classical to Art Deco and reflecting the same architectural periods and styles found outside the cemetery walls.

The most majestic tombs, mausoleums and crypts date back to the late 19th and early 20th century, many of them designed by renowned Italian sculptors. Ornaments on these tombs (broken columns, obelisks, trees, skeletons and skulls) are often of pagan origin, but by the end of the 19th century Christian imagery came into fashion with a profusion of angels, cherubs and crosses. Angels that weep, brandish a sword (angels of death) or blow a trumpet (to announce Judgment Day) act as guides to lead the souls of the dead heavenward. Doves represent a soul's flight to heaven, while sheep are associated with the child Jesus. Upside down torches and white sheets draped over crosses refer to the end of life, a truncated tree symbolizes a life cut short, while hourglasses indicate the limited time given to each of us.

In addition to the old European stone palaces, there are hundreds of modern-day rustic cabins, concrete bunkers and even suburban homes built by non-professional architects. Adorning these low-rent tombs, homemade crosses made from cheap metal, rusty pipes, scraps of wood or even bathroom tiles grace the graves, while jerry-rigged cages or fences protect many a family's significant real estate investment. The sculpted busts and statues of past centuries have given way to framed photographs of the deceased or hand-painted portraits. Visitors come not only to mourn their dearly departed but also to clean house and to offer maintainence of their real estate properties, for which brooms, buckets, paint cans and brushes are common sights in the cemetery.

The Panteón de Dolores is perhaps the most democratic of all urban spaces within Mexico City. Within its confines there is a no-rent district populated by all those killed by violent means or without family or loved ones to claim them, working-class neighborhoods dedicated exclusively to bakers, teachers and machinists, European neighborhoods (a German and an Italian section), and elegant, exclusive neighborhoods, such as the Circle of Illustrious Men where internationally famous artists, including Diego Rivera, David Alfaro Siqueiros and José Clemente Orozco, as well as the composer Agustin Lara, the poet and Nobel Laureate Octavio Paz, the comedian Cantinflas and the actress Dolores del Rio, are buried.

A Dying Business

Although it's hard to believe, there are more human beings living in Mexico City today than have lived in the city throughout its whole history. The great majority of these millions of human beings will also die here. As death lasts longer than life, a person's final abode is more important than any real estate they might possess while still alive. Depending on the size of the land, the exclusivity of the plot and the elegance of the construction, a grave can be more expensive per square meter than most houses outside the cemetery walls.

Although the Panteón de Dolores is the largest cemetery in Mexico it has run out of space, and no new graves have been dug since 1975. Only families that bought plots before that year may still bury their deceased there, but even they often must stack family members on top of each other, five deep being the current legal limit. Dozens of ads to sublet or sell plots appear in the real estate sections of newspapers each day, and those lucky enough to buy plots when they were still available can now sell them off at a good profit.

There are slightly more than one hundred registered cemeteries in Mexico City, but thirty-two of these have already reached capacity and in just a few years most of the others will, too. Once cemeteries fill in all their graves they no longer generate profits, and thus they are usually left to deteriorate and the monuments and gravestones are condemned to languish in a slow death. The government has tried to end the practice of eternal resting places by promoting exhumations and cremations of corpses after just a few years of rest within the earth, but this policy hasn't yet been implemented.

Cremation came into vogue in Europe and the United States at the end of the 19th century, but it took much longer to catch fire in Mexico. Despite the fact that it is inexpensive, takes up much less room and is much more city-friendly, the practice of burning corpses had to overcome strong resistance from the Church, which managed to delay its implementation for hundreds of years. In addition to the Biblical injunction to bury one's dead, the Church encouraged its followers to fear death and the afterlife, and the image of being buried in a tight box six feet under where worms devour your flesh served this purpose perfectly. (Even though it resembled the flaming tortures of Hell, the Church felt that cremation was too easy an exit from a lifetime of sin.) Anthropologists also objected to cremation because it deprived them of important raw material for future studies, and police and legal authorities worried that relevant forensic evidence would be destroyed along with the body. To remedy this situation, police are now allowed to photograph dead bodies and anthropologists can request the skeleton or skull of an already-buried corpse before it is to be cremated.

The first crematorium in the Panteón de Dolores, installed inside a macabre building with a façade in the shape of the face of an Aztec emperor, incinerated over 18,000 bodies in the first ten years. Today, an average of seven cremations are performed each day inside the basement of a modern building within the cemetery. The original German ovens operated with logs cut from trees from the Chapultepec forest, while today Canadian ovens burn up to 200 pounds of coal a day at a temperature of 1,500 centigrade. A normal cremation lasts about two hours and the ashes obtained weigh around 3 kilos. The human ashes spewed out by the 90-foot-high brick chimney, the tallest structure in Chapultepec, have for decades served to fertilize the trees and plants in the park, although they have also pumped large quantities of human remains into the lungs of millions of *chilangos* living or working nearby.

It wasn't until 1983 that the Catholic Church in Mexico City finally decided to allow its congregation the option of cremation, not for any spiritual reason but rather because it represented a profitable business venture. The Metropolitan Cathedral recently underwent a major renovation to compensate for how unevenly the building had sunk over the years. Even more important than keeping the building level, the new renovation created 11,000 niches in the basement. Given that they measure only six square feet and that they cost only around $40 dollars to construct, niches that are sold for over $2,500 (plus a modest maintenance fee) make these basement death lockers a wonderful investment for the Church and one of the most profitable real estate investments in all of Mexico.

Around 50,000 human beings die in Mexico City each year and each of these deaths generates a profit. Even though it is doing brisk business with the dead these days, the Catholic Church no longer monopolizes death these days. Four hundred licensed private funeral homes currently operate within the city, handling both funeral services and burials. Being that a large number of deaths occur in medical institutions, funeral homes tend to cluster around clinics and hospitals, especially in poorer neighborhoods. Informal agents with connections to several funeral homes prowl emergency rooms in search of those who have lost (or are about to lose) a loved one, offering to handle all the paperwork and funeral arrangements in their moment of need. These agents get commissions from the funeral homes, but they also tend to tack on fees and exploit the grief of family members and their ignorance of funeral procedures (the reselling of used coffins is a common practice).

Cremation, the cheapest option, can cost as little as two hundred dollars, and an urn where the ashes can be deposited costs $150 and up. Even with the bureaucratic fees, the cost of a coffin, the transportation of the corpse and the funeral service, a funeral ceremony in Mexico City can go for as little as $300. If a family chooses the option of an open casket, however, costs increase greatly, for besides the rental of a special coffin the deceased must be made presentable to appear in public one last time.

Extreme Makeover

Although it is shunned in most of the world, both amongst the most traditional cultures and the most modern, embalming is widely practiced throughout the Americas, and most funeral homes in Mexico City push this service on their clients for the extra profit to be made but also due to the lack of space and technology (such as industrial refrigeration) needed to keep a body from rotting.

When someone purchases a funeral package that includes embalming they usually imagine that the body of their loved one will undergo only a superficial cosmetic procedure. In fact, embalming is the most extreme makeover anyone can ever receive.

Embalming begins with up to two gallons of formaldehyde and artificial color injected into the major arteries to help preserve the body's natural color and to stop the organic processes of decomposition that occur after death. After this, a needle-like tube attached to a suction pump is inserted beneath the lowest left rib, and the tube is then jabbed into the lungs and heart, reducing them to tiny pieces that can be sucked out along with the body's fluids, gases and solids. The intestines, kidneys, stomach, bladder, uterus, ovaries, and other organs are then removed. After the body has been hollowed out from within more embalming fluid is pumped in, and the anal and vaginal cavities are plugged with a giant screw and penises stuffed with powdered cotton to seal off the urethra.

The body is then laid out on a stainless steel table and washed with an antibacterial, perfumed soap, not just from head to toe but also inside the mouth, gums, tongue and nasal passages. Large quantities of cream are slapped on to soften and shape the skin and rigor mortis is relaxed by massages, although if tendons and muscles don't respond they are cut in order to be able to stretch the body out in a casket. Cotton gets shoved up the nose of the corpse and the eyes are sealed shut, often with glue, which is also used to keep the fingers in a natural position. The mouth is propped in place with a mouth guard and the throat is sealed with cotton in order to keep any vomit from escaping. A screw is set into both the upper and lower jaw and the mouth is wired shut while the lips are glued tightly together.

The final, artistic touches, including make-up, fingernail paint and hairdressing, are applied and the body is then clothed, often in a suit or dress that merely covers the front part of the body. The final color and texture of the skin is brushed on with a colored liquid.

Although many families like the idea of being able to pay their last respects to their dearly departed, mourners are often horrified at the result. Embalmed corpses often wind up looking like zombies (although with the current mania for plastic surgery and Botox injections there isn't always that much of a difference). To make matters worse, the beautification of a corpse leads to extreme environmental contamination, for instead of human life energy returning from whence it came, a body bag filled with embalming fluid (a toxic time bomb waiting to explode) is buried in the earth.

On Maggots And Mummies

Families often choose embalming because they feel they are helping their deceased avoid the horrible processes of decomposition, but unlike stuffed animals and mummies that can survive for centuries, embalmed human beings decompose just as much in the end as untreated corpses. By repelling most insects and by fixing cellular proteins that normally act as food for bacteria, embalming can delay the decomposition of a human body up to six months but things eventually fall apart.

Natural decomposition begins with the death of a human being (although for some it can start even while they are still alive), as corpses are an ecosystem unto themselves. The bacteria inside a corpse feed off of the contents of the deceased's intestines, then the intestines themselves, and then they move on to consume the other internal organs. When cells and tissues are broken down by the chemicals, enzymes and microorganisms already present in the body, gases such as hydrogen sulfide, methane, cadaverine and putrescine are released that swell up the corpse.

Larger living creatures, especially insects attracted by the released gases, dig in, as well. Flies and maggots deposit their eggs within all the bodily orifices of the dead body. Young maggots move as a mass in order to benefit from communal heat and shared digestive secretions, and they spread bacteria, secrete digestive enzymes and rip tissue with the hooks in their mouth. The flies and beetles that arrive next feast on both the decaying flesh and the maggots and wasps use the maggots as a breeding ground. The corpse's skin eventually breaks and its bodily fluids spill out, leaving a flattened, blackened bag of bones. The part of the body in contact with the earth becomes colonized by mold, which in turn helps the corpse's fermenting process.

In addition to exposure to insects and animals, the speed with which a body decomposes depends on the temperature and humidity, while the exposure to air is also an important factor. In extremely dry environments, a body exposed to certain gases or chemicals within the earth can become mummified. A substance called grave wax occasionally appears about a month after death in the fatty parts of the body (that is, cheeks, stomach, butt and breasts). This white, soapy wax is produced by a chemical reaction of fat, water and hydrogen and can actually help preserve the body against the onslaught of decomposition.

Mummies from the state of Guanajuato are a national icon and have inspired dozens of local horror flicks, but Mexico City has a few of its own. Twelve patrons and priests of a convent in the San Angel neighborhood were buried in the church over 300 years ago, and exposed to gases in the earth that acted to freeze all bodily decomposition, their bodies and even their clothes became mummified. Discovered in 1916 by soldiers in Zapata's revolutionary army digging for buried treasure in the basement of the church, they are now displayed inside sealed glass coffins in the basement of the building.

Newborn babies who have never eaten solid food and therefore whose bodies are free of the microbes involved in the decomposition process, can often, in moderately dry conditions, become mummified. This special biological status of newborns might have given rise to the cultural phenomenon of *La Niña Muerte*

(Infant Death). According to the Catholic Church, all infants who die after being baptized but before being able to speak (or, perhaps more accurately, before they start shitting solid) are free of original sin, need no final communion and are considered angels.

When these *angelitos* (little angels) die they go directly to heaven, and thus their funeral is meant to be a joyous occasion. Baby girls are dressed as the Virgin of the Immaculate Conception and the boys as Saint Joseph, crowns are placed on their heads and flowers in their little fists. Family and friends visit the dead child in the parents' home, and the next day the child is put into a small, white coffin wrapped in ribbons and taken to the cemetery. Up until the mid 19th century, paintings were commissioned of deceased children, but with the rise of photography, studio portraits were taken of the dead child. Mexico is the only country in the Americas where paintings and photographs of dead children are common in graveyards.

Dead Days On the first day of the annual holiday celebrating the dead, the Aztecs mourned their deceased children and on the second day their adults. Family members installed an altar with the bones, ashes and hair from the deceased and adorned it with incense, food, flowers, tobacco and alcohol, and chickens, butterflies or rabbits were sacrificed in the deceased's honor. The whole city was allowed and even expected to get drunk as well as to dance, cry and sing to their hearts' content during the funeral celebrations, as this was a way to establish contact with both the gods and the spirits of the deceased.

After the Conquest, the Aztec practices of human sacrifice, cremation and burying the remains within one's house were prohibited by the Church, although the drinking, dancing and crying at funerals and religious holidays continued. In order to gain control over the way the indigenous population mourned its dead, the Church promoted the Christian holidays of All Saints Day and All Souls Day. Established back in the year 835 as a revival of an earlier celebration of the Maccabees (Jewish patriots considered martyrs by the Church), All Saints Day was held on the first of November to celebrate the anonymous saints and martyrs not blessed with their own holiday, while All Souls Day, celebrated the following day, commemorated all the souls still wallowing in purgatory.

The day before the celebration priests made their rounds of the neighborhood to collect donations of the food and drink to be offered to the dead (although much of it had a way of winding up on the priests' dining table). Usually resistant to Church ceremonies that demanded such offerings, the natives living in Mexico City freely gave food and drink to their local church for this celebration. At first pleased but then suspicious, the Spanish priests finally realized that the natives were surreptitiously smuggling their pagan funeral rituals into these Catholic ceremonies. Fearful of the excesses of these celebrations, and seeing signs of the handiwork of the devil, the authorities began to punish the drunken revelers with fines and jail time, criticizing the natives for neglecting their daily labors and Christian responsibilities. Nonetheless, these holiday celebrations expanded beyond the control of the Church and, after Mexico gained independence from Spain, the Days of the Dead became the most popular holiday within Mexico.

Churches displayed their collection of relics to the general public only during this holiday, and thus Mexicans visited as many churches as they could and touched as many relics as they could since each relic offered a set amount of years of forgiveness for their dearly departed. The Metropolitan Cathedral was often the last church visited, and mourners bought bread or sweets shaped as skeletons or relics to be blessed by a priest and then taken back home to the family altar. Once the Church no longer monopolized the burial places within the city, cemeteries became the main destination during this holiday for family members to offer their dearly departed food, liquor and music.

For more than one hundred years after Independence from Spain, the dead were celebrated with allegorical pageants and markets set up in the main plazas and parks of Mexico City. The food and alcohol stalls that sprung up one month before the Days of the Dead in the Zócalo and in the Parque Alameda soon became a problem for the city, provoking congestion and offending the sensibility of the upper classes, and police were often sent into the plazas and cemeteries to subdue the wailing and drunken masses.

Many still celebrate the Days of the Dead in their homes by building altars decorated with a Christian cross, statues or images of the Virgin Mary, photographs of their deceased relatives and often famous public figures, sprinkled with orange flower petals and lit by candles. Public schools install elaborate altars and invite parents and neighbors in, as do many governmental offices, although these altars tend to be free of religious symbols.

Several respectable industries depend upon this celebration of the dead for their livelihood. During the Days of the Dead, markets, stalls and street vendors do brisk business selling flowers outside the gates of all city cemeteries. Bakeries sell *pan de muerto*, a sweet egg bread often decorated with sugar bones and skeletons, and sugar skulls are made especially for the holiday. Soft drinks and fried foods are sold everywhere outside and inside the gates of the cemeteries, while beer and tequila sales reach yearly highs around this time of the year. Musicians of all styles, especially mariachis and *norteños*, are hired to serenade the deceased.

Many people, both in Mexico and outside the country, believe that Mexicans have a privileged relation to death, and that this festive holiday is living proof of this fact. Yet Argentina, Chile, Peru, Sicily and even Japan all have a millennial tradition of honoring their dead with altars in their homes, and there are rambunctious celebrations of the dead in Haiti, the Philippines and in Brazil, as well. Tombs uncovered beneath the Vatican attest to the fact that ancient Romans also mourned their dead relatives with altars, the burning of incense and animal sacrifice (they even shared food and drink with their dearly departed through tubes stuck into the coffins). Perhaps the only truly Mexican aspects of its Days of the Dead celebration is the amount of sugar consumed and the tradition of ending the celebration lying on the street dead drunk.

To claim that all Mexicans share the same attitude toward death (as popularized by the Day of the Dead ceremonies) is not just a folkloric cliché it is also a denial of the profound class, racial and cultural differences that exist within Mexico. These days, the younger generations' relation to death comes more from TV, Nintendo and Hollywood than from any Mexican cultural traditions.

After the Revolution, in an attempt to appropriate this originally pagan and then Catholic celebration, the Mexican government promoted the Day of the Dead (now celebrated as a single day) as a consolidation of Mexico's national character, a mix of indigenous and Hispanic traditions. With generous government funding, intellectuals and artists such as Octavio Paz, Diego Rivera and Frida Kahlo did their part to promote the celebration as the single most important tie to pre-Hispanic culture, claiming that death had always been the essence of Mexican's identity.

By the 1960s, however, the Day of the Dead celebration had lost much of its festiveness and the support of both the Church and State, as well. It wasn't until the gringo celebration of Halloween, the nemesis of the Day of the Dead, entered into Mexico in the 1970s and awoke a heated reaction against it that the Day of the Dead was once again promoted as a nationalistic, traditional celebration. Although most kids in Mexico City dress up in mass-produced Halloween monster or horror costumes and ask for money and candy on the night of October 31 (and the next two nights, as well), the Day of the Dead celebration has come back from the grave, its imagery and advertisements once again seen throughout the city.

Regardless of whether it is indigenous or Catholic in origin, and regardless of whether or not it is a true expression of culture in Mexico or merely folklore created by upper-class cultural figures, the association of the identity of Mexico with its celebration of death has been perhaps the greatest tourist promotion any country ever created.

The Art Of Death

Despite Mexico's reputation for having a special relationship to death, newspapers have no obituary section. Instead, when an important businessman, politician, public figure or member of a wealthy family dies, *esquelas* are placed in the major newspapers. These paid announcements express the survivors' loss in standardized poetic terms ("...participate with deep pain in the sensitive passing away..." or "...unite in the pain that overtakes..."), and the design is somber, usually in black and white, illustrated only with a single cross (the printed equivalent of a headstone). The person's actual death is never referred to directly, the cause of their demise never mentioned, and the only information to be gleaned is family relations or place of employment (*esquelas* often seem more like advertisements for the company that placed the notice than tributes to the dead).

A much more popular, personal and public display of mourning can be found throughout Mexico City on sidewalks, traffic islands and alongside highways where handmade crosses are hammered into the concrete and are accompanied by handwritten text (which often includes the deceased's name, date of birth and death, cause of death, personal notes or even a poem), photos, candles and flowers. Unlike tombstones that indicate where a person's bones or ashes lie, these crosses mark the site where someone was killed. Like the memorial murals painted in honor of fallen gang members, these crosses are public displays of mourning, testaments of the crimes of the city, protests against government injustices and warning signs that signal where social conditions or traffic flow is most hazardous to human life. If a map were to be made of the location of all these crosses, it would faithfully illustrate the geography of violent death in Mexico City.

Regardless of how Mexicans personally handle death, public art in Mexico has always reveled in death, the more gruesome the better. Mexico has one of the longest traditions of mega-death and hardcore gore imagery of any country. Much of this gore comes from the *art brut* of the Aztec codices and murals that graphically depict battles, human sacrifices, cannibal rituals and torture (with plenty of red ink splattered across the pages and the walls), and from the *tzompantli* (rows of skulls) that can be seen as one of the earliest art installations in the Americas.

Spaniards have always been fanatics of gore, as well. The religious artwork brought over from the Old Country or crafted within Mexico under the guise of Catholic priests (especially the figures representing the crucifixion of Christ) is bathed in blood and guts. Medieval textbooks from the 15th and 16th century called *Ars Moriendi* (The Art of Dying), containing images of the agony of death, were brought the New World to help convert pagan souls into good Catholics. The depictions of gruesome tortures and bloodcurdling murders (as extreme as any contemporary gore flick or crazed Japanese *manga*) are common in many of the paintings and installations in the Metropolitan Cathedral, and several classical paintings in the Chapel of Relics portray saints and religious martyrs in the act of being beaten with sticks, stabbed or beheaded.

The Catholic Church revels in the assassination and mutilation of its most holy figures: Saint Sebastian shot through with arrows, Saint Peter chopped in the head with an axe, and the eyes of young Saint Lucy gouged out and served on a platter. The *milagritos* (little miracles), metal figures of legs, arms and hearts used to ask for favors or miracles, can be seen as the by-products of saintly dismemberment. Jesus Christ is the posterboy of Catholic sadomasochism, and within the Cathedral he can be seen hammered to a cross, his forehead dripping blood pricked by a crown of thorns, his body shrunken and black after being poisoned, and his back literally flayed opened from a whipping he received.

The artistic figures exhibited in churches throughout the city are gruesome enough on their own, but given the fact that they accompanied one of the most savage genocides on this planet, that they were the visual icons used by an especially sadistic Inquisition during its public displays of the beating, whipping, stoning, hanging and dismemberment of sinners, that they were literally shoved in the faces of millions of natives dying in the streets from bloodcurdling plagues, and that they stood on church altars surrounded by dead bodies, these images were extremely effective vehicles for putting the fear of God and the horrors of Hell into the Aztecs.

The greatest modern inheritor of the Aztec and Catholic gore aesthetics is without a doubt José Guadalupe Posada. Although best known for his dancing skeletons that illustrate verses of grave humor and political criticism, and acknowledged as one of the main influences of contemporary Day of the Dead imagery, his less well-known illustrations of everyday acts of meaningless cruelty and violence published in daily papers were, in fact, his greatest contribution to Mexican gore. Posada also illustrated and wrote scathing obituaries of famous personages, very much in the tradition of the early evangelists in Mexico who brought with them medieval paintings on wood called *danzas macabras* that mocked the vanity of public figures when confronted by their own death. Perhaps the greatest Mexican artist ever, Posada died in 1913 and was buried in a common grave in the Panteón de los Dolores, not too far from the monumental tomb of Diego Rivera, the man most responsible for popularizing Posada's least violent death images as tourist advertisements for Mexico and its Day of the Dead celebration.

Nota roja (red note) are news stories and photographs of criminal acts, disasters, accidents and death in all its incarnations, pumped up with psycho-sensationalism and splashed upon the page with lurid headlines. *Nota roja* is a particularly Mexican genre (even though it now exists in other countries in Latin America, especially Colombia), the legitimate offspring of both the writing and artwork of Posada. The Mexican *nota roja* magazine with the largest circulation and the longest tradition is *Alarma!* With print runs up to 2 million, *Alarma!* has brought its particular style of blood and guts to all of Mexico, as well as major cities across the US. The magazine was first published in 1963 and, except for a five year hiatus at the end of the 1980s, has remained true to its editorial penchant for gore. During the five years it ceased to publish, its style of slash-and-burn news reporting was imitated by several other magazines, such as *Alerta* (Alert), *El Arma* (The Weapon), *Angustia* (Anxiety), all of which disappeared from the scene as soon as *Alarma!* returned to the newsstands (due to legal restrictions it is now called *Nueva Alarma!*).

Perhaps the most famous visual chronicler in the *nota roja* press was Enrique Metinides, a photographer who documented crime scenes from the 1940s all the way into the early 1990s, almost exclusively for the newspaper *La Prensa*. At a very young age, Metinides began photographing fatal automobile accidents on the streets of his neighborhood. Later, by following police radio reports and chasing ambulances, he became one of the great chroniclers of death in the whole city (much like Weegee in NYC).

While *nota roja* is part of the Mexican tradition of gore art, it is also the direct expression of the modern experience of life in Mexico City and its particular forms of violent death, and is thus the equivalent of street crosses. In addition, *nota roja* photographers fulfill the function of the forensic photographers working in the city morgue who document all the violent death within Mexico City.

Requiem For A Morgue

A monumental statue of the Aztec goddess of death stands in front of the building that only recently housed the old Mexico City morgue. Cuatlicue (her head and skirt made from snakes and with a skull on her belt) died by her own hand, and had she lived in modern Mexico City, her death, like the death of all those who have met a violent end in this city, would have landed her here in this building.

The city morgue opened its doors to the dead in 1960. Before this building was constructed, the morgue was located in a chapel behind the graveyard of a hospital where doctors and army generals performed autopsies. The building is a squat, square, somewhat ominous construction (it looks Aztec but was actually inspired by the old New York City morgue), with two murals on its façade representing birth and death. Inside, the fluorescent lighting, the long, narrow hallways, the small rooms and the white walls make it look like a public elementary school. Sliding metal cabinets in the basement of this three-story building stored up to 70 corpses at any one time, although bodies were mostly kept in the cabinets on the second floor as they were nearer the autopsy room and amphitheater. A new building, painted mostly orange and with several post-modern details, much in the style of a mall or convention center, is now located next door to the old morgue and has taken over all of its forensic functions.

Over five thousand corpses are brought to the Mexico City morgue each year, an average of over fifteen bodies a day. Most corpses arrive at night and are brought directly to the amphitheater to be identified. If they have no ID, the bodies undergo genetic, dental and fingerprint examines and the results are checked against criminal records. Afterwards, photographs are taken (over 75,000 photographs in a single year) of all lesions and traumas to serve as the basis for the determination of time and cause of death. All objects of value (watches, earrings, cell phones, etc) are handed over to the family, while all bullets taken from the bodies are sent to the police.

All bodies undergo autopsies in which the brain matter is removed from the skull, the neck is opened to search for lesions of the trachea, esophagus and the main arteries, and the thorax is cracked to inspect the heart, inner organs, veins and nerves. Inside the abdomen, the investigation starts first with the liver, gall bladder, the kidneys, bladder, pancreas and the veins, with the stomach and intestines inspected last, as they contain gastric or intestinal waste that could contaminate the other organs. Once the autopsy has been performed on a corpse, the inner organs are returned to their place of origin. The brain, given its tendency to melt, is placed with the rest of the viscera inside the abdomen, which is then sewn up, transforming the corpse into its own body bag. The samples of blood, urine and skin tissue taken from all corpses undergo toxic and pathological studies. (Most of the sophisticated machines in the pathology laboratory serve to detect controlled substances and alcohol, present in the bloodstream in the great majority of all the corpses brought to the morgue in the last few years.)

The city morgue has a strict door policy, allowing in only those who have met their end through violence. Those killed in or by cars represent the number one cause of violent death in Mexico City, after which come homicides, followed by accidents that occur in the home, suicides, and accidents in other places. The number of men killed in homicides is three times greater than that of women and the same for traffic accidents. Traffic accidents and homicides occur most often in men between 20 and 30 years old who are married, employed and have attended school at least through junior high (not one single person with a postgraduate degree in Mexico City has died violently in the last couple of years, a fact which comforts me at night). Men die in accidents in public places fifteen times more often than women. The most common homicide occurs during hold-ups or robberies, followed by fights, and most homicide activity happens late Saturday night. For suicides, men represent five times more deaths than women, and occur most frequently in men over 65 years old suffering from depression, schizophrenia and/or alcoholism. Asphyxiation by hanging is the preferred method of suicide, followed by the use of weapons, rat poison or other toxic substances, and jumping off high structures, and the most common place for suicides is at home or in a hospital.

In its 40 years of existence within this building, the Mexico City morgue had to handle some of the country's biggest tragedies: the student massacre of 1968; a subway accident at the end of the 1970s; a Western Airlines plane crash (piles of corpses were laid out in the hallways and only photographs and fingerprints were taken before the bodies were burnt); the 1985 earthquake (there were so many dead bodies that a nearby baseball field was used as an extension of the morgue); narco-satanic murders in 1989; and a fire that consumed a discotheque at the beginning of this millennium.

In the 1985 earthquake, several government buildings surrounding the old city morgue collapsed. The morgue building held up, although it was left teetering to one side, designated as being at risk of falling in the case of another earthquake. Although it officially ceased to operate in 2009, the old morgue still stands, a monument to death in Mexico City.

Life Insurance

After life, some human beings, the privileged ones, can atone for their sins and set their life right in an act of final redemption. This has nothing to do with the Church's rites of confession or absolution, but rather with life insurance. If a person dies in the possession of an excellent life insurance policy, properly made out in the name of those that survive them, their sins tend to be forgiven at the moment their loved ones cash in the policy. In this way, the insurance industry believes (much like the Aztecs and the Catholic Church) that what is important is not what one does while alive but how one dies.

Unfortunately, life insurance is a luxury that most in Mexico City can't afford. Even if they could afford it, not everyone has what it takes to be allowed to purchase a policy, as there are strict rules and membership requirements. Life insurance coverage can be obtained only by those not afflicted with any major chronic disease, thus excluding a large percentage of the population (my colitis would either disqualify me or raise the payments prohibitively), and there exists great age and gender discrimination within the industry, as well.

Even if a person qualifies for life insurance, redemption is not guaranteed, as some deaths are better than others. Most insurance policies will not pay out if a person takes their own life (at least not during the first year of two of the policy). If someone should die while in the act of committing a felony the policy becomes invalid, and if they should be killed while breaking the law, or if they get arrested and then die in jail, for whatever reason or from whatever cause, their beneficiaries will not receive a peso. If a policyholder dies in a war, civil uprising or riot (a common occurrence in Mexico City) most insurers won't pay up, and the same holds true for many Acts of God (including the natural disasters that take the lives of so many of the city's inhabitants).

Many life insurance policies pay benefits only if the insured died in an accident. Given that the vast majority of *chilangos* die from disease, the payouts don't reflect the actual situation and thus don't cover the majority of cases. Although they are the most reliable (and at times profitable) way to go, accidents themselves are actually a tricky business. Insurance companies often refuse to pay claims by arguing that a death was not accidental if the deceased's actions in any way recklessly endangered their own lives. By this logic, payouts on life insurance policies can be denied if a policyholder had been drinking or driving in an unsafe way at the moment of their demise. Being that alcohol is involved in the majority of deaths (accidents, homicides, suicides and even most fatal illnesses) and that everyone who drives within the city exceeds the speed limit as often as they can, insurance companies can refuse to pay life insurance policies for a large number of 'accidental' deaths. The insurance industry's ideal customer would thus be someone who lives a long, prosperous life, paying a substantial amount of their annual income to their friendly local (or these days, global) insurance company, and then dies a death whose circumstances justify their insurer's refusal to pay.

Most violent deaths in Mexico City, however, are not 'accidental,' just as diseases are no longer 'natural.' The over-emphasis on cars, the poor quality streets, traffic signals and inadequate infrastructure, added to the permissiveness of drinking and speeding, makes automobile-related accidents (the number one violent form of death in the city) anything but accidental. As far as diseases go, given the genetic make-up of much of the population and the increased health risks associated with the consumption of huge quantities of fat, sugar, processed foods and alcohol, deaths from tumors, circulatory diseases, cirrhosis and diabetes, are all avoidable deaths.

Despite what most human beings are taught to believe, life is not only about getting paid, and death shouldn't only be about money, either. Like most Mexicans, I don't own a life insurance policy and thus can't hope for the final redemption of a good payout to my family. Nonetheless, I hope my death won't be judged only by the profit/loss it generates for my loved ones. All that I ask is that I meet my death with some dignity and style, perhaps even with a sense of humor, that I don't get run over or shot in front of my sons, and that I check out of this world before I lose control of my body and mind. For me, that, added to a life well lived, would be a death worth dying. ✝

ADIOS

Invasion of the Culture Snatchers

Mexico City is currently undergoing a painful transition from an underdeveloped economy to a post-industrial society dependent upon and at the whim of a much more powerful economy. (As the saying goes: Poor Mexico, so far from God and so close to the United States.) Like the united front of European microorganisms, plants, animals and human beings that invaded, conquered and colonized the New World, US corporations and their consumer products are taking over Mexico, and at least half of all food, alcohol, cigarettes and hundeds of other basic products consumed in Mexico City today comes from the US.

In addition, many areas of the city have cloned the American way of life, including several suburban zones, financial centers and trendy neighborhoods. The recent transformation of the Condesa into an international-style neighborhood is in no way a natural event. The greediness of the local government and its business of taking bribes in exchange for liquor licenses paved the way for the rapid expansion of the neighborhood's alcohol-based service sector economy. Local magazines and guides packaged and sold the Condesa life-style, directing consumers to the new restaurants, bars and cafes, while dozens of US newspapers, glossy magazines and books by gringos puffed up the neighborhood as an artsy tourist destination.

Despite all the hype, the Condesa represents the avant-garde not of Mexico City culture (which is to be found in lower working class barrios such as Tepito) but of US franchises and imported consumer goods. The recent, widespread penetration into Mexico City of multinational corporations has restructured the service sector in the neighborhood, substituting global goods for local ones. Today, three Starbucks, two Wal-Mart supermarkets, a couple of Crispy Cremes and Subways, a GNC, one MacStore, a couple of Blockbusters, as well as Nike, Converse and Adidas

241

stores ply their goods in my neighborhood. These companies spend millions of dollars on marketing campaigns, their ads and logos stamped large on clothes, the sides of buses and across the facades of buildings, with billboards that advertise the American Dream refashioning Mexico City›s skyline. Now subsidiaries of multinational corporations, the artisanal packaging and labels of local beers, cigarettes, snack food and candy that have long defined the visual culture and national identity of Mexico have almost all been replaced by global digital designs.

A large sector of Mexican society has always been *malinchista*, a term derived from Cortés´ indigenous translator and lover that refers to the fact that Mexicans prefer foreign culture to their own (which is often dismissively referred to as *naco*, that is, with roots in rural, indigenous culture). Even after hundreds of years, however, European cultural domination reached only the upper classes and swanky neighborhoods (a tiny fraction of the city), leaving the working classes to their own devices. The current US cultural invasion, however, is more widespread than anything in Mexico City´s past, infiltrating all classes and neighborhoods, and supplanting local industrial and cultural production.

Like a cancer, globalization is metastasizing and spreading throughout the city. The Mexico City I fell in love with when I arrived twenty-three years ago has mostly been killed off in my neighborhood and in surrounding areas. The social centers for Mexico City working class society, that is, traditional old cinemas, pool halls, *pulquerías*, public baths, porn theaters and dance halls, many of which had been around for more than half a century, have mostly disappeared throughout the city, replaced by bowling allies, sports bars, cafes or malls. Even with the influx of trendy international locales and foreigners, there is less cultural diversity in Mexico City now than when I first arrived, and much of the city, especially the Historic Center, has been transformed into a museum of extinct culture.

Although Mexico City is still located within the same mountain valley and although the majority of those who live here still retain genetic material inherited from original cultures, a large segment of its inhabitants (especially the new generations) have lost all connection to traditional Mexican culture. *Chilangos* are now being born into globalized neighborhoods and live gringo lifestyles without even realizing the radical cultural displacement that has occurred there. By eating instant noodles sold in 7/11´s, renting Hollywood films from Blockbusters, downloading US pop music from ITunes on their IPhones, wearing the latest outfits from American Apparel while sipping on a frappuccino at a Starbucks, or drinking Bacardi rum mixed with Diet Coke in a Hard Rock Cafe, most *chilangos* today have much more in common with consumers all over the world than they do with their own cultural past.

To gauge the profound transformations that living the American Dream has had on life in Mexico City, you need only look at the city´s mortality rates. Up until a few decades ago, Mexicans, like human beings throughout history, died mostly from diseases related to parasite infection (that is, natural deaths). Today, in their desire to be thoroughly modern and international, most *chilangos* now die slow deaths related to the consumption of alcohol, cigarettes, processed foods, pesticides, medicine and cars that are manufactured and imported mostly from the United States.

The American way of dying, that is, in a hospital connected to a life support system, with a foreign-owned funeral home in charge of disposing of the body and with international life insurance covering the costs, has become the most sought-after way to go in Mexico City. Along with its consumer products, the US now also exports its own brand of death to Mexico, and like much else these days, even dying in Mexico City is no longer Mexican.

Until Death   A few years ago, a friend who saw how emaciated and paranoid I´d become sent me to see his homeopathic doctor. From the moment I stepped inside his clinic (complete with a cafe and a store that sells New Age books, Indian elephant figures, incense and crystals) it was obvious that he was just another quack. I was asked to remove my shoes and turn off my cell phone before I entered his office. Inside, Gregorian chants bathed the airwaves, two large anatomical posters of the human ear were nailed to the wall, and several *Virgen de Guadalupe* figures sat on the bookshelves. Just the right elements to raise skeptic hackles all down my spine. I lay down on an examining table and Richard, a tough-looking Serbian with a shaved head, handlebar moustache and sandals, questioned me about my medical and personal history. Afterwards, he took my pulse with one hand while waving filters above my ear with the other, then jabbed a metal prong into delicate parts of my earlobe and discharged currents of electricity into my body. Convinced that it was all a waste of time, I nonetheless took home the homeopathic cures he prepared for me (mixed with *Oso Negro*, a cheap Mexican brand of vodka), just waiting to add this to the long list of bogus treatments I´d received so far.

After just a couple of visits, though, something strange happened. I ran to the bathroom less frequently, with less phlegm and blood in my shit. I no longer had a constant low-grade fever and didn´t feel so drained all the time. I stopped getting colds every month. I gained back some of the weight I had thought was lost forever. I even eventually stopped taking cortisone without any adverse effects.

Did his homemade homeopathic remedies ease my colitis? Did his probing into my early emotional traumas free me from the inner stress that had caused my intestinal meltdown? Did zapping my ears kill off parasites lodged deep inside my gut? Who knows? What I do know is that instead of viewing my body as defective, instead of isolating my large intestine from the rest of my body, instead of trying to suppress symptoms and hunt down all the creatures crawling around inside me, Richard boosted my body's defenses, reestablished a healthy intestinal flora and got my immune system up and working again.

I'm not yet normal and I probably will never be (my colitis will accompany me all the way to the grave). I still get the bad shits every time I eat out in Mexico City, but I can usually get my shit together after a few days and my vital fluids no longer dribble uncontrollably out my ass. My body can now almost fend for itself. I am no longer an open wound helplessly exposed to the aggressive environment of the city. The colitis-scope I had this year found no polyps or tumors, giving me a clean bill of health for a couple more years. I'm still in debt and see no way to improve my future finances, but I'm more relaxed and more productive, less paranoid. I know I'm going to die one day (not even so very far in the future) but having focused on death in general for this book I don't obsess about my own death so much any more.

It's possible that I might get run over while out walking my dogs, crash into a lamppost while driving at night in the rain after drinking one too many mezcals, get hit by a falling concrete slap from a construction site or be shot during an argument on the street over a fender-bender. It is much more likely, however, that my end will come from the long-term, intimate interaction between my body and Mexico City. Although I have always believed that I am much more than the sum of my body parts, as I get older the abuse to which my inner organs have been subjected will surely shape my death. Stress, bouts of frustration, rage and depression, added to high altitude and lower levels of oxygen, have all taken their toll on my circulatory system, increasing the possibility of heart attack or stroke. My lungs have been bombarded with serious amounts of pollutants and toxic particles, as well as viral and bacterial infections, making my lungs likely candidates for cancer. My large intestine, ravaged by colitis and cortisone for so many years, is undoubtedly the weakest link in my chain of being, a prime target for malignant tumors.

My death could come in any of many ways, but however it does happen it will most likely be caused by the accumulation within my inner organs of man-made substances from Mexico City air, water, food and alcohol, and will happen when my defenses are breached and the outer mega-city overwhelms my inner-mega-city. The number of years that I can keep all these potentially lethal diseases at bay depends in large part on my defenses. So long as my body doesn't freak out and start attacking them again, so long as I avoid the weapons of bio-mass destruction the medical-industrial complex is intent upon selling me, there are trillions of microscopic allies inside my body that will do everything they can to keep me healthy and strong and help me defend against all the worst Mexico City can throw at me.

Mexico City will surely shave years off of my life, but I can live with that. A longer life isn´t necessarily a better life. Despite all the ugliness that has descended upon my neighborhood in the last few years, the quality of life is still good. My wife and kids are happy here in Mexico City, perfectly adapted to their city. My wife works, takes her yoga classes and has a large group of friends in our neighborhood. My kids walk to school, bike to parks, play in rock and funk bands and practice martial arts in the neighborhood. Within my neighborhood there still exists an incredible biodiversity: hummingbirds flit around my patio and lizards and exotic insects crawl all around my house. All around my neighborhood there is great racial diversity (including millions of descendants of the Aztec civilization), a rich cultural diversity of immigrants from all parts of the country and continent, and a huge working class and lower working class within the city that ensure the production of local culture for many years to come.

I am a product of mega-cities, my consciousness is an urban creation, and my creative output has always been based on urban culture. Although it will be the death of me, Mexico City has as much life as any other mega-city on this planet. Mexico City is the best of cities and it is the worst of cities, the city I most love and the city I most love to hate. It is my city, for better or worse, for richer or poorer, in sickness or health, until death (my own or the death of the local culture) do we part. *Adiós.* ✝

RIP

Maki

(2005-2012)